BENIN · THE CONGO · BURKINA FASO

W9-ATF-835

Marxist Regimes Series

Series editor: Bogdan Szajkowski,
Department of Sociology, University College,
Cardiff

Further Titles

BENIN
Chris Allen

THE CONGO
Michael S. Radu and Keith Somerville

BURKINA FASO
Joan Baxter and Keith Somerville

Economics, Politics and Society

 Pinter Publishers, London and
New York

© The authors, 1989

All rights reserved. No part of this publication may be reproduced, stored in a retrieval system, or transmitted by any means without the prior written permission of the copyright holder. Please direct all enquiries to the publishers.

First published in Great Britain in 1988 by
Pinter Publishers Limited
25 Floral Street, London WC2E 9DS

British Library Cataloguing in Publication Data
A CIP catalogue record for this book is available from the British Library.
ISBN 0-86187-481-1
ISBN 0-86187-482-X (pbk.)

Library of Congress Cataloging-in-Publication Data
Available from the Library of Congress
ISBN 0-86187-481-1
ISBN 0-86187-482-X (pbk.)

Typeset by Joshua Associates Limited, Oxford
Printed in Great Britain by SRP Ltd, Exeter

Contents

Editor's Preface

The three West African Marxist regimes featured in this volume have much in common. They share the French colonial experience which contributed greatly to their political cultures and all had multi-party systems at the time of their independence from France. However, subsequent intensification of ethnic rivalries, which served as the main background of the post-colonial struggle, led to the emergence of military dictatorships under the guise of Marxist ideology. All three polities are unstable and increasingly economically dependent on France. But they also display major differences in the way that various policies on agriculture, religion, education and trade, to name just a few examples, have been implemented. The ideological shape of these regimes is also far from uniform.

This volume, apart from giving a comprehensive account of the working of these regimes and evaluation of their policies, also allows the reader to embark on a broad comparative exercise of the social, economic and political processes taking place in the three Marxist regimes of Francophone Africa. Although each part has been written separately, the volume as a whole provides a uniquely collaborative exercise giving for the first time in one book an analysis and an in-depth appraisal of military Marxist experiments in power. It also gives the reader a stimulating insight to the problems, dilemmas and limited options facing numerous countries in the developing world.

This volume is a timely and very important contribution to the overall analysis of Marxist experiments, the study of which has thus far been equated with the study of communist political systems. There were several historical and methodological reasons for this. For many years it was not difficult to distinguish the eight regimes in Eastern Europe and four in Asia which resoundingly claimed adherence to the tenets of Marxism and more particularly to their Soviet interpretation—Marxism-Leninism. These regimes, variously called 'People's Republic', 'People's Democratic Republic', or 'Democratic Republic', claimed to have derived their inspiration from the Soviet Union to which, indeed, in the overwhelming number of cases they owed their establishment.

To many scholars and analysts these regimes represented a multiplication of and geographical extension of the 'Soviet model' and consequently of the Soviet sphere of influence. Although there were clearly substantial similarities between the Soviet Union and the people's democracies, especially in the initial phases of their development, these were often overstressed at the expense of noticing the differences between these political systems.

It took a few years for scholars to realize that generalizing the particular, i.e., applying the Soviet experience to other states ruled by elites which claimed to be guided by 'scientific socialism', was not good enough. The relative simplicity of the assumption of a cohesive communist bloc was questioned after the expulsion of Yugoslavia from the Communist Information Bureau in 1948 and in particular after the workers' riots in Poznań in 1956 and the Hungarian revolution of the same year. By the mid-1960s, the totalitarian model of communist politics, which until then had been very much in force, began to crumble. As some of these regimes articulated demands for a distinctive path of socialist development, many specialists studying these systems began to notice that the cohesiveness of the communist bloc was less apparent than had been claimed before.

Also by the mid-1960s, in the newly independent African states 'democratic' multi-party states were turning into one-party states or military dictatorships, thus questioning the inherent superiority of liberal democracy, capitalism and the values that went with it. Scholars now began to ponder on the simple contrast between multi-party democracy and a one-party totalitarian rule that had satisfied an earlier generation.

Despite all these changes the study of Marxist regimes remains in its infancy and continues to be hampered by constant and not always pertinent comparison with the Soviet Union, thus somewhat blurring the important underlying common theme—the 'scientific theory' of the laws of development of human society and human history. This doctrine is claimed by the leadership of these regimes to consist of the discovery of objective causal relationships; it is used to analyse the contradictions which arise between goals and actuality in the pursuit of a common destiny. Thus the political elites of these countries have been and continue to be influenced in both their ideology and their political practice by Marxism more than any other current of social thought and political practice.

The growth in the number and global significance, as well as the ideological, political and economic impact, of Marxist regimes has presented scholars and students with an increasing challenge. In meeting this challenge, social scientists on both sides of the political divide have put forward a dazzling profusion of terms, models, programmes and varieties of interpretation. It is against the background of this profusion that the present comprehensive series on Marxist regimes is offered.

This collection of monographs is envisaged as a series of multi-disciplinary textbooks on the governments, politics, economics and society of these countries. Each of the monographs was prepared by a specialist on the country concerned. Thus, over fifty scholars from all over the world have contributed monographs which were based on first-hand knowledge. The geographical diversity of the authors, combined with the fact that as a group they represent many disciplines of social science, gives their individual analyses and the series as a whole an additional dimension.

Each of the scholars who contributed to this series was asked to analyse such topics as the political culture, the governmental structure, the ruling party, other mass organizations, party-state relations, the policy process, the economy, domestic and foreign relations together with any features peculiar to the country under discussion.

This series does not aim at assigning authenticity or authority to any single one of the political systems included in it. It shows that, depending on a variety of historical, cultural, ethnic and political factors, the pursuit of goals derived from the tenets of Marxism has produced different political forms at different times and in different places. It also illustrates the rich diversity among these societies, where attempts to achieve a synthesis between goals derived from Marxism on the one hand, and national realities on the other, have often meant distinctive approaches and solutions to the problems of social, political and economic development.

University College   *Bogdan Szajkowski*
Cardiff

Part I
Benin

Chris Allen

Contents of Part I, Benin

Basic Data

Official name	People's Republic of Benin
Population	3.34 million (1979); 4.24 million (est. 1988)
Population density	30 per sq. km.
Population growth	3.1% p.a. (1985)
Urban population (%)	39 (in towns over 10,000; 1979)
Total labour force	1.78 million (1980)
Life expectancy	49 years
Infant death rate	115 per 1,000
Child death rate	19 per 1,000
Ethnic groups	Fon (47%); Adja, Aizo, Yoruba/Mahi, Bariba, Somba, Peulh
Capital	Porto Novo 132,000 (1979)
Largest city	Cotonou 327,000 (1979), 606,250 (1987)
Land area	112,600 sq. km.
Official language	French
Other main languages	Fon, Yoruba, Bariba
Administrative divisions	Provinces: 6; Districts: 84
Membership of international organizations	UN since 1960; IBRD and IMF; OAU; ECOWAS, OCAM, Conseil d'Entente, CEAO, CEDEAO, EEC-ACP
Foreign relations	16 States represented in Benin (including Soviet Union, China, GDR, North Korea, Cuba, Libya). Benin represented abroad in 26 states, some jointly, plus UN, EEC.
Political structure	
Constitution	As of September 1977
Highest legislative body	Revolutionary National Assembly of 196 members
Highest executive body	National Executive Council
President	Mathieu Kérékou (since 1972)
Prime Minister	No such position
Food self-sufficiency	Achieved in 1980s; deficient in basic tubers and grains from mid-1960s to late 1970s

Growth indicators (% p.a.)
GDP	2.3% (1960–85); 3.4% (1980–5) (real GDP growth rate −2%, 1982–6)
Industry	13.5% (1980–5)
Manufacturing	7.2% (1980–5)
Agriculture	0.9% (1980–5)
Food output p.c.	−0.4% (1960/62–1978/80)

Exports	$129 million (1986), but note high levels of unrecorded re-exports
Imports	$541 million (1986)
Exports as % GNP	Meaningless
Main exports	Cotton, palm products, karité
Main imports	Food, 12%; fuel, 5%; machinery and vehicles, 17% (1985)
Destination of exports	Non-socialist countries: 94% (1986); socialist countries: 6%
Main trading partners	West Germany, France, United States, Holland, UK, China, Japan; neighbouring states
Foreign debt	$1.07 billion (end 1986, OECD estimate)
Foreign aid	$141 million (1986)
Foreign investment	
Main natural resources	Palm oil groves; cotton, etc., oil

Ruling party	People's Revolutionary Party of Benin
President of the Party	Mathieu Kérékou
Party membership	Unknown but small
Armed forces	Army 3,800; airforce 350; navy 160 Gendarmerie 2,000; militia 1,500–2,000 (1987)

Education and health
School system	6 years primary (5–11); 2 × 3 years secondary (11–17)
Primary school enrolment	64% of age group; male 84%, female 42%
Secondary enrolment	19% of age group; male 28%, female 11%
Tertiary enrolment	6,300 (1986)
Higher education	University of Benin
Adult literacy (%)	Not available
Population per hospital bed	550 (1979)
Population per doctor	17,000 (1981)

Economy
GDP	CFA fr. 558 billion ($1.8 billion) (1986)
GDP per capita	CFA fr. 138,000 ($400) (1986)
Budget (expenditure)	CFA fr. 53.7 billion ($170 million, 1988)
Defence expenditure as % of budget	20.6

Monetary unit	CFA (Communauté financière d'Afrique) franc; tied to French franc, at CFA fr. 50 — 1 French Franc
Main crops	Yams, cassava, maize, millet
Land tenure	Communal, and private freehold
Main religions	Animism (60%), Catholicism (18%), Islam (15%), Protestantism (4%)
Rail network	Main line (440 km.) Cotonou/Parakou; two minor coastal lines to Bopa and Sakate; total length 580 km.
Road network	Tarred roads: 800 km.; all roads 7,300 km.

Population Forecasting

The following data are projections produced by Poptran, University College Cardiff Population Centre, from United Nations Assessment Data published in 1980, and are reproduced here to provide some basis of comparison with other countries covered by the Marxist Regimes Series.

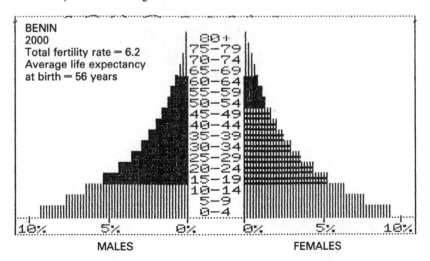

Projected Data for Benin 2000

Total population ('000)	6,757
Males ('000)	3,349
Females ('000)	3,408
Total fertility rate	6.22
Life expectancy (male)	53.9 years
Life expectancy (female)	57.5 years
Crude birth rate	44.9
Crude death rate	12.1
Annual growth rate	3.28%
Under 15s	47.07%
Over 65s	2.80%
Women aged 15–49	22.19%
Doubling time	21 years
Population density	60 per sq. km.
Urban population	54.4%

List of Abbreviations

ACR	*Africa Contemporary Record* (London)
ARB	*Africa Research Bulletin* (Exeter)
BAN	*Bulletin d'Afrique Noire* (Paris)
BCEAO	'Indicateurs économiques béninois', *Notes d'information et statistiques* (Dakar: Banque centrale des états de l'Afrique de l'ouest)
CAETS	Coopérative agricole expérimentale à type socialiste
CARDER	Centre d'action régionale pour le développement rural
CDR	Comité pour la défense de la révolution
CEAO	Communaté économique de l'Afrique de l'ouest
CEAP	Comité d'état d'administration de la province
CFA	Communauté financière d'Afrique (see Basic data: currency)
CFDT	Companie française pour le développement du textile
CMV	Comité militaire de vigilance
CNR	Conseil nationale de la révolution
COF	Comité d'organisation des femmes
CRAD	Comité révolutionnaire d'administration du district
CRL	Comité révolutionnaire local
ECOWAS	Economic Community of West African States
EOM	*Europe Outremer* (Paris)
FACEEN	Fronte d'action commune des élèves et des étudiants du Nord
FLRD	Fronte de libération et de rehabilitation du Dahomey
FUD	Front unique démocratique
GRVC	Groupement révolutionnaire à vocation coopérative
GV	Groupement villageois
IMF	International Monetary Fund
JIR	Jeune instituteur révolutionnaire
JUD	Jeunesse universitaire du Dahomey
MDD	Mouvement démocratique du Dahomey
MTM	*Marchés tropicaux et méditerranéenes* (Paris)
OAU	Organisation of African Unity
OCAM	Organisation commune africaine et malgache
OFRB	Organisation des femmes révolutionnaires du Bénin
OJRB	Organisation de la jeunesse révolutionnaire du Bénin
ONEPI	Office nationale d'édition, de presse et d'imprimerie
PCD	Parti communiste du Dahomey
PDU	Parti dahoméene d'unité
PRD	Parti republicain du Dahomey
PRPB	Parti de la révolution populaire du Bénin
QER	*Quarterly Economic Review: Togo, Benin, Niger, Burkina* (London:

	Economist Intelligence Unit); now named *Country Report: Togo, Benin, Niger, Burkina*
UDD	Union démocratique dahoméene
UGEED	Union générale des étudiants et élèves dahoméenes
UGTD	Union général des travailleurs du Dahomey
UMOA	Union monetaire ouest-africaine
UNSTB	Union nationale des syndicats des travailleurs du Bénin
UPD	Union progressiste dahoméene
UVS	Unité villageoise de santé
WA	*West Africa* (London)

Glossary

cadres	senior officials
comité de direction	management committee
féticheur	animist religious leader
groupuscule	small grouping
hommes de main	stalwarts
notables	persons of standing

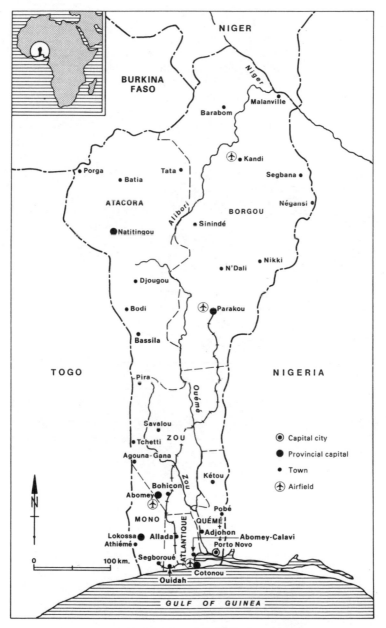

People's Republic of Benin

Introduction

This study of the People's Republic of Benin has three main goals. It provides the first detailed account of the politics of Benin (formerly Dahomey) since the coup in 1972 which established the present regime.[1] The only other accounts are either brief, like those by Decalo or M. L. Martin (see Bibliography) or narrower, like the monograph by Francine Godin, which is an attempt to understand the nature of the Beninois state and its relations with social classes, using neo-Marxist theories (Godin, 1986). It also attempts to explain the origins and nature of the political system of Benin, and in particular its transformation from an unstable polity marked by coups and increasingly intense regional conflict, to a stable system within which regional and ethnic rivalry exists but does not threaten to develop into conflict. Finally this study attempts to assess the regime's frequent claims to being socialist (for which see Chapter 3), and to determine whether it is appropriate to apply the term 'Marxist regime' to Benin.

This last question is discussed primarily in Chapters 4 and 5, which deal respectively with the development of the economy and economic policy, and with foreign policy, education and health. Changes were introduced in the aftermath of the coup, primarily in social policy and in the political structure, and following the adoption of socialism as the official development path late in 1974, a move symbolized by the change in name from Dahomey to Benin. I have used this symbolism in my own text, by continuing to refer to the pre-1975 state as 'Dahomey', and reserving 'Benin' for the post-1975 period. I argue that neither the changes in policy nor the changes actually carried out in the 1970s can be seen as socialist. Instead it seems more reasonable to regard them as attempts at realizing three features of the loose civil-military alliance that assembled in 1972–3 behind the then and present head of state, Mathieu Kérékou. These were: its nationalism, especially in the sense of a rejection of what was deemed excessive involvement by France in Dahomean affairs and institutions; its egalitarianism, especially expressed in the critique of the education system as designed for urban elites, and of the political system as excluding participation; and its radicalism, stemming less from socialism (though this had some influence) than from the broader currents of ideas about educational theory, health care delivery, etc., that had emerged globally in the 1960s. While there were major changes in the political system and in education (but to a lesser degree in health), and a greater role for the public sector in the economy, the extent of change overall was limited both by a basic want of resources in the 1970s and even more by the economic decline of the 1980s, a decline that still continues and is shared by most other African states. This decline, analysed in detail in Chapter 4, was in part due to the changes introduced in the 1970s (notably the development of the public sector and of parastatals), and has brought about the rejection of the statist economic strategies of that period, as well as a reduction in nationalism, egalitarianism and radicalism. I therefore argue that it is inappropriate to conceive of Benin as a Marxist regime at any point in its history, despite the arguments advanced in Szajkowski (1982) and Young (1982), which are considered in Chapter 6.

Chapter 6 also considers the question of stability, arguing that Benin's political system can be understood as one case, perhaps a particularly clear case, of a general phenomenon in the majority of African political systems: the shift from clientelist politics to centralized bureaucratic systems focusing on a strong executive presidency.[2] I discuss the nature of clientelist politics in Chapter 2, in which an account is given of the development of Dahomean politics from 1945, and especially of the growth of regionalism, corruption, state incompetence and political instability. These I argue were all caused by the resort in the early 1950s to clientelism as a means of recruiting electoral support, in a society in which there was but modest differentiation into classes; and they created continual crises reflected in frequent military interventions. What marks the Kérékou regime is its confronting of clientelist politics, its attack on the institutions that supported clientelism, and the creation of a new centralized political system in which the Presidency, the bureaucracy and limited local-level participation play key roles. The detail of these changes is provided in Chapter 3, which discusses the formal political structure, and Chapter 2, which provides a chronological account, albeit one shaped to stress certain themes and features and which does not purport to provide a complete political history. Chapter 6 then draws together this material by explaining the significance of the changes in the system, and the extent to which such changes can be seen as a general African phenomenon.

I have not devoted a separate chapter to society and social change, in part because of the difficulty of assembling material on this field compared to that on political and economic change. Instead Chapter 3 includes a section on the relationship between the state and certain social groups, notably women, workers, the military and religious groupings (where a brief discussion of the anti-witchcraft campaign of the 1970s is provided). At the end of the chapter I consider to what extent the regime should be considered repressive and hostile to human rights, a theme recalled in the Conclusion. The remaining material on Beninois society is in Chapter 4, where I attempt to provide a statistical picture of the main social categories, and to assess the relationships between the government and the peasantry (drawing on an earlier account of rural policy) and between government and the petty bourgeoisie. In each case I conclude that a compromise has been established, in which in return for abandoning certain policies harmful to the interests of peasants or petty bourgeois the government is allowed to govern without disruption. Such an accommodation is more difficult to reach with students and workers, whose interests are particularly threatened by policies adopted in the 1980s, and those which would be imposed under a structural adjustment programme arising from IMF assistance, for which requests have been made. Herein lies a possible cause of future instability for a regime which can count that stabilization of the political system as one of its main achievements.

Notes

1. For a study of similar length of the 1945–73 period, see Ronen 1975.
2. But not, as Jackson & Rosberg (1982) argue, on a strong individual as president, helpful though that may be.

1 Background

On 30 November 1975 the Republic of Dahomey became the People's Republic of Benin, a name symbolizing a sharp break with the country's past history. This history, together with its human and natural endowment, had made Dahomey one of the poorest Third World states—it nestled in World Bank statistical tables fourteenth from the bottom—as well as the least stable of all African polities.[1] This brief chapter surveys that history and endowment, while Chapters 2 and 4 detail the origins and implications of instability and poverty.

Benin extends 700 kilometres northwards from the West African coast, bounded by Nigeria to its east and Togo to the west. Only 120 kilometres wide at the coast it expands to 150 kilometres in its southern half and then again to 350 kilometres above latitude 10 degrees, making its shape oddly but inappropriately like a fist pointing at the Sahara. Its location, size and shape have each had several implications. That much of southern Benin is only a short distance from Togo and especially from Nigeria has encouraged the development of cross-border trade and migration, which became highly important after independence in 1960 (see Chapter 4). Benin is well placed to play an entrepôt role not only for Upper Volta (Burkina Faso) and Niger to its north, but also for Nigeria, through the port of Cotonou, which was expanded and modernized in 1959–65 and again in 1979–81 (allowing it to handle well over a million tonnes of freight in the early 1980s). The port connects with Niger first by rail—an eight-hour trip to Parakou 440 kilometres away—and thence by road. This road and the coastal highway that connects to Lomé and Lagos make up the bulk of the country's 800 or so kilometres of tarred roads; communications within Benin, and especially within the north, are thus poor.

Benin runs almost due north from the coast, dividing the country into two basic climatic and agronomic zones. The south is hot and humid with relatively heavy rainfall and two dry seasons. Apart from the 300,000 hectares of natural oil palm groves which stretch across the south, this zone is an area of maize, yam and vegetable production, and of fishing (mainly artisan). Here live a little more than half the population, on a tenth of the land, making it relatively densely populated, even allowing for the presence of Cotonou (606,000 inhabitants) and of the capital, Porto Novo (132,000) (see Table 1.1). This dense population and the existence of land owned (but not cultivated) by absentee landlords make this area also one of intense cultivation, especially

Table 1.1 Population of Benin, 1961 and 1979

Province	1979 Population	% total	% 1961	Annual growth rate	Density per sq. km. 1979
Atacora	481,500	14.4	14.9	2.4	15
Borgou	490,000	14.7	14.5	2.7	10
Zou	569.500	17.1	20.2	1.6	31
Mono	476,500	14.3	13.8	2.8	125
Atlantique	693,300	20.8	14.7	4.6	215
Ouémé	627,100	18.8	22.0	1.7	133
Benin	3,338,200	100.0	100.0	2.6	30

Source: 1979 Census.

in Atlantique Province, with subdivision of plots and growing rural landlessness.

The northern provinces—Atacora and Borgou—make up three-quarters of the land area of Benin, and have 29 per cent of its population. Land is underutilized, though since it is poorer in quality than southern areas and rainfall is low and unreliable, intensive cultivation could have severe ecological consequences. Apart from cotton and groundnuts grown for export, the area's main crops are the local staples, millet or sorghum; cattle and smaller livestock are also kept. The province of Zou, in the centre of Benin, has more rain than the north, and produces similar crops.

Other features do not represent so tidy a north–south division. While Christianity is mainly confined to the coastal area, animist beliefs and Islam are found throughout Benin, the latter strongest along the border with Nigeria and among the Yoruba and Bariba. Similarly, although Dahomean politics came to pivot around a three-way contest between north, south-east and south/centre, the ethnic distribution to which political regionalism is sometimes linked by analysts is far more complex and owes much more to Dahomey's precolonial kingdoms. The largest single ethnic groupings are the Fon, estimated in 1961 to be 47 per cent of the population and located like the Adja (12 per cent) and Aizo (5 per cent) in the south-west, location of the old Danhomé, Abomey and Allada kingdoms. To their west, and with ties across the border into Nigeria, are the Yoruba and Mahi (9 per cent), and the Goun (3 per cent), associated with the kingdoms of Kétou and Porto Novo.

The main northern group are the Bariba (10 per cent), former rulers of three kingdoms (Kandi, Nikki and Parakou) in the north-west, and thus also overlords of the Fulani or Peulh (4 per cent). The north-east, home of the Somba (5 per cent) and several smaller groups, never came under Bariba authority despite lacking any powerful states.[2]

What is now Benin did not exist as a political entity before colonial rule. Even the name 'Dahomey' is a corruption of the name of one of the area's kingdoms, Danhomé, which covered part of what is now southern Benin. Thus the precolonial history of the area is that of several groups of states or smaller units, their eastern and western neighbours, and the impact on them of the Atlantic slave trade and its successor, the trade in palm oil and other products.[3] The two key groups of states from the sixteenth century onwards were those of the Adja peoples (the Fon and Goun) in the south-east and coastal zone, and those of the Bariba in the north. Both overlapped the present boundaries of Benin, extending eastwards into 'Togo' and westwards into 'Nigerian' Borgou, while the Yoruba kingdoms associated with the Oyo empire of the late eighteenth and early nineteenth century (notably the kingdom of Kétou and Sabé) extended into what is now western Benin. Large areas lay outside these state systems, notably north-eastern Benin, and had only limited political contact with them.

The Bariba states, known collectively as Borgou, lay between the River Niger and the Atacora mountains in the northeast of Benin, on a flat ill-watered plain of scattered settlements. Their origins lie in the sixteenth century, or possibly earlier, when the four principal states were formed: Bussa (the oldest), Illo and Wawa (all now in Nigeria), and Nikki. Further expansion eastwards produced states which while acknowledging the overlordship of Nikki were in practice independent. These states included Kaiama, powerful and prosperous in the early nineteenth century but now a relative backwater in Nigeria, and Kandi, Djougou, Kouade and Parakou. All these states shared a social and political organization centred on the *wasangari* (or freemen) and two subordinate groups, the relatively mobile Fulani and the settled *gando*, effectively slaves. Trading networks connected them to Hausa states (and later the Sokoto Caliphate) to the west, and to the trans-Saharan markets. Trade to the south existed also, but largely in the form of slaves which the Bariba ruling families sold in the eighteenth century. Contact with Europeans was slight until late in the nineteenth century, and was then sudden and disastrous. The French rapidly conquered the area in the late 1890s, and—as they did elsewhere in Dahomey—established the old kingdoms as administrative units, thus making the former kings, now chiefs, or equal status. They also freed the *gando*, thus weakening the economic and political power of the *wasangari* ruling families, though they retained influence and status throughout the colonial period.

The southern kingdoms had a similarly early origin being formed by a series of migrations of Adja groups, initially from Tado (in Togo) to Allada, then from there to Abomey, Porto Novo and Hueda (Ouidah). During the seventeenth century Abomey developed separately, to form the kingdom of Danhomé, while the other centres grew increasingly independent of Allada. Finally Danhomé conquered Allada (in 1724), as part of a long campaign that united the western Adja states within the Danhomé kingdom. The expanded kingdom remained dominant for the rest of the eighteenth and most of the nineteenth centuries, though obliged to pay tribute to Oyo until the latter's disintegration after 1800. It was able to adapt readily to the slave trade, in part because warfare provided a ready surplus to be traded, but also because the sale of slaves was a relatively small part of its economy and largely in the hands of the ruling family. None the less, Manning shows that the rates of population loss for the Adja were subtantially greater than for any other population group in West Africa in the eighteenth century, leading to population decline and a lower rate of growth (Manning, 1982, pp. 32–3, 49–50). After 1840 export of slaves declined and their labour was diverted into cultivation of palms and production of palm oil, which became the economic basis for the kingdom for the remainder of the century.

Those who prospered from the production of palm oil were the ruling family (as major producers) and the merchants (often freed slaves, known as 'Brazilians') who sold and exported the oil. French conquest was first to limit and then undermine both their wealth and their power. The French had acquired a measure of political control over the coast through trade and treaty, from 1850. By 1890 this conflicted sharply with the economic interests of the Danhome kingdom, as did the kingdom's authority with France's claim to the entire area: conquest followed swiftly in 1893. During the rest of the decade the French attempted to break up the kingdom, first by restoring to life its historic components ('recognizing' kings for Abomey, Allada and Kétou) and then by deposing the king of Abomey and not allowing a successor. As in the north, the kings were also soon downgraded to chiefs. The economic impact of French rule is discussed in Chapter 4.

Politically, three themes stand out in the colonial period to 1940: the long rearguard action of the southern merchants, planters and ruling families against French economic and political domination; resistance from below against colonial exploitation; and the rise of the Dahomean intelligentsia. All three came together in 1914–30 when popular resentment of forced labour, taxation and wartime recruitment of troops produced a series of revolts and strikes, allowing the merchants and their intellectual allies to attack both the colonial state and the chiefs with some success.[4] The years of the Depression and of the Second World War saw, by contrast, a strengthening of the colonial state both as an economic and as a repressive organ, and a corresponding weakening of the Dahomean merchants. Their movement split into sections either supportive or critical of French rule, and by 1945 it was their educated relatives from the liberal professions who were to lead the nationalist movement. The merchants and planters had lost, and reached an accommodation with the state allowing it the predominant economic role, an accommodation which still holds.

If for nothing else, the current regime in Benin should be famous for its stability. While there has been a continual change in the personnel of government, with only a handful of the president's original colleagues now even at the fringes of power, the same government has ruled Benin since 1972 (when it was still called Dahomey). President Kérékou, then a major, took power through a military coup in December 1972; it was the sixth such coup since 1963, and in the six years of civilian rule before the first of them there had been nine distinct governments.

This sharp contrast is a symptom of the change in the nature of the political systems enjoyed or suffered by Dahomey/Benin since the 1950s, rather than the key to it. The system that dominated in 1957-72 grew out of the form taken by decolonization in French West Africa, in combination with Dahomey's social structure and the activity of its nationalist parties. The system that has with several adaptations dominated since the mid-1970s can be seen as a direct response to the inherent features of the earlier system, and especially to the contradictions of its principal component, clientelist politics.

Decolonization: 1945-57

Like the other territories of French West Africa, Dahomey acquired direct representation (through a single deputy) in the French National Assembly[1] and its own territorial council in 1946. The latter had little power, though it was directly elected by two distinct groups, those with French citizenship, and a second more motley collection of Africans with some official standing or recognition such as ex-soldiers (over half of the group), those with permits or licences, chiefs and employees (especially civil servants). The deputy—in this case Sourou-Mignon Apithy, a member of the Goun ethnic group from the Porto Novo area—had greater influence. With only limited electoral competition and a small electorate—60,000 or so in the 1940s—early party organization was minimal, and candidates relied on their connections with chiefs, merchants and other 'notables' (including trade-union leaders) to mobilize votes.

This situation was decisively changed by two reforms of the 1950s which in 1951 increased the electorate six-fold and made it largely rural, and then in 1957 doubled it and created a powerful territorial assembly. These changes, common to all of French West Africa as part of the process of decolonization, had two effects. Would-be national politicians now had to find ways of mobilizing rural electorates; and local leaders were offered something new with which to bargain for local facilities: the votes of their communities. With the 1951 reforms announced only weeks before the elections, national politicians had no recourse but to attempt to recruit ready-made blocks of local votes. In this they could use contacts built up through family, education, occupation or membership of the Catholic Church (influential in the south); but most important was the use of clientelism.

Clientelist politics is essentially the exchange of blocks of votes, usually communities or organizations, for valued goods such as a school, piped water or a pay increase. These goods are provided (or promised) from state resources by national politicians and channelled through local or sectional leaders such as chiefs, merchants, union leaders, priests etc. The exchange helps to confirm the local leader in his leadership status and provides the politician with votes. In the case of colonial Dahomey it was the colonial state that provided the goods, at the urging of national politicians. As a means of mobilizing an electorate, especially a new electorate, clientelism has few equals; its drawbacks for Dahomey became clear in the 1950s, and especially after 1957 when Dahomean politicians themselves controlled the main source of goods, the state.

The 1951 elections were immediately preceded by the fission of the main nationalist organization of the 1940s, the UPD (Union Progressist Dahoméenne), a loose association of wealthy and/or educated notables, in which only one significant figure was not from the coastal area: Hubert Maga, a teacher based in Natitingou.[2] This southern domination reflected the pattern in education and economic development within Dahomey as a whole, and led in 1951 to Maga presenting his own list of candidates for the Assembly elections, appealing overtly to regional resentment at material neglect—and with the backing of some French administrators (Ronen, 1975, pp. 89–92). Maga's network of ex-pupils, chiefs and others gave him the bulk of northern votes—indeed in seven of the nine northern districts he took 80 per cent or more of the poll. Apithy, who had also left the UPD, polled almost as well in the south-east and especially in his home town, Porto Novo. The UPD rump, now led by Emile Zinsou, was left with a handful of districts mainly in the south-west. Elections for the territorial assembly early in 1952 showed a similar regional pattern, modified by the success of independents and local parties.

By 1957 the regional pattern was firmly established. Both Maga and Apithy built their parties around a core provided by ethnic organization and the ruling families of the chiefdoms or the precolonial kingdoms of their areas. They extended their support from these cores—Porto Novo for Apithy, the north-west for Maga—by alliances with local leaders (often known as *grands électeurs*). Such alliances were also used in attempts to weaken rival parties in the peripheries of their regions, as with Maga's link with Faustin Gbaguidi of Savalou, a region in the centre of Benin.[3] The regional pattern was in turn based on an intense localism.[4] Candidates of whatever party were drawn from the locality and usually chosen by local notables to act on behalf of their locality. The parties can then be seen as regionally based coalitions of local interests, an image confirmed by their failure to present candidates other than in their own regions (and peripheral areas of neighbouring regions), their lack of organization and their lack of activity between elections.[5] It proved impossible to sustain a party on any other basis, as the history of the Union Démocratique Dahoméenne (UDD) indicates.

The UDD was founded in 1955, well after Maga's Mouvement Démocratique du Dahomey and Apithy's Parti Républicain du Dahomey had established themselves. It presented itself as a mass, national party and included within itself both trade unionists (notably from Cotonou) and the small group of younger radical nationalists and student leaders. It established a formal national organization and at first spread swiftly, mobilizing groups that felt excluded from (or alienated by) the existing division of power. At the same time, the UDD can be seen as yet another coalition of local leaders and interests. Even its most radical 'national' figure, Alexandre Adande, was a highly influential member of a leading Porto Novo family. His running mate for the 1956 French National Assembly elections, Justin Ahomadeghe, was also from a ruling family and had headed a successful local party in Abomey which had won all four local seats in the 1952 territorial assembly elections.

At first the UDD polled well throughout the south and centre, collecting between 14 per cent and 59 per cent of the vote in each district in 1956; in urban areas it became 'a real competitor with Apithy's PRD' (Staniland, 1973, p. 492). Yet it was forced to mirror the strategy of its rivals in order to compete effectively in the 1957 territorial elections. First it agreed not to contest northern seats in return for Maga's MDD standing down in Savalou (allowing the UDD to win this district). Then it had to 'sacrifice . . . educated and experienced candidates for the sake of attracting rural support' (Staniland, 1973, p. 500) by adopting local men. Eighty-six per cent of PRD candidates in 1957 were local; the same proportion of UDD candidates were local, although fewer were local residents. Finally the electoral system itself aided regionalism. In each of the ten districts the party winning most votes took all of the seats so that the UDD's urban support—clearly reflected in its control of municipal councils in 1957—was 'swamped by numerically weightier, rural majorities for the PRD' (Staniland, 1973, p. 503). Thus the UDD emerged from the 1957 election as the party of the residual regions, the south-west and centre.

1958-65: from Decolonization to Crisis

In 1958 Dahomey achieved internal self-government. Africans were appointed to ministerial positions and now controlled the single most important source of patronage: the state, its offices and revenues. This change led in turn to a series of developments in the political systems which were to force a limited military intervention in 1963 and a fullblown military coup in 1965. Those developments arose from the reliance of politicians on clientelism as their sole or principal means of mobilizing electoral support, and from the impact of access to state resources on the elite stratum of Dahomean society.

Clientelism, though an extremely effective means of gathering support, at the same time creates or exacerbates phenomena which undermine the stability of regimes and ultimately of political systems founded upon its use. Politicians at regional and national level gained and reproduced the support of local leaders by allocating to them state resources over which they had influence or control. Each attempted to maximize this support and his access to resources in competition with rival politicians inside and outside his own party. In expanding their bases of support individual politicians used existing groupings, sometimes formal organizations like trade unions or cooperatives, but more commonly local communities, ethnic or religious groupings. In the process, and especially as competition for resources increased, the divisions between these groupings became politicized, leading to the emergence of regionalism and tribalism within Dahomean politics.

This process was already visible in the early 1950s and became institution-alized after 1958. Each of the parties functioned as a regional party, able to mobilize the majority of votes in its own region but often not even standing in other regions. Instead, support was offered to local opponents of rival parties, as in 1958 when the PRD backed independent candidates standing in northern districts against Maga's party. This tactic had considerable success, as the independents won two-thirds of the seats. The regional strength and exclusiveness of each of the three main political parties also meant that no one of them could form an administration on its own. Coalitions were essential, yet the partners in each coalition continually attempted to gain the greatest advantage from the coalition, while the excluded party manoeuvred to enter the coalition by replacing one of its members. Governments thus tended to be unstable, while the party scene was marked by a series of attempts to unite two or more of the rivals, only for the resulting united party to divide again in the following months.

A second 'contradiction' inherent with clientelist politics arose from the need for material resources for distribution downwards to the electorate. These resources were necessarily limited, but expansion and retention of support implied an ever-increasing pressure for the allocation of resources. This could only be done by denying resources to other communities and areas. Thus while Maga was the dominant leader in the 1960-2 coalition, 'northerners in large numbers were promoted throughout the entire governmental system' (Decalo, 1973, p. 458), at the expense of southerners. Another means was for the whole range of potential state resources to be pressed into service as rewards or inducements for support, so that the pattern of public spending came gradually to be determined by its implications for generating electoral support. Finally, the size of the public sector and of public spending generally was expanded, to create more rewards. Dahomey's public sector posts increased by 20 per cent in 1960-5 and its budget (the greater part of which went on salaries) by 40 per cent. Since Dahomey's budget and balance of trade were permanently in deficit and grants from France were required to balance the former, this upward pressure on public spending made the viability of clientelist politics highly vulnerable to even modest economic reverses, while the diversion of resources from developmental activity into clientelist spending made such reverses more likely.

The final contradiction of clientelism lay in its sociology. Depending from each regional or national politician was a network of local leaders through whom the distribution of rewards occurred. These leaders required rewards of their own, provided once again through access to political office and state resources. Not only did this encourage corruption, but since no other means of obtaining wealth was so swift or so certain, it created a second source of increased demand for clientelist spending. This form of spending, however, inevitably competed with spending on the reproduction of electoral support, and since the elite control both forms, the tendency was for the latter to suffer as the costs of clientelism rose or resources dwindled. The result was a drying up of individual benefits and collective services at the local level and reductions in real incomes for the poor at the national level through wage freezes, tax increases and reduced prices for export crops.

Clientelism thus encouraged and politicized communal divisions, resulted in the misallocation of resources and in corruption and ultimately came to alienate rather than reproduce popular support for the regime. The retention of power was, however, essential to sustain the flow of rewards to supporters, even though this had become attenuated at the base. The regime's response was to attempt to prevent loss of power through electoral competition, by coercive means such as the banning or jailing of opponents, by the rigging of elections and potentially the abandonment of competitive elections, and the creation of a single party state. The opposition, and in turn the regime, were forced to have increasing recourse to violence in the attempt to gain or retain power.

The resultant 'crisis of clientelism' can be seen in Dahomean politics in the mid-1960s. Maga's period as president in 1960–3 was marked not only by discrimination towards the north but by increasing authoritarianism and abuse of powers. In 1961 the opposition paper *Daho-Matin* was banned, the trade unions forced to combine in a single national centre (the UGTD, Union Générale des Travailleurs du Dahomey) and Ahomadegbe and ten others arrested for 'plotting' against Maga. With the formation of a united party, the PDU (Parti Dahoméen d'Unité), from the coalition partners (PRD and UDD) *de facto* single-party rule was introduced (Thompson, 1964, pp. 231–4). Maga's attempt to minimize Apithy's role in government and in the PDU only weakened the coalition, and his government was increasingly seen as corrupt and wasteful, symbolized by the construction of a flamboyant presidential palace at vast cost while cutting public-sector pay.

In October 1963 a general strike was called by the UGTD against continued austerity policies in the public sector, following a week of demonstrations against Maga in Porto Novo. Under pressure from civilian leaders the army commander, Colonel Christopher Soglo, suspended the constitution and thus ended the Maga government. A month later, another 'plot' was announced, this time against Soglo. Two former ministers were detained and Maga placed under home arrest, effectively excluding northern politicians from the new regime. Apithy and Ahomadegbe promptly announced the creation of a new united party which alone contested the 1964 elections, described by Ronen (1975, p. 196) as a 'mockery of democratic processes'. Rioting against southerners broke out in the northern town of Parakou in March, and several more northern political leaders were jailed.

In the new regime stemming from the 1964 elections Apithy became president, sharing power with Ahomadegbe who became vice-president and head of government. Conflict was inevitable and against a background of hastening economic decline the two leaders manoeuvred to achieve pre-eminence. As the two mobilized factional support within the administration, the functioning of government was itself impeded. One of the few measures that was taken proved ultimately fatal: a 25 per cent salary cut for the public sector, designed to reduce the large and growing budget deficit but which only antagonized the unions and reduced the regime's popular support still further. As competition between the president and vice-president increased, Ahomadegbe first manipulated the PDU executive into calling for Apithy's resignation as president,and then tried to evict Apithy from the presidential palace built by Maga. To do this he used troops under the command of Lieutenant-Colonel Aho and himself put on uniform—to the disgust of the armed forces commander, Colonel Soglo (Glélé, 1969, pp. 289-95). Soglo, supported by his senior officers, then dismissed Apithy and Ahomadegbe from government and installed the president of the National Assembly, Tahirou Congacou, in their place. At this stage the military had no intention of taking power. The refusal of the three civilian leaders to cooperate in attempts to create a new constitution and new regime, together with similar popular pressures as in 1963, finally induced them to do so just before Christmas 1965.

1965-72

The taking of power by the army failed to resolve the inherent crisis of clientelist politics. Instead, Soglo's regime and its several successors only reproduced and intensified the features of earlier regimes. Political life became even more a contest for control of state resources between the three regional factions, in which the temporary winner(s) sought to monopolize the spoils, a system we may call 'spoils politics'. The officer corps and with it the army as a whole were drawn into spoils politics, divided into factions based on religion, rank and ideology, and politicized. These processes underlie the 1972 coup in which junior officers overthrew not only a civilian government but also most of the senior officers involved in coups and governments of the preceding seven years.

At first Soglo attempted to rectify some of the abuses of the earlier period, appointing a government drawn from administrators and other technocrats, and attempting to reduce overspending through yet another austerity package including a 25 per cent 'solidarity tax' levied from September 1966. The tax proved very unpopular with the unions, and as urban and southern pressures on the regime increased Soglo was driven to rely even more on 'politicians', several of whom joined the government in 1967, though Maga and his two rivals remained in self-exile in Paris. Within the officer corps a

Table 2.1 Coups and governments in Dahomey, 1965–72

Nov. 1965	Col. Soglo overthrows Maga/Apithy government; Congacou becomes acting head of government
Dec. 1965	Gen. Soglo removes Congacou and becomes president
Dec. 1967	Maj. Kouandété overthrows Soglo; Col. Alley becomes president
July 1968	Power transferred to Emile Zinsou
Dec. 1969	Lt.-Col. Kouandété overthrows Zinsou; military triumvirate installed
May 1970	Maga becomes president after elections annulled
May 1972	Ahomadegbe becomes president, in rotation
Oct. 1972.	Major Kérékou overthrows Ahomadegbe

clique of southern officers grew up around Lieutenant-Colonel Aho (Minister of Internal Affairs, and Defence), a member of the senior Abomey ruling family; it included Majors Adandejan, Hachémé and Sinzogan. In response a second clique collected around Major Maurice Kouandété, uniting the small group of northern officers (a fifth of the officer corps), but with the support of many junior officers from all regions.

The officer corps, as with other West African armies,[6] was divided not simply by region or personal ambition, important though these proved. The more senior ranks were increasingly prone to corruption (see for example Lemarchand, 1968, p. 52) which itself promoted rivalries. They were also divided from the more junior officers by their lesser education (the most senior were indeed former NCOs), by lower social status and by their creation of promotion blockages for the juniors. The latter tended also to be more conscious of the army as a professional and corporate body with its own integrity, which they saw as threatened by involvement in government and spoils politics. Their political beliefs were in turn more radical, stemming in part from their closer contact with Dahomey's student radicals and intellectuals.[7] In an attempt to exert some control over Soglo as his regime became visibly more corrupt and incompetent the junior officers pressed for a Comité Militaire de Vigilance (CMV) to be established, drawn mainly from the junior ranks and NCOs. The CMV, however, became itself little more than a vehicle for personal gain and the political ambitions of the southern clique; nine of its fifteen members, and all of the most senior among them, were Fon.

Later in 1967 the unions again pressed for an end to austerity measures. Soglo vacillated, eventually compromising in the face of a threatened general strike, and removing a recently imposed ban on union activity. Two days later Major Kouandété seized power, backed by several junior officers including the then Captain Mathieu Kérékou. There followed a prolonged struggle for control between Kouandété and Lieutenant-Colonel Alley, Soglo's chief of staff. Alley, though a northerner, had the confidence of the southern 'Abomey' clique and acted briefly as head of state. His provisional government was largely of northern origin, however, and Kouandété slowly gained the advantage, aided by the dismissal of several southern officers for corruption, including Majors Hachémé and Chasmé (Lemarchand, 1968, p. 53). Neither the junior officers nor civilian leaders wanted another military government, however, and after an attempt to hold elections from which the three regional leaders were debarred—which simply resulted in 72 per cent of the electorate joining a boycott—the army appointed a conservative politician from the 1940s, Emile Zinsou, as president.

Zinsou lasted one year and a half. Like Soglo he attempted to reduce public spending, thus antagonizing not only the unions but also the southern elite and merchants. And like Soglo again, his regime was undermined by internal conflict within the army, arising from Kouandété's downgrading of Alley and pursuits of northern interests. Alley, given six months' 'leave of absence' in 1968, was offered the post of military attaché in Washington and then dismissed when he refused it. Two months later an attempt was made to kidnap Kouandété, and Alley and many fellow officers were arrested and tried. Alley was sentenced to ten years' imprisonment; both Decalo and Ronen argue that Kouandété had wanted a death sentence but had been prevented by Zinsou's insistence on the use of a civil court. Zinsou thus lost Kouandété's support. Earlier in 1969 he had lost that of the unions, students and the urban middle class. Attempts by Zinsou to palliate the impact of austerity measures seem only to have antagonized Kouandété further, and in December 1969 he overthrew Zinsou.

In so doing Kouandété acted without consulting his fellow officers whose support he needed. They refused to allow him to become head of state appointing instead a military directorate of three—Lieutenant-Colonels de Souza, Sinzogan and Kouandété. This directorate called an election, inviting the exiled leaders to participate, a course Kouandété had successfully opposed in 1968. The elections were held over three weeks and contested region by region; they were marked by 'intimidation, mass bribery and illegal distribution (and non-distribution) of electoral cards' (Decalo, 1970, p. 454) and by open involvement by rival factions of officers. The results reflected the regional pattern of clientelist politics. Zinsou, who lacked a mass base, received 3 per cent of the vote, while the others carried their regions with ease (see Table 2.2).

The last region due to vote was Atacora where Maga would inevitably have received a huge majority, enough to make him president. There had, however, been violent clashes in Atacora as Ahomadegbe's party attempted to capitalize on the erosion of clientelist spending at the base of the system which in some areas had alienated local support for Maga.[8] De Souza cancelled the Atacora election, and while Apithy and Ahomadegbe attempted to create a southern–based coalition government, northern leaders threatened secession and resident southerners were attacked in northern towns. Regional conflict had reached a new level of intensity, with civil war a possibility. A resolution was reached; but one that formalized spoils politics. The three rivals made up a presidential council; each in turn was to be head of state for two years, starting with Maga. Ahomadegbe promptly aligned his supporters with Maga, austerity politics were abandoned (assisted by increased aid and receipts from smuggling to Nigeria) and the distribution of offices and spoils began (Ronen, 1975, pp. 220–2). The senior officers were themselves rewarded by the creation of new posts, even for those dismissed in 1968.

Political and military life became increasingly violent. In May 1971 an attempt was made to ambush Ahomadegbe and other southern politicians on their way to a rally in Abomey. Several mutinies occurred, including two at the Ouidah artillery base (March 1971 and January 1972) and in February 1972 a complicated coup attempt (in which de Souza was to have been killed) did not succeed. Kouandété and more than twenty others were tried for this: ten were jailed and six condemned to death, including Kouandété. All of these events were seen by politicians as part of military manoeuvres against

Table 2.2 1970 elections in Dahomey, regional votes (%)

Region	Ahomadegbe	Apithy	Maga	Zinsou
Ouémé	8	82	5	3
Atlantique	51	35	6	5
Mono	43	27	8	6
Zou	73	19	5	3
Borgou	2	–	97	–
Atacora	Election cancelled			

them (see for example Decalo, 1973; p. 475; *ACR* , 1972-3, B578-80). Despite this, and continued conflict with students and teachers, Ahomadegbe peacefully succeeded Maga as chairman of the presidential council in May 1972, only to be faced by an alliance of Maga and Apithy which prevented even an effective change in ministerial appointments. In October his impotent regime was overthrown by junior officers including several involved in the Ouidah mutinies and led by Major Kérékou (who had been involved in the 1967 coup). This time however the junior officers did not surrender power to their seniors; instead they removed them from command positions and established their own regime. This regime, in various guises, has ruled ever since.

1972-5: Taking and Keeping Power

The 1972 coup had contradictory features. Like the earlier interventions it was a response to the instability of regimes based on the politics of clientelism and spoils; and it reflected the personal and corporate ambitions of a faction of officers hitherto excluded from significant political and military power. At the same time it also reflected the junior officers' distaste for what had happened to their army and their seniors as both became caught up in spoils politics. Like many other coups of the 1970s and early 1980s, this coup can therefore be seen as an attempt at rectification. Similarly, civilian attitudes towards the political system had changed (Decalo, 1979, p. 236). The continual excesses of both civilian and military government, the endless failure to deal with economic problems,[9] the erosion of participation and the democratic process and the breakdown in clientelist distribution had combined to produce an alienation from the existing political system, most marked among the opposition groupings of the 1960s (union, students, intellectuals) but also present among rural communities.[10] These groups were to press for reforms in the system and in policy which helped to bring about Dahomey's radicalization and a decisive break with the old system symbolized in its change of name to Benin in November 1975.

The first three years of the new regime were years of struggle over the controls of the state and the direction of policy between (and within) three rival groupings: factions in the officers corps, the residues of the old political system including former rulers and the civilian supporters of political and policy reform. By the end of 1975 Kérékou had established himself as the dominant military figure, had routed the former politicians and undermined the political system that supported them and had neutralized and come to

terms with his civilian 'left'. In the process the policy stance had shifted from
a mildly radical nationalism to the espousal of a socialism strongly flavoured
with nationalism. In November 1974 an official announcement was made of
Dahomey's adoption of socialism. It was followed by a year of political crisis
and attempts to overthrow Kérékou in which all three categories of claimants
to power were involved. Kérékou's ability to confront and defeat these
challenges was the more remarkable in that previous regimes had all
collapsed in such circumstances. Apart from the nature of the opposition to
Kérékou, the explanation for his survival lies largely in the policy initiatives
of his regime, in its association with themes of 'revolution' and 'renewal' and
in the creation of new political institutions especially at local level. Thus,
while in 1977 opposition reappears briefly in the form of a mercenary
invasion, the main themes of the second half of the seventies are those of
building the state and building 'socialism'.

Opposition to Kérékou in the military came from those officers directly
involved in the coup and from the senior officers associated with past regimes
and against whose abuses the coup was in part directed. The coup was
instigated not by Kérékou but by more junior officers, notably Captains
Aikpé, Assogba and Badjogoume and Major Michel Alladaye. Kérékou,
whose ties were as much with senior officers as with juniors and who was
Kouandété's cousin, was invited to join the conspirators only shortly before
the actual coup. The coupmakers were all present in the initial government
which consisted largely of captains with a leavening of three gendarmerie
majors. All the members were under forty years old and only four had any
experience of government (under Kouandété). Broader representation, again
leaning towards the lower ranks and NCOs, occurred in the fifteen-man
Comité Militaire Révolutionnaire and in the advisory Conseil National de la
Révolution of sixty-seven members established in September 1973.

The senior officers were in a weaker position. Several of the key figures of
the 1960s, like Soglo and Aho had retired by 1972. Most of the remainder—
three colonels and four majors—were immediately put out to grass as heads of
parastatals, notably De Souza, Alley and Sinzogan (*WA*, 1972, p. 1576);
Kérékou took over from De Souza as chief of staff. This attempt to
marginalize the older officers was not however entirely successful: early in
1973 Alley and Hachémé were implicated in the first of the plots to
overthrow Kérékou, along with one of Maga's key supporters, the wholly
corrupt Pascal Chabi Kao.[11]

This was the sole attempt by the senior officers to regain any influence.
Within the government however there were major differences in ideology—
between the wealthy and conservative Major Barthélemy Ohouens and more

radical officers—and conflicts over authority between Kérékou and the coupmakers. Kérékou increased his own power by a series of administrative changes that strengthened the powers of the presidency and gradually downgraded or removed the coupmakers and their supporters in government. Early in 1973 Captains Beheton and Badjogoume were dropped,[12] while late in 1974 Captain Assogba was demoted from Finance to Labour. Into government came Kérékou's supporters, notably Lieutenant Martin Azonhiho, destined for rapid advancement.[13] In 1975 Assogba and Aikpé were to try to reverse this decline in influence and take power; both failed.

Dealing with the old political system proved easier. The former heads of state and ministers were placed under arrest at the time of the coup, except for Zinsou who was in France. Gradually the ministers were released, usually once they had returned some of their corrupt gains; thus Arouna Mama, former Minister of the Interior and a Maga supporter, 'repaid' CFA fr. 6.6 million, about £100,000 (see *WA*, 1974, pp. 107, 417). The politicians' clientelist networks had already been partially detached from them and had begun to disintegrate, due to the ravages of spoils politics and neglect of the networks. The new regime moved quickly against the local representatives of the networks—chiefs, priests of local animist cults (*fêticheurs*; see also Chapter 3), and other rural notables—denouncing their past role and reducing their power. At the same time it attempted to create rival holders of power attached to the new regime, through reforms in local government and by promoting the political activity of subordinate groups like youth and women. Subsequent attempts by exiled politicians to regain power, if indeed that is what happened in 1975 and 1977, were ineffective; if anything, they increased the regime's support and legitimacy.

The most difficult opposition to confront came from the regime's civilian supporters. It arose from the implications of the general desire for a restoration of political participation and a reduction in austerity and rural exploitation. While widespread, these desires were expressed particularly by three groupings notable for their opposition to previous regimes: organized labour (and especially union leaders in the public sector), students and Dahomey's left, which overlapped considerably with student groups like the League of Patriotic Youth (the *Ligeurs*) and the northern-based FACEEN.[14] These groups wanted more than the adoption of particular policies by the new government: they wanted a different, civilian, popularly based regime.

The general desire for reform could be satisfied by the regime introducing new policies and institutions, discussed below, and by the relaxation of past austerity measures. Thus salary increases arising from promotion but frozen after 1966 were now partially paid and wage levels generally increased. The union leaders, tied as many of them had been to Ahomadegbe and Lieutenant-Colonel Alley, were more cautious in their support, as were student organizations. There were some 300 of the latter, the majority small with a local or ethnic basis. The largest of the nationally based unions, UGEED (Union Générale des Etudiants et des Elèves du Dahomey), active in Paris as well as at home, had been banned by the Maga government. The ban was lifted by the new military government in January 1973, and the union's leadership like that of other radical student unions became involved in attempts to radicalize government such as the anti-French demonstrations of February 1973 which followed the abortive coup attempt of Alley and Hachémé. These demonstrations (which developed into rioting and attacks on foreigners) were organized by the student-dominated FUD (Front Unique Démocratique), which called significantly for a 'mass party to unite progressive military officers, trade unionists, workers and left-wing intellectuals' and for the democratization and civilianization of the regime. Kérékou dismissed the call brusquely (*ACR*, 1973-4, B632), but left the student organizations and the FUD alone until January 1974 when students struck over conditions and over what they saw as the regime's conservatism.[15] Of the student organizations, 180 were dissolved and some students were drafted into the army increasing the intensity of protest. Kérékou later denounced students as 'anarchists playing the game of anti-revolutionaries . . . polluting the national atmosphere' (*WA*, 1974, p. 651). UGEED was banned and plans made to impose a single, official student union (a process that took several years, in practice).

While Kérékou was determined not to allow the left, such as it was, to replace or control his government, his own rhetoric and actions were by no means 'conservative'. At their core was a militant nationalism reflecting a common belief among Dahomey's urban population, and especially the left, that previous governments were too closely aligned to France and to French interests—diplomatic, cultural and commercial. Kérékou's first major speech, in November 1972, announced a programme of 'national independence' with policies representing national—and mass—interests and the ending of foreign influence in education and culture (GMR, 1972). While the speech also implied action over the economy little specific was promised, and Kérékou was careful to conciliate local French businessmen after the February 1973 riots. Not until two years later was there any official mention of socialism or moves to nationalize foreign businesses. What radical moves there were tended to be modest in scope, like the opening of diplomatic relations with China, North Korea and Libya, or merely empty gestures.

Yet the government was not inactive.[16] A major reform in the educational system was discussed and begun, designed to erode its urban, metropolitan and elitist biases (see Chapter 5). In the political sphere, in parallel with changes that strengthened the presidency, attempts were made to create representative institutions, especially at the local level. The CNR, representing as it did all ranks and factions in the army and the urban activists, quickly became an arena for ideological and factional conflict. To contain this, its membership was changed and its policy-formulating functions transferred to a small political bureau drawn from the CNR but largely made up of Kérékou's supporters. A year before these events, in 1973, a national seminar of administrators had drawn up plans for the reorganization of regional and local governments, plans swiftly implemented in early 1974. The old boundaries of administrative units were retained, but directly elected local revolutionary committees were to be created at village, town and commune level, replacing but not wholly eliminating the appointed chiefs. Above these were to be district and provincial councils, their membership largely appointed. By the end of 1974 1,500 local committees were claimed to exist. In addition to these largely rural revolutionary committees, two urban participatory institutions were initiated in 1974: Committees for the Defence of the Revolution (CDRs) at places of work or residence (*ARB*, 1975, p. 3475), and workplace *comités de gestion*. As Leymarie (1977, p. 56) points out, these measures amounted to an attempt to revive representation and to ensure that it would no longer be by wealthy or educated notables, but by ordinary citizens—not that this attempt was always successful (Godin, 1986, p. 168–9).

The last event of 1974 was Kérékou's dramatic announcement in November that Dahomey was to adopt Marxism–Leninism as its ideology and create a socialist state and society (see summary in Ronen, 1979, pp. 135–6). The speech was in part a reiteration of the theme of his 1972 speech, for much of the text was strongly nationalist. Now however the nationalist goals were seen to require a socialist strategy. Most interpretations of the speech (for example Decalo, 1979; Ronen, 1979; Godin, 1986; Ronen, 1987) see it as attempting to create legitimacy for the new regime and as designed to placate and demobilize pressures from the left for further radicalization. In the year following however it had neither result, for 1975 marked the regime's biggest crisis: the death of Captain Michel Aikpé and the eruption of internal and external opposition that followed it.

In part the November 1974 declaration itself created problems. It was followed by nationalizations, at first almost token (private schools and the minuscule oil sector) but later included insurance, major banks and other foreign companies. There was a modest outflow of foreign capital but more important—especially in the light of the need to compensate owners for the assets expropriated—was the threat by France to discontinue aid. France was then, as always, Dahomey's largest donor and trading partner: its grants and loans in the early 1970s were each year worth far more than the value of the assets nationalized (CFA fr. 2 billion, or £3 million). The government had already already reintroduced some austerity measures in September 1974 in response to a budget deficit of over a billion cfa francs, the largest deficit since the coup. In February 1975 the university student maintenance grant was cut by 55 per cent, civil service salaries were frozen and overtime payments ended. The government seemed to be returning to the policies of Soglo, Zinsou and others.

Alienating trade unionists, civil servants, students and even many teachers (through the education reform) worsened the effects of military factionalism. In January Captain Assogba, a coupmaker but not a radical, attempted to overthrow Kérékou, accusing him of corruption (*ACR*, 1974–5, B624). He failed and his attempt provided a pretext for a trial in which he and Zinsou (the latter *in absentia*) were condemned to death; five others including Zinsou's brother and a former minister were jailed for life. Six months later the third of the four coupmakers was eliminated. Captain Michel Aikpé, Minister of the Interior, was shot by the Presidential guard, made up of northern troops loyal to Kérékou. He had been discovered, according to the president, in bed with Kérékou's wife. Few believed this account[17] and for the rest of June there were large demonstrations against Kérékou which were met with harsh repression and resulting in several deaths. The unions, many of the urban revolutionary committees and CDRs, and members of the CNR joined in the protests and accusations of murder, and a general strike was called. It was repressed and many trade unionists arrested. Kérékou withdrew to Cotonou barracks, made his close ally, Azonhiho, Minister of the Interior and another ally, Captain André Atchadé, commander of the key Ouidah garrison. From the barracks he ruled without reference to the CNR which, like the civil service and Aikpé's paracommando corps, was purged of suspected opponents.[18]

The death—or murder—of Aikpé was seen also in regional terms, as yet another southern officer removed by the northern Kérékou. Southern civil servants, already antagonized by an inflow of northerners into the administration, began to resign, as did fifty-three Dahomean diplomatic staff abroad. in July the exiled politicians, civil servants and intellectuals formed a Front for the Liberation and Rehabilitation of Dahomey (FLRD) in Brussels, led by Gratien Pognon, former ambassador to the EEC, and Zinsou. With the discovery of a 'plot' by this group to use mercenaries to overthrow the government yet another change to purge opponents was created (*WA*, 1975, 1288). Those deemed responsible were tried in February 1976, many *in absentia*, and were condemned to death or long terms of imprisonment.

In earlier periods such events had signalled the fall of governments; what, then, allowed Kérékou's not only to survive but also to do so with relative ease? Such a question assumes that the political situation in 1975 was in essence the same as in the crises of 1963–72, and that Kérékou's regime was at this point just another of the many brief regimes since independence (as Decalo, 1976 seems to imply; see especially pages 80–5). In two important ways, however, this assumption is false: the opposition was weaker and the regime both stronger and different in character. None of the likely contenders for power could take and keep hold of it. Thus Kérékou's military rivals were dead, detained or marginalized, and he had built up a considerable following of his own. The option of a restoration of one of the former rulers was also precluded for not only were they highly unpopular and in exile or detention, but their local supporters had been specific targets of campaigns to render them powerless. The left, while more in tune with popular sentiments, had little mass support as its easy defeat in 1973 had indicated— and its leaders had the attractive alternative of cooptation by the regime, a path followed by virtually all the student radicals.

The government by contrast had strengthened its position since 1972 in two ways. It had created a degree of popular consent to its rule not enjoyed by its recent predecessors through the impact of policies and of increased participation; and it had begun reforms of the political system, reforms which elsewhere had been associated with increased stability. Thus while some teachers disliked the implications of the changes in education, for villagers they promised education or schools where there had been none previously, just as the medical reforms also discussed in Chapter 5 promised better medical care. To a limited degree both promises appeared to be being met in the mid-1970s; it was later that the faults in both reforms began to be exposed. A similar pattern arose with participatory structures: for all their weaknesses the new institutions did provide some degree of participation, and were welcomed for that (see Chapter 3).

Both participation and lessening of exploitation were combined in a further policy measure: rural literacy campaigns.[19] These did not cover more than a limited area, and were mostly found in the north and especially Borgou. In several cases they were more associated with voluntary associations (like the student organization FACEEN) and funded externally, rather than being official campaigns. Their impact, however, was felt crucially in 1973–6, and the government shared in the credit. For the peasants involved literacy had economic benefits, giving them greater control over the incomes from their crops and hence closely associated with the development of *groupements villageoises* (discussed in Chapter 4), and allowing them to finance schools and other local services (see for example Auroi, 1977–8, pp. 111–18). Politically it encouraged participation in local institutions and strengthened peasant capacity to resist administrative pressure and run their own affairs. Auroi (1977–8, p. 103) quotes one letter to the monthly magazine for newly literates: 'It is thanks to the literacy class (*l'école en boko*) that we have been able to set up cooperatives and have peasants leading the *groupements villageoises*.' Benini, writing on the same campaign, comments that peasants hoped literacy would empower them, and allow them 'to get rid of the *intellectuels*, the agents of the state commanding French as a source of power that they were unable to control' (Benini, 1980, p. 289). The letters quoted by Auroi also make it clear that the new government got a least some of the praise for the programmes—ironically, since that same government was to close down most of them, 'their place being taken by more institutionalised and more authoritarian methods of adult literacy, ie. schools' (Giesecke & Elwert, 1983: p. 267).

Since much of the next chapter, and of Chapter 6, concerns the institutional reforms that began in 1973 and helped transform the political system into a centralized and stable bureaucracy, it is not necessary to go into details here. Their influence on the government's capacity to survive the 1975 crisis cannot have been determinant, since most of the reforms occurred after Aikpé's death; but it is reasonable to argue that what had already been accomplished by 1975 contributed to the stability of Kérékou's regime even then.

1976–9: Building the State and Building 'Socialism'

One regular commentary on Dahomey/Benin refers to 1976 as 'an unusually quiet year' (*ACR*, 1976–7, B549). Compared to 1975 so it was, but the absence of coup attempts, strikes and the like conceals key events in the institutional sphere. In November 1975 Dahomey became Benin and the creation of the long-awaited official political party was announced, with the CNR's political bureau becoming its interim central committee. Also announced was an operation to 'cleanse' the Committees for the Defence of the Revolution from which much of the new party's membership was to be recruited, and which had revealed too much independence of action and critical sentiment during 1975. In May 1976 the new party (PRPB, People's Revolutionary Party of

Benin) held an extraordinary congress and elected a twenty-seven-person central committee. This had a clear civilian majority, albeit like the Political Bureau mainly of Kérékou supporters, and was the first key institution since the coup not to be dominated by army members.

Less public changes designed both to strengthen Kérékou's position and even more to centralize power and authority in the presidency included the expansion and elaboration of the security apparatus (divided among several junior officers all responsible to the president and Azonhiho), a reorganization of ministry boundaries and a reorganization of the military and para-military forces. In the last three commands were created, two covering the largely civilian militia and the public security force. The third and largest covered the army, gendarmerie, national police, customs and some minor forces. These processes of institution-building and centralization were to continue for the rest of the decade, amounting to the beginnings of the creation of a modern state.

There was to be one final act in the surge of opposition that followed the coup. The last occasion on which Kérékou's rule was seriously threatened, it consisted of a tragicomic mercenary invasion of Cotonou. Led by a French secret service officer then working for the Government of Gabon, Gilbert Bourgeaud (alias Bob Denard), a mixed group of Europeans, African mercenaries and a few Dahomeans numbering about 100 in all arrived by air on the morning of Sunday 16 January 1977. Despite the lack of military opposition the group confined itself to machine-gunning a few buildings between the airport and the centre of Cotonou, and withdrew after three hours leaving behind arms, bottles and documents. Eight people were killed including two mercenaries, and one mercenary, a Senegalese, was captured.[20] The motives for the raid and the reason for its extraordinary casualness and inconclusive outcome remain unclear. A subsequent United Nations' inquiry indicated that both Gabon and Morocco were involved in the attempt, and argues that Zinsou was its main initiator. More significant were its effects, felt both in domestic and in foreign affairs (see Chapter 5).

Outside Benin, and especially outside Africa, few took the invasion seriously. Inside Benin however neither the townspeople nor the government doubted its reality or its importance. Nationalist anger was fuelled by radio broadcasts, and justified restrictions on foreigners. It also increased the government's popularity and even its legitimacy, while ending for ever the prospects of a return to power of the former leaders. Within the government it encouraged three interlocking responses. The simplest was a defensive and repressive reaction to external threat symbolized best by an absurd trial of those deemed responsible, at which virtually all the accused were absent.

Name	1975 Jan	1976	1977	1978	1979	1980 Feb	1981	1982 April	1982 Dec	1984 Aug	1985 June	1987 Feb
Mathieu KÉRÉKOU	D											
Martin AZONHIHO	INF	I/INF				INF						RD
Barthelémy OHOUENS	J	IND				*						
Michel ALLADAYE	FA							*	INT	E2		
Isidore AMOUSSOU	F					J		*	*			
Feweis KOUYAMI	L/CS	Y										
Djibril MORIBA	RD	J										
Issifou BOURAIMA	H											
Vincent GUEZODJE	E	E1				INT			*	H	E	
André ATCHADE	IND/T	T										
Leopold AHOUEYA	PW/TPT	TPT								L	H	*
Michel AIKPÉ	I											
Adolphe BIAOU	Y/C	L/CS				L		*	*	RD	RD	
Richard RODRIGUEZ		PW										
François DOSSOU		P				TPT						
Philippe AKPO		RD										
Soule DANKORO						T		H	*	E1	*	*
Gregoire AGBAHE						TOUR		*	*	T	*	PW
Gado GUIRIGUISSOU						PW		*	*	*	*	T
Moussa ALI TRAORE						E1		*	*	Y	*	
Edouard ZODEHOUGAN						E2		*	*	INT	*	*
Armand MONTEIRO						E3		*	*			
Paul KPOFFON						H						

PORTFOLIOS:

C   Culture
CS   Civil Service
E   Education
E1   Basic Education
E2   Secondary Education
E3   Higher Education
F   Finance
FA   Foreign Affairs
H   Health
I   Internal Affairs
Ind   Industry
INF   Information
J   Justice
L   Labour
LIT   Literacy
P   Planning
PW   Public Works
RD   Rural Development
SC   State Corporations
SF   State Farms
T   Trade
TOUR   Tourism
TPT   Transport
Y   Youth
*   Portfolio continued

Sanni Mama GOLMINA	T		
Simon OGOUMA	FA		
Gratien Tonakpon CAPO CHICHI	C/LIT	*	
Francois Codjo AZODOGBEHOU	RD		
Aboubacar BAEA MOUSA	P		
Roger GARBA	SF		
Manasse AYAYI	SC	T	
Tiamiou ADJIBADE	FA	FA	*
Alidou BA BOUKARY	SF	SF	*
Justin GNINDEHOU	Y	Y	RD
Kifouli SALAMI	P	P	* ... * ... *
Alidou KOUSSEY	SC	SC	
Gédéon DASSOUNDO	RD	RD	
Amidou BABA MOUSSA	INF	INF	*
David GBAGUIDI	Y		
Paul AWHANGOU	SC		
Taofiqui BOURAIMA	TPT		
Ali HOUDOU	INF	INF	*
Frederick AFFO	FA	FA	
Didier DASSI	J/SC	J/SC	
Hospice ANTONIO	F	F	
Ousmane BATOKO	Y	Y	
Nathaniel MENSAH	L	L	*
Barnabe BIDOUZO	F		
Guy Landry HAZOUME	FA		
Saliou ABOUDOU	J/SC		
Ibrahim SOURADJOU	P		

Figure 2.1 National Executive Council: Composition 1975-87

Ex-President Zinsou and many others were, yet again, sentenced to death. The army was expanded from 1,650 to 2,100, and the three separate commands within the People's Armed Forces were unified, with Kérékou becoming chief of the general staff as well as taking charge of the militia. Less benignly, complaints of torture of detainees began (*WA*, 1977, p. 532).

Benin also retreated into partial international isolation, relying more on its links with Libya and other 'radical' African states such as Algeria, and distancing itself from Gabon, the Ivory Coast, Togo and several other African states seen as involved in the invasion or more generally with the exile opposition (for whom Togo was a convenient base). Since President Bongo of Gabon was then the OAU chairman, Benin's relations with the OAU worsened while France withdrew its ambassador in January 1978 after a curious interlude of four months in which Benin, having asked for his withdrawal, simply treated him as absent. French aid—not at this stage particularly generous—was reduced, although by 1979 a new ambassador had arrived and a modest flow of loans resumed.

The final effect on the regime was internal. The invasion seemed to confirm the analysis offered by the left within the party leadership, and especially by the *Ligeurs*, that Benin's socialist strategy was valid and under threat from imperialism as well as exiled Dahomean politicians and their internal class allies.[21] The most visible consequences were rhetorical but the invasion temporarily strengthened the tendency to rule from the centre and by decree; and it made more powerful the position of Martin Azonhiho, minister of the interior.

The processes of institution-building, and of the gradual displacement of military by civilian authority, continued although at a lessened pace. A new constitution was drafted, formalizing and adding to the reforms and changes since 1972, and then opened to two months of active public debate organized by the new local government system and the PRPB. Subsequently, 115 amendments, none fundamental, were approved and the draft was adopted on the fifth anniversary of Kérékou's November 1972 speech. Implementation was slow. There were few institutional changes in 1978[22] and the elections due under the new constitution were postponed until November 1979. A single national list of candidates was presented in these elections, chosen to represent the different strata and groupings within Beninois society and selected from lists of potential candidates at meetings in villages, towns and at district level after more central vetting, a process not unlike that adopted a little earlier in Mozambique.

As the elections were being prepared a quite different and no less significant participatory exercise was being realized, one that indicated some of the trends of the 1980s. Concerned at the reluctance of many senior administrators and other intellectuals to join the PRPB, and no doubt well aware that many of these had already left Benin following 1975 events, Kérékou called a meeting of some four to five hundred administrators to discuss the issue (*MTM*, 2 Nov. 1979; 21 Dec. 1979). At the meeting 'participants criticised the regime and freely vented their own grievances' (*ACR*, 1979–80, B471), which were in essence that many of the reforms were ineffective and damaging, notably those in education, that some of the campaigns undertaken and especially that against *féticheurs* (see Chapter 3) were harmful and repressive; and that the regime ruled too much from above and failed to listen to others—or at least to the educated elite. These criticisms drew on both radical and liberal critiques of the regime and thus cannot be seen simply as an attack from left or right; and they echoed the more self-interested complaints of students in tertiary education. For the first time since 1975 there had been a student strike, in response to a typically heavy-handed reception given to protests over late payments of grants and lack of teaching staff. Students were also critical of the educational reforms, in part because they were now obliged to teach in the new schools for a year to make up for the lack of qualified teachers (see further in Chapter 5).

A month after this meeting the PRPB held a congress with delegates echoing the administrators' comments and adding their own. Kérékou denounced the 'leftists in our midst'. But at the same time the membership of the Central Committee was virtually doubled (from twenty-five to forty-five) as was that of its Political Bureau (seven to thirteen), creating space for critics to gain access to seats on these hitherto tightly controlled bodies. This expansion also allowed in more civilians, as did the formation of a new government early in 1980, an act which marked a new stage in the political development of Benin.

The 1980s: Responding to Failure

The 1980s have been marked in Benin by a sense of decline and failure, both in the economy and in the changes in structure and policies made in other areas. Thus the main theme of the history of the last seven years has been the response to failure, and particularly the shift towards liberal policies and Western alignments. Much of the discussion of this response is in later chapters; at this stage I shall deal only with the way in which the response was organized, and with changes in government and the political system. In all three areas one can see two phases: 1980–3, in which there is a sense of attempting a positive, internally determined response; and 1984–7, in which reaction is more haphazard, externally determined and pessimistic in tone. The period ends with a debt crisis imminent, the IMF at the gates and strongly influencing policy and Kérékou seemingly losing hold of the stabilizing techniques of 1975–80 and relying more on older and more risky forms of politics.

The 1979 'conference of cadres' referred to above forced the government to take seriously widespread administrative and popular discontent with the impact of 'socialist' reform. Over the next three years a process of self-examination and internal debate took place covering education, the parastatals and administration generally, rural development and the new political institutions, particularly those at the base. Most of this examination was carried out by administrators and members of government, or by assembly committees. Thus it was the six political commissioners who reported on the functioning and economic activity of parastatals late in 1980, and a committee of the assembly that discussed the working of the constitution in 1983. There was also, however, some broader debate. The state newspaper *Ehuzu* began to carry more critical material in 1982 and the failings of the new educational system were opened to general discussion in 1981, after a year of internal debate in government and the ministries.

These reports and debates showed that many of the seventies' reforms had been at the least ineffective, and that those responsible for administering them were all too often incompetent, indolent and corrupt (see for example *WA*, 1980, 1817–18, 2201; *WA*, 1981, 272). There is little evidence that the administrators suffered any greater penalties than vague denunciation by the president and sideways transfer in postings, but there were major changes in education policy, parastatal organization and economic policy. There was also a sense of optimism aided by French, World Bank and other donors' appraisals of Benin. The idea that a reconsideration of policy and structures could reverse economic decline lasted until 1983 when the 1983–7 plan was presented to a donor conference but failed to raise more than a third of requested aid. Thereafter, as accumulated debts, declining production and failure to control imports drove Benin's economy closer to crisis, the sense of optimism was lost. Initiative for change, and thus the content of policy, began to come increasingly from outside and especially from the World Bank and the IMF, with which Benin began negotiations in 1985. From within Benin, by contrast, there are only speeches from Kérékou outlining the perilous state of the economy or berating the merchants for not investing in productive sectors (see for example *WA*, 1985, p. 542; *Courrier*, May–June 1986).

From 1975, after the death of Aikpé, to early 1980 there were no changes in the National Executive Council and a few in the Central Committee, Political Bureau or the Prefectorate. The 1980s, by contrast, have seen two major upheavals, and virtually annual reshuffles reminiscent of 1972-4. These changes are often understood either as a process in which Kérékou replaces older and independent individuals with younger men (never (1) women) who owe their promotion and earlier advancement to him; or as a process in which Kérékou attempts to balance the rival regional and (2) ideological factions in government, and especially the *Ligeurs* (or orthodox left) against the nationalist and conservative groupings.[23] There is some apparent merit in each interpretation. Thus in 1980 seven of the fifteen members of the National Executive Council were dismissed; most had been members since 1974. Twenty-three new appointments were made in 1980 and 1982, almost all men unknown before 1972. Between 1982 and 1985 such veterans as Barthélemy Ohouens, Isidore Amoussou, Michel Alladaye, Issifou Bouraima and François Dossou were replaced by younger men. The 1982 changes can also be seen as weakening the *Ligeurs* since several of their key members were dropped, including Simon Ogouma (Foreign Affairs), Simon Kpoffon (Health), François Codjo Azodogbehou (Rural Development) and Sanni Mama Gomina (Commerce). Two years later it was apparently the turn of the right.

Such interpretations are however too narrow. They fail to consider the long-term pattern of change, and they concentrate too much on the council. The shake-up of 1984, in which only Kérékou and Kifouli Salami (planning) kept their posts, not only saw the demise of Ohouens and Amoussou but also of many of the new younger men introduced in 1980 or 1982. Indeed of the twenty-three 'new men' only four survived into 1985 (and one of those was dismissed later that year). Similarly Martin Azonhiho, downgraded in 1980 and dismissed in 1982, reappeared in 1987 in much the same way as Philippe Aho (dismissed 1980, reappointed 1982) and André Atchadé (dismissed 1980, reappointed 1984). Furthermore, while some of those dismissed were put out to grass in comfortable sinecures, many simply shifted to other powerful locations. In addition to the ministerial members of the council there are six prefects, reporting directly to the president and who are ex-officio members of the council; Azonhiho became one when he ceased to be Minister of Information, as did Azodogbehou in 1982. The Central Committee of the party has become too large (forty-five member membership in itself to be significant but its Political Bureau is small and powerful. In 1985, after several of its members had been removed at the PRPB congress, it included Simon Ogouma and Sanni Mama Gomina (dropped from the Council in 1984) and Azonhiho.

The pattern of shifts is thus more complex than consideration of each set of changes in council membership in isolation would suggest. The factions are more stable in their influence and less vulnerable to entry and exit at the whim of Kérékou; instead Kérékou balances and mediates between factional pressures and uses transfers between powerful posts of differing status as a means of control as much as he uses dismissal. Equally, there are policy-related reasons for many of the changes. The wholesale shifts and dismissals of 1980 and 1984 marked the new direction of policy away from that set in 1974 and the realization that the 'reconsideration' of 1980-2 had been ineffective. More specifically one can see in the frequent changes in personnel at rural development (five ministers in 1980-7) and state corporations (four ministers) a frustrated response to the intractibility of the economic problems for which those ministries take responsibility. Similarly, in the wake of student problems in 1985 Michel Alladaye lost his post as education minister, and Ali Moussa Traore was dropped from the ministry of youth, culture and sport. This last pattern, of dismissal for failure, has become more common since 1983 and can perhaps be seen as a symptom of a loss of a sense of capacity by government.

Although the political system was also the subject of enquiries, such as those by the party into its own functioning and by the assembly into the first three years of the new constitution, the extent of significant formal change is far less marked than in the policy fields. Some minor changes in this period can be seen as part of earlier processes—like the continuing accretion of power by the presidency including the transfer to it of oil revenues in 1984—or as implementation of earlier discussions. Thus the creation of people's courts with a largely lay judiciary in 1981 was a constitutional requirement. Other changes were attempts to respond to criticism. The Central Committee's enquiry revealed that political life at the base of the party and especially in the party auxiliaries and the CDRs was moribund (*ACR*, 1981, B90). The measures agreed, internal party and auxiliary elections to be held in late 1981, seem to have had no effect at all, as is shown by the auxiliaries' passive reaction to the 1985 protests, discussed below. Similarly although a fairly full report on the workings of the constitution, based in part on popular consultation, was produced for the assembly, the debate on it resulted only in decisions to extend the life of the assembly to 1985 and to reduce its size from 336 to 196 deputies (or commissioners). While this did imply that many deputies would inevitably lose their seats at dissolution it had little other significance. The elections, held in June 1984, followed a pattern similar to 1979, with local meetings choosing members of an electoral college which in turn selected candidates as representatives of twenty-two different social or political categories. There were changes in the categories, with more representation of peasants and party officials, and certain new categories added (teachers, magistrates and pensioners), plus direct representation of the women's and youth organizations. Since, however, the assembly now functions neither as a source of initiative nor as a means of representation, these changes also have limited importance.

Economic decline seems to have resulted more in a slow distancing of the population from the regime than in active protest. Since the institutions through which such protest would normally be articulated have been suppressed by or incorporated within the government this is scarcely remarkable. In one group for which there is a degree of autonomous organization—students—there has been protest, casting light on the regime's attitude to dissent. In the aftermath of the 1979 protests several dozen students were detained. At the same time an inquiry was set up by the Political Bureau which concluded that many of the students' complaints were justified. Grants were increased by 22 per cent and better transport provided. This conciliatory approach tended to characterize the early 1980s.[24] Although some students remained in detention, trade unionists associated with unofficial workers' organizations and those who were arrested in November 1980 were released early in 1981. The three former heads of state under house arrest were released in April 1981 and the majority of political prisoners were given amnesty in August 1984. The amnesty included about thirty trade unionists detained in mid-1983 for membership of an unofficial union (the Centrale Syndicale des Travailleurs du Bénin) and the students. Also released were many figures from the past, such as Lieutenant-Colonel Alley, Captain Janvier Assogba, Major Hachémé and others involved in the 1973 and 1975 coup attempts, but not those jailed after the 1977 invasion.

The amnesties mark a high point in the gradual loosening of the repressive measures associated with the late 1970s and Azonhiho's tenure of the ministry of the interior. Since then both overt protests and detentions have resumed, particularly of students and those suspected of membership of the tiny Parti Communiste du Dahomey which has some backing among younger intellectuals and trade unionists but functions mainly abroad. A few students were again detained soon after their release in 1984, but far more after student action in May 1985. Following student criticism of their official union as unrepresentative, the university authorities agreed to allow elections for a new independent union (or cooperative), seemingly with the connivance if not the official blessing of the Minister of Education, Alladaye. The election, however, resulted in a minor political crisis, as much due to the government's inept response as the election itself. Five former detainees were among the eleven students elected, and the period of the election also saw student demands for greater freedom of expression and a less authoritarian regime. Equally important, perhaps even more important in mobilizing discontent, was student anger at the ending in April of the virtual guarantee that all graduates would get public-sector jobs, a change affecting even those with scarce professional skills, like doctors.

Kérékou treated the events as a student revolt. He ordered the new cooperative to be dissolved, and transferred administration of the university to the ministry of the interior; later four senior university officials including Jean Didier Alavo, a member of the Political Bureau, were dismissed. As students struck in response, and as the action spread to schools, there were clashes with police and Kérékou ordered toops to 'shoot on sight' striking students; there were two deaths. On 6 May the university and schools were closed, reopening on 10 June, when classes resumed peacefully. In all about a hundred students were arrested, and eighteen were permanently banned from campuses as the political bureau took stock (*Amnesty International Report*, 1986, p. 24). The ripples from the events spread widely. Apart from the arrests and dismissals of officials, two ministers closely involved were deemed responsible and dropped: Michel Alladaye (education) and Ali Moussa Traore (youth). They were in turn removed from the Political Bureau at the PRPB second congress held later in the year.[25]

While about fifty of the students arrested were released in September 1986, twenty-two were still detained and there were further demonstrations in 1987 and 1989, over conditions and the lack of jobs. These, as before, were met by repression. Rumours of discontent in the army became more common, as did unconfirmed reports of arrests for 'plotting coups' (see for example *Africa Now*, April 1986). Kérékou, however, had enough confidence to retire from the army in January 1987, and to concentrate on the economic crisis. The cabinet changes of February 1987 reflect this concentration. Three economic ministers left the government: Kifouli Salami (planning 1982-7), Hospice Antonio (a university economist, and Minister of Finance from 1984) and the veteran Adolphe Biaou, a minister since 1975 and who had been allocated the risky portfolio of Rural Development. Azonhiho returned from the Prefectorate to take the Rural Development post, Finance was filled by the experienced banker Barnabé Bidouzo, and Ibrahim Souradjou (another technocrat) took Planning. Two other ministers were dismissed. Frédéric Affo, a former ambassador to Cuba who had become Minister of Foreign Affairs in 1984, was replaced by the ambassador to the United States, Guy Hazoumé; and Didier Dassi (Justice) stood down for the ambassador to the EEC, Saliou Aboudou. The new government contained only one military officer, Squadron-Leader Edouard Zodehougan (Interior) and but one *Ligeur* (Guirigousou Gado, Commerce). In its civilian, technocratic and pragmatic character it stood in sharp contrast to its counterpart of ten years before, but so in many ways did Benin itself.

These manœuvres had little effect. In March 1988 there was a pre-empted coup attempt involving mainly junior officers led by Captain Jean Hountoundji of the Presidential Guard, together with the older and more senior Lieutenant-Colonels Francis Kouyami and Hilaire Badjagoume. Both senior officers had been involved in the 1972 coup and Kouyami was chief of staff of the paramilitary forces while Badjagoume commanded a military camp. The reasons for the attempt—and most of the details—remain unclear but several factors have been suggested (*WA* 1988, 2183; *ACR* 29 April 1988; *QER*, 1988/2). They include: regional divisions (since the 170 or so arrested were mainly from Abomey, Porto Novo or other parts of the south/centre); personal interests (the Presidential Guard's allowances had been recently cut, as part of general austerity measures); and a left-wing response to the regime's shift to right-wing economic policies (an interpretation based on some of the officers arrested having been trained in Libya and Madagascar, and on unsupported assumptions about Kouyami's political views).

The coup attempt was followed a month later by Benin's share in the West African toxic waste scandal, in which *Africa Analysis* claimed that Benin had agreed to allow the dumping of several million tons a year of chemical waste at $2.50 a ton (an astonishingly low price), together with radioactive waste from France (for $18 million). This was initially to be buried near Abomey, though this site was apparently abandoned after strong protests including those of the Health Minister, André Atchadé. The continuing failure to reverse economic decline reflected in this willingness to accept toxic waste led to another round of ministerial dismissals in July. Bidouzo (Economy & Finance) and Ibrahim (Planning), both of whom were involved in the toxic waste negotiations, were dropped, as were Atchadé and two others. Simon Ogouma returned to become Minister of Planning as did Didier Dassi, who had been dropped in 1987 as Justice Minister and was now landed with the Finance portfolio. Kérékou remained, apparently still in control of the political system if not of the economy.

3 The Political System

This chapter is about formal institutions, and the relationship between state and society, which is also discussed in Chapter 4. Analysis of the general nature of the political system is made in the final chapter.

The Constitution

Benin, which has had nearly as many constitutions as heads of state since 1958, adopted its present constitution a decade ago. Drafting was done by a small committee including senior jurists and lawyers, whose work once reviewed by the Central Committee and the National Executive Council was widely publicized and opened to public debate (*ACR*, 1977-8, B615). Amendments arrived from the large numbers of public meetings organized to discuss it, from the diplomatic corps and from individuals. Most were rejected, including attempts to avoid characterizing the state as multinational (article 3) or extending the period for which president and national assembly were elected, which was of course done expediently in 1983. Some amendments were accepted, weakening parliamentary immunity slightly (article 50), guaranteeing the right to trade union activities (but also limiting that right; article 128) and modifying the equality of women (article 124). This last provision attracted much dismal criticism asserting that woman's equality within the family was unthinkable. Two extra clauses were added, one saying blandly that 'the unity of the family must always be safeguarded', the other promising the state would act so as to 'create progressively the conditions for this right [equality] to be enjoyed' (Olodo, 1978, pp. 764-9; Paraiso, 1980, pp. 415-16).

The Constitution in its final version of 160 clauses was adopted on 9 September 1977 (the text appears in *Ehuzu*, 29-30 August 1977; and in Olodo, 1978). It combines three sorts of clause: those with orthodox functions setting out basic institutions, rights and obligations; those which confirm and celebrate achievements and institutions already created (such as local government); and those which set out a sort of manifesto programme. This last includes the regime's formal commitment to socialism: 'In the People's Republic of Benin the development path is socialism. Its philosophical foundation is Marxism–Leninism, which should be applied in a living and creative way to Beninois realities' (article 4). Unlike all other clauses, this is precluded from revision (article 154); the rest may be amended by a two-thirds majority of the assembly's membership. As Lavroff (1978) points out, the constitution, especially its programmatic clauses, borrows heavily from socialist models, notably that of the Soviet Union. It also draws on French constitutional practice, as have many francophone African states, and there are important variations from the Soviet model; the state is seen for example not as the state of the working class, or even the working people, but as the state of a broad class alliance that excludes only the bourgeoisie (article 2).

The greater part of the Constitution (articles 30–120) is concerned with the main political institutions: a directly elected Assembly; a president elected in turn by that Assembly and chairing a National Executive Council (a cabinet) responsible to the Assembly; 'local organs of state power', combining representative and administrative functions; and the judiciary. Other articles (121–51) guarantee basic human rights: equality before the law, freedom of working, expression, association etc., as well as the rights to education, work, leisure and forms of social security including free medical care. These are modified and limited in other parts of the constitution as I shall show below. The early articles, finally, establish the basic character of the state (socialist and democratic), of the army and of external relations and set out the state's role in and conception of economic development, in the course of which the right to private property is established (articles 18–28).

The Presidency

Unlike many other African constitutions, Benin's makes the Assembly rather than the presidency the key institution. None the less the president does enjoy considerable power as head of state and by virtue of also being president of the Central Committee of the PRPB (as the constitution mentions but does not formally establish; see Paraiso, 1980, p. 423). In theory, the president executes decisions of the Assembly, which is supreme. In practice, the office has been made central to the political system, initially through Kérékou establishing his personal political authority during 1973–5, and then through the deliberate strengthening of the formal and informal powers of the presidency and the president's office (as distinct from Kérékou's own power). Three bases to this power exist: the constitution, the administration and the organization of government.

As head of state the president has few independent powers assigned him; but as party president he is in a position to influence or make a wide variety of appointments as well as to intervene in the selection of candidates for the

Assembly. He is also head of the armed forces, giving him formal control over such appointments as chief of staff or the command of such key garrisons as Ouidah barracks. As head of the administration he appoints the prefects of the six provinces who are directly responsible to him, and to whom are responsible in turn their lower-level counterparts as well as the regional and local representatives of all the ministries. Thus the president heads the system which controls the flow of resources downwards towards the localities.

The president is also part of the government, not simply in discharging the prime ministerial role within the National Executive Council, or as Minister of Defence (which he has been since 1972), but also through the concentration of functions and resources within the president's office. Attached to this office since late 1974 have been the Ministry of the Interior (sometimes including Information) and the Ministry of Planning. This concentrates the entire repressive apparatus in the hands of the president, while the planning function also covers foreign aid, which in 1980-3 for example totalled $600m and thus matched the size of the recurrent budget. Since 1975, a number of less significant additions have been made to the power of the presidency including the allocation of oil revenues to that office from 1984. The actual revenues earned have been small, but at 1984 prices and the planned rate of output, they would have constituted a major part of state revenues.

Thus despite the relative weakness of his constitutional position the president has a similar concentration of powers and resources as the Senegalese or Zaïrean presidencies (see Schumacher, 1975; Callaghy 1984). As I shall argue later this is a determinant feature of the Benin political system as a whole, and one that it shares with a large number of stable African states.

The Party and Mass Organizations

It is the party statutes (*Ehuzu*, 5 August 1977) that determine who is to be president, notably article 29: 'all the organs of the revolutionary state are under the exclusive control of the Party. To that end, the President of the Central Committee of the Party is Head of State and President of the National Council of the Revolution' (later National Executive Council). It is therefore the Central Committee that formally proposes its own president to the Assembly, for election as state president. This formal supremacy of the party is barely mentioned in the constitution (Paraiso, 1980, pp. 404-5) but is reflected in its actual role, especially that of its Political Bureau. This is the most powerful institution in the political system, responsible for key debates and decisions and for all major appointments. The larger Central Committee (now having forty-five members, but originally twenty-five) is less powerful and the locus more of factional conflict than of policy determination, as for example in the conflict over policy in 1979, when the Committee and the Bureau were increased in size to allow for new tendencies to be represented without having to go through the difficult process of removing members of powerful factions. The Party Congress, held so far only three times (1976, 1979 and 1985) functions mainly to hear policy announcements and to ratify them: thus the 1985 Congress confirmed the decision to approach the IMF for standby credits, a process that had already begun.

The party itself was not created until November 1975. Its creation had been mooted by Kérékou a little over a year before as a means of transforming and revitalizing its unreliable National Revolutionary Council. A Political Bureau of thirteen was created soon after, and was to become the Central Committee of the new party. Actual recruitment of members, apart from being guided by a set of exclusions common to all of Benin's major institutions,[1] seems to have been limited to those already having influence. There was no process of the presentation of candidates for membership and of public scrutiny (as for example in Angola and Mozambique) and no recruitment campaign, just as there was no formal process of selection of delegates to May 1976 Extraordinary Congress. One effect has been that the party remains small, even for a democratic-centralist vanguard party (as it is officially described). Decalo (1982, p. 95) quotes a figure of 6,000 by 1978 and even this he sees as 'likely to include a sizeable inactive contingent'. There are no publicly available official details of the party's membership.

Another effect has been the continual weakness of the party at the base. In the 1970s this gap was to be filled by the local Committees for the Defence of the Revolution, established in 1974. As has occurred elsewhere (Ghana, Burkina Faso, Angola, Ethiopia) the committees provided an excellent means for opposition organizations and the various different factions involved in the regime, notably the Liguers, to establish a political base. On several occasions, and most visibly in the aftermath of Captain Aikpé's death in 1975, the committees articulated hostility towards the Kérékou regime, defending a quite different revolution (*WA*, 1975, 1288). By 1980 such opposition had been dissipated, but at the cost of inertia in the party, prompting the Central Committee to investigate party functioning, and 'in particular the need to broaden the basis of its support' (*ACR*, 1981–2, B400). The same problem preoccupied the 450 delegates to the 1985 congress who received a Central Committee report which stressed 'the very small number of members ... [which] has not yet allowed the setting up of the proper party structures at all levels' (*EOM*, 1986, 15). The party thus remains more a private club for the powerful and influential than the directive and mobilizing force that it should be.

Similar problems arose with mass organizations and their relationship with the party. As I point out elsewhere both the student organizations and to a lesser degree trade unions continued to play the role of popular opposition to which they laid claim before the 1972 coup. The party made a series of efforts to exert control over these organizations and convert them into party anxiliaries. In addition it had to create a woman's auxiliary, which proved the least of its problems. Establishing control was a long process, combining the elimination of independent leadership through arrest and (sometimes brief) detention, the banning of some student organizations and a slow centralization of the remainder and of the unions. In 1978 the Central Committee announced its decision to create a single national women's organization and youth organizations for each of four age groups 'to enable the party to establish close control and to concentrate organisation nationally' (*WA*, 1978, 769). A single trade union centre had already been established and in 1979 the UNSTB (Union Nationale des Syndicats des Travailleurs du Bénin) was made a party auxiliary; it held its first congress in 1981. A women's organization, the Organisation des Femmes Révolutionnaires du Bénin (UFRB) followed, and finally a single youth organization, the OJRB (Organisation de la Jeunesse Révolutionnaire du Bénin) was created in August 1983 (although the University students retained their own officially recognized student cooperative). The OJRB's leading member, and vice-president, is the not exactly youthful Minister of Information, Ali Houdou. None of these bodies has functioned as an effective auxiliary. There has been no revival of party life, and in 1985 during the student strikes Kérékou denounced the leaders of all three organizations for 'passivity, lethargy and "delighting in bureaucracy"' (*ACR*, 1985–6: B4), an excellent epitaph.

The Assembly

Benin's legislature, the Revolutionary National Assembly, was the last of its formal institutions to be established, some seven years after the coup. The drafting process for the constitution provoked debate about the title of the assembly's members, for 'deputy' smelt of the past, and about their term of office, limiting to three years though many favoured a longer term. There was also strong support for the principle of an elected majority though the method of election seems not to have been criticized (Olodo, 1978, p. 766). The basis of candidate selection is corporatist: each major social category and the key institutions (party, bureaucracy and army) was to be represented by a quota of 'people's commissioners' within the total of 336. The following categories were established (*Ehuzu*, 31 May 1978), reflecting the very limited exclusions from office practised in Benin (only the rich and former office holders or leading figures):

Peasants	84
Workers	33
'Middle classes'	8
'Leading cadres'	20
Civil servants, other	60
Teachers	25
Army	33
Party	21
Affiliated organizations	46
Religious organizations	6

The distribution clearly overrepresents workers and underrepresents peasants, as did the legislatures of Angola and Mozambique elected at about this time (Munslow, 1983, p. 177; Somerville, 1986, p. 110).

The process of selection allowed some public participation. In both the 1979 and 1984 elections possible candidates were nominated by the party, and initially discussed at meetings held at village, ward and enterprise level. In 1979 the resulting nominations were then more thoroughly discussed at local meetings where candidates had to justify themselves and which weeded out unsuitable individuals –usually those known to be corrupt or with strong links with former regimes (the old *notables*). Final scrutiny was by the Central Committee which produced a single national list. This received the inevitable massive majority in the formal election, which 71 per cent of the electorate ignored. There was however a review process early in 1980 at which forty-five protests against those on the list or against having been excluded from it were heard by the National Executive Council. The exclusions stood, but seven of those elected were judged to have been improperly included (*ACR*, 1979–80, B472).

The assembly having extended its own life by eighteen months in February 1983, the next election was held in mid-1984 with a similar selection procedure varied only in that the initial discussion of nominations resulted in the choosing of an electoral college which in turn selected the final list for approval by the Central Committee (*WA*, 1984, 1089). This narrower participatory procedure was applied to a smaller and differently composed list, the assembly having also decided to cut its size to 196, and to alter the categories and distribution of numbers. There were now more categories—twenty-two in all—and various hitherto neglected groups such as women, the national bourgeoisie (replacing the vague category of 'middle class'), retired people (actually former army officers and civil servants), lay magistrates (from the 1981 judical reform) and students were deliberately included. The proportion of peasant seats arose from 25 to 40 per cent and of party officials from 6 to 16 per cent. This time, according to official figures, the population flocked to the polls, turnout being 93 per cent and a mere 28,000 voting against the list. Half of those selected to stand were new to the Assembly, indicating some level of popular judgement (*ARB*, 1984, 7271; *ACR*, 1984–5, B427–8).

The Assembly is constitutionally supreme, the central organ of the political system (Lavroff, 1978, p. 120). It makes laws and votes budgets, and the president and National Executive Council are responsible to it, acting to execute the decisions. In practice it meets only twice a year for relatively brief periods and exercises no obvious initiative or authority of its own. While not in session its functions are discharged by a fifteen-person permanent committee (chosen by the PRPB Central Committee), whose president is a figure of some standing who acts for the head of state in his absence; the current occupant is the head of the trade union movement, Romain Vilon Guezo.

Participation and Penetration at Local Level

There were local representative bodies much earlier than the Assembly. Their creation was the new regime's first structural reform, coinciding with the changes in education. At independence the Maga–Apithy government had kept the old colonial boundaries for the six departments and retained their elected councils, but allowed them only weak powers compared to those of the administrative hierarchy. As central governments changed year by year so also did the structure of local government but with one consistent trend: the erosion of its representative function. Elected councils were deprived of their power, replaced by appointed councils, or simply dissolved (Ayo, 1982, pp. 47–86); in 1970–2 the Maga government even failed to install them until just before the coup (*ACR*, 1972–3, B582).

The new regime saw the existing structures as out-dated and over-centralized, too colonial; and it called an administrative seminar in November 1973 to propose new arrangements. The result was a structure which combined centralization and decentralization, and representation and administrative penetration. The provinces and their prefects remained, as did the subprefectures (now districts), their officers (now district heads) and communes. To these were added a new village/ward level corresponding to relatively small communities, though with a minimum of 300 inhabitants. At each level there were three institutions: a revolutionary council largely or wholly elected; an administrative organ; and a single official responsible for directing local administration and activity (see Figure 3.1). The four layers divide in practice into two, province and district, and commune and locality. The former can be seen essentially as a deconcentration of central authority and as a means of efficient exercise of central power, but the latter contains the potential for a decentralization of power and for a degree of local participation and representation.

The Provincial Revolutionary Council at first consisted of five delegates elected by each district (that is thirty-five to fifty in all), the prefects and the local heads of the security services, together with all members of the corresponding administrative organ (the CEAP). The district councils had a similar structure. In 1981, in a reform meant to link the council system more closely to the party and mass organizations, council memberships were altered (de Gaudusson, 1981). Provincial councils were now to have only two from each district together with two representatives each from the armed forces, and from organizations representing university students, workers, youth, women and Committees for the Defence of the Revolution. Again members of CEAP were ex-officio members of the council. The eighty-four (formerly fifty) district councils have a related membership: up to thirty delegates distributed 'judiciously' according to population among the local communes and elected by their executive secretariats from among the commune councillors; two each from the same mass organizations and the army; the members of CRAD (see below); and any resident members of the National Assembly not part of its permanent committee.

These large bodies provide no evidence of exerting authority. They meet only twice a year for two weeks at most and are in any case limited to giving advice. They cannot debate most topics without prior permission from the government of the assembly's permanent committee (for details, see *ibid.*, pp. 86–8). The real holders of power are the corresponding administrative organs, the prefect and the district head. The Comité d'état d'administration de la Province (CEAP) consists largely of ex-officio members (the prefect, the local heads of services including security, a secretary appointed by the National Executive Council). There are also two representatives of the armed forces and a mere seven from the Provincial Council, two appointed by the Central Committee and five elected by the council. The district counterpart,

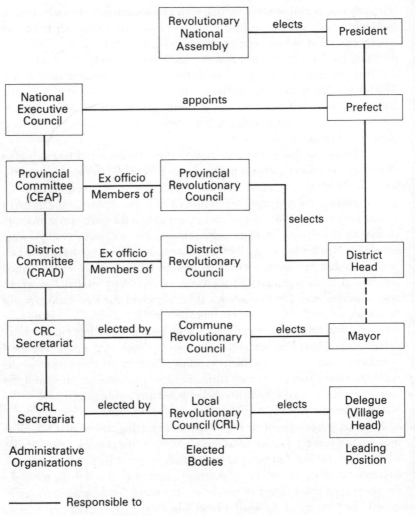

Figure 3.1 Administrative structure

CRAD (Comité revolutionnaire d'administration du district), has fewer councillors (just two appointed by the Central Committee) but is otherwise similar. CEAP and CRAD work with the two appointed officials, the prefect (elected by the Assembly but selected by the Political Bureau) and the district head (elected by the Provincial Council on the nomination of the Central Committee). The district head is responsible to the prefect, rather than to the District Council or committee over both of which he presides. The prefect, also independent of council and committee, is responsible to the president. Prefects are also members of the National Executive Council, and so are powerful political figures, usually becoming or in some cases having been ministers. It is this hierarchy that oversees all government activity whether concerned with policy implementation, political tasks, mobilization or service delivery. It therefore decides on the allocation of services etc., the components of patronage, to lower levels as local and national politicians had done before 1972.

The two lower levels have different structures, less tightly linked to administration. At the village/ward level the Comité Revolutionnaire Local (CRL) originally met monthly and had fifteen members elected by the local organizations for young men, elders and women. A deliberate attempt was made through this structure to play upon local generational and gender divisions, for political power had hitherto been limited almost entirely to male elders, a not unfamiliar situation even outside Africa. Now elders were limited to but four seats on the council, with women taking three, and eight going to the 'youth'. These councils in turn elect seven of their members to be a secretariat, including the village head, or délégué. It is the secretariat (and especially the village head) that takes responsibility for local administrative and political tasks. Since 1981 the composition of the CRLs has been more complex: ten representatives chosen by youth organizations (now simply the OJRB), six by women's bodies (now the OFRB) and six representing peasants, craftsmen or workers. The village or ward elect these representatives from among candidates nominated by the mass organizations (de Gaudusson, 1981, p. 84).[2]

Commune councils meet quarterly and consist of up to thirty delegates from CRLs, distributed roughly by population between the villages and wards involved. It was intended that at least one-fifth should be women, but initially this did not occur: Brand (1977–8, p. 78) reporting on a district in Ouémé in 1976 asserts that no women at all were elected to commune or district councils. Like the CRLs, the commune council elects a seven-man secretariat, whose secretary becomes the mayor. Thus unlike their district and provincial counterparts, who are appointed, the administrative heads at the lower levels are elected and in principle responsible not to central government (or the party) but to their local communities.

Before dicussing the extent to which the lower councils are representative, I shall outline the powers and responsibilities of each level. According to the constitution these are broad: there is very little division of powers, each council having essentially the same general remit at its own level with a small range of particular powers. Two factors however exert a strong practical influence on the exercise and distribution of power: the authority of upper level over lower, and finance. Virtually all the actions of lower-level councils and committees are subject to prior permission, validation or review by higher levels, making them more an instrument of central government than a source of local autonomy. Finance exerts a similar influence. A province gets its funds mainly from the centre or a portion of the funding of projects executed at provincial level, like most rural development projects. For the rest it must rely (apart from fees, gifts etc.) on the head tax, CFA fr. 1,710 in the 1970s. Only some adults pay this tax, and then with reluctance; it is frequently paid late and has always been unpopular (see Wong, 1977). The district, which collects it (another task for the district head), keeps 70 per cent but even this amounts to relatively little. For a district like Adjohon in Ouémé, with 114,000 people in 1976, maximum revenue would have been CFA fr. 30 million. Allowing for tax evasion (around 30 per cent) likely income would be about CFA fr. 20 million or £45,000. Districts thus possess some means, albeit very limited, to influence local social and economic development, but the funding arrangements for commune councils and CRLs are much worse. A CRL with an average population—about 1,200— might raise from its 10 per cent share of the tax a mere CFA fr. 30,000 (£65). A commune, of which there were 303 in 1974 and 580 in 1979[3] might hope for CFA fr. 300,000 to 600,000 francs (£650–1,300). It is scarcely surprising that these institutions should have been forced to rely on voluntary labour for development input and that according to Ayo 'a minimal proportion of these funds is reserved for executing development projects', revenue going instead on the running costs of the council, its office and its entertainment budget (Ayo, 1984, p. 371).

Literature on the councils as representative organs is very scarce, and concerned entirely with the lower levels, which alone are designed for this function. Early comment tended to contrast their behaviour with implicit models of revolutionary institutions active in organizing and mobilizing the population for social and economic transformation. Thus Michael Wolfers, writing a few months after the councils were established, commented that 'current government practice is rather to issue instructions to local, district and provincial committes than to seek guidance from the new institutions' (*WA*, 1974, 1515). Morgan (1977) makes the same comment, saying of the CRLs that 'they have been by-passed. Instructions are issued to local, district and provincial committees instead'. Brand, who worked in Ouémé in 1975-6 talks of a 'certain inertia' setting in among the new councils and accuses the majority of lacking revolutionary consciousness (Brand, 1977-8, 79-87).

Perhaps one should not be contrasting the councils (still less the committees) with such models, or even with the rhetoric of the regime. From the perspective of central government the committees and councils did not exist to provide guidance. They were a means of administrative penetration, especially the prefects and district heads, within a system that provided very limited means of exerting influence at local levels. Apart from the elected administrators like village heads the only representatives of central government to be found at local level were police (at times), extension agents and teachers; and the teacher might well be the village head (see for example Wong, 1977, p. 17). The elected lower councils did exist to carry out instructions, given that their structure included executive organs subordinate ultimately to government; indeed as Lachenmann (1982, 266) points out there was often no one else to carry out local tasks. As with the new schools and health units discussed in Chapter 5, the danger then arises that central government will fail to support the activity of local councils—in for example digging wells or building a school—with the necessary resources (pipes or a teacher's salary). The community becomes alienated, perceiving what were intended to be local self-help organizations merely as devices for reducing costs (for example Lachenmann, 1980, pp. 141-7).

Did the CRLs and commune councils perform any representative functions? One can find examples: thus Germaine Kora (1979, 177) notes that during the 1977 production campaign in Borgou many CRLs decided to reduce rather than increase export crop production, to do away with work on communal fields and to use centrally provided inputs like fertilizer to grow food.[4] The councils were here acting as representatives of community interests in the face of the state, bargaining with its local representatives, exchanging continued support or at least consent for a community good. Brand's study shows a similar pattern. His 'active' councils had similar community-based goals (a school to be built and a teacher provided) and sought to use the new structures and the increased role of youth within them to secure their goals. What we see here is behaviour very similar to that of local *notables* (the chief for example) bargaining with party politicians of the previous era for local spending in exchange for votes. Given that a form of clientelist politics survives at local level it is not surprising to find that Brand's village heads behave as *notables* and are treated as such by villagers. Equally, when Brand says rather plaintively that 'the initial drive for renewal declines and is replaced by two attitudes: inertia towards actions that government urges, and a scepticism that in some councils and CRLs leads to criticisms of central authority' (Brand, 1977–8, 80), we can again see behaviour appropriate to clientelist politics when the government's side of the bargain seems slow or unlikely to appear.

   Thus I would argue that the local councils could and did provide a limited degree of representation and participation, using various means including clientelist techniques to attract resources from (or defend the community against) new administrative and political structures that had replaced and eradicated the patronage-based networks of the old political leadership. Some confirmation that the councils have been found to have value can be found from two sources, ten years apart. Philippe Leymarie (1977, p. 56) in a somewhat uncritical piece says

it is not uncommon to witness in Benin today public sessions of criticism or self-criticism on a particular problem or the conduct of a particular councillor. For the first time in recent history, men (and also youth and women) are representing their villages and communities . . . without having to be also rich, notables, educated or familiar with French culture.

Ten years later the local council elections were still keenly contested. Thirty-five per cent of mayors lost their positions, and among the very many local councillors who wished to be renominated, 30 per cent failed to be selected again as candidates and 40 per cent were not re-elected (*EOM*, 1986, p. 16). The electorate is critical, certainly, but not indifferent, as is also the case with the single-party general and local elections in Cameroun, Tanzania and Kenya (Hermet *et al*. 1978).

Ideology

Kérékou's November 1974 speech in which he announced the official choice of a socialist development path and a Marxist–Leninist ideology was, as Crawford Young says, 'a dramatic ideological reversal and a complete surprise' (1982, p. 43). There existed, as there did in most of francophone Africa, a radical or even socialist tradition of thought among intellectuals and educated trade unionists; and some junior officers were in touch with current exemplars of this tradition. But according to Decalo (1976, p. 83) who interviewed some of them in 1971 (or perhaps 1972; see Decalo 1979, p. 236), the coup-makers had little or no interest in ideology of any sort. Kérékou's first major speech, the 1972 *Discours-programme*, is nationalist and anti-colonial in content as were the policy measures of 1973, and in mid-1973 he is recorded as saying 'our earnest desire is that the Dahomean revolution will be authentic. It should not burden itself by copying foreign ideology. You see we do not want communism or capitalism or socialism. We have our own Dahomean social and cultural system, which is our own' (*ARB*, 1973, 2885). The 1974 speech does reassert the nationalism of 1972 and makes it no less prominent than socialism. Thus along with the tasks of inculcating Marxist habits of thought, mastering the knowledge of the revolution and scientific organization of the masses to defend the revolution, we find 'reliance on our own strength, on our own resources', revival of national culture and languages and the ending of foreign domination (see the useful summary in *ARB*, 1975, 3457-58).

This eclecticism shows itself in other ways. As Young points out Benin is typical of several 'Afro-Marxist' states in the selectivity of its borrowings from Soviet models and even more in its actual practice (Young, 1982, pp. 27-32, 43-50; contrast Obukhov, 1978). Similarly while the constitution, party statutes and administrative structure are replete with borrowings, other models intrude powerfully. De Gaudusson (1981) stresses how much French constitutional and administrative theory shaped the reform of local adminis-tration, and even Lavroff (1978) concedes that the constitution diverges frequently from the Soviet model.[5] As subsequent chapters on policy show, actual practice embodied not so much Marxist models as nationalist goals or borrowings from ideas common among radical professionals in health and education, linked by the slogans of self-reliance and grassroots democracy.

Marxism itself makes its appearance much more frequently in rhetorical forms: Marxist habits of speech rather than of thought have been inculcated. Every visitor to Benin stresses the ubiquitous excesses of official language even down to revolutionary equivalents for the courtly phrases beloved of French civil servants (see for example Langellier, 1976; Weiss in *EOM*, 1986). Decalo (1979, p. 46) comments on the extent to which factional conflict, and the regime's analysis of dissent have been phrased in terms of 'ideological deviation', 'infantile leftism' etc., just as the contest with former power-holders at local level was presented through the medium of a crude class analysis and as a 'fight against feudalism and religious observation' (*ACR*, 1976-7, B549-50). The rhetoric and the denunciations remain, as any recent speech or interviews of Kérékou's will show (see for example *EOM*, 1986). The stress on Marxism as a guide or on the socialist development path has declined since 1979, when the '*conference des cadres*' argued that the masses 'had become disgusted with Marxism–Leninism and even with the revolution itself' (*The Guardian*, 18 February 1974).

What then accounts for its adoption in 1974? Three interrelated factors seem to have been important: the attempts to gain support, to gain legitimacy and to discover a framework for development. Thus Young (1982, p. 45) argues that 'it offered the hope of disarming the union and student militants'[6] a point made earlier by Decalo (1979, pp. 237, 244), and that it offered 'a means of distinguishing the incumbent regime from the discredited past'. Also discredited in the eyes of the regime were the previous development strategy and political system, and Marxist analysis and the socialist development path appeared not only to illuminate the failings of the past but to suggest measures that could be taken to avoid or eradicate them. As Kérékou put it in 1974, 'without this doctrine Dahomey has no other way of rapid development'. It is the failure of those measures in turn, as much as the original 'imposition' of Marxism that has led to its tacit abandonment in the 1980s.

State and Society

This section is concerned not with the class basis of the state (see Chapter 3) but with relationships between certain groups in civil society—women, the religious, workers etc.—and the state, and the degree to which these relationships are authoritarian.

Religion

Most Beninois are animists, adherents of a variety of indigenous religions notably Vodun (see Desjeux, 1984), whose priests exert considerable local influence. Among the Yoruba and in the north-west Islam is widespread and 15 per cent of the whole population count themselves Muslim. In the south where missions have been active since the seventeenth century (though ineffective until the nineteenth) about a third of the population are Christian, four-fifths of these Catholic. The Catholic Church retained until independence a largely expatriate priesthood, and there were only forty-four African priests in 1960, the year in which the first African Archbishop, Monsignor Gantin, was installed (Thompson, 1964, p. 202). Of the three religions, the Catholic Church has also had most social influence (through its schools which before 1974 provided half the places available at primary level) and national political infuence, notably through education and the activity of its priests.

Thus the best known, Father Aupias, was reported to have chosen Apithy as his running mate in the 1945 French Constituent Assembly elections (in which Dahomey had two seats) thus starting Apithy on his long if not wholly distinguished career. At local level the leadership of each religion tended to become involved in local competition between parties or party factions, being solicited for support on clientelist lines, or hoping themselves to use the support of politicians to secure advantage in local disputes, often internal to their religion (see for example Brand 1977-8, pp. 83-6). Similarly political leaders activated the support of the *grande féticheurs*, the senior leaders of certain indigenous religions, often miscalled witches.

This association between the old system and religious organizations strongly influenced the Kérékou regime's attitude towards them, especially during the mid-1970s when it felt more under threat from internal forces. Thus the constitution, while guaranteeing freedom of belief (articles 135 and 12), goes on to say 'no one may preach against the Beninois revolution on the pretext of defending a religion or its special or peculiar interests'. On this basis the tiny Jehovah's Witness sect was banned and its expatriate leadership deported for '"blocking the revolutionary process", refusing to respect the new national colours and hymn, and encouraging political "and matrimonial" disobedience' (*ACR*, 1976-7, B554). There were also clashes between Catholic priests and central government as the latter sought to secure its political authority, especially against residues of the old system. Among those arrested (and condemned to death) after the Assogba coup attempt in 1975 was the prominent Catholic Abbé Alphonse Quénum; he was detained until 1984. The most serious of these conflicts, however, was with the fetishists, culminating in a long anti-witchcraft campaign in 1976-7.

The constitution is all too clear on such matters: 'all obscurantist practices created by feudalism to terrorize, oppress and exploit the masses under the guise of religion are vigorously forbidden' (article 12). In practice the 'antifeudal' fight combined different national and local objectives. At the national level the new regime sought to deprive opposition of a potential rural organizational base, while creating a rival set of institutions in the local councils, Committees for the Defence of the Revolution, and the party and mass organizations. It was for this reason that not only the fetishists but also a variety of local 'secret societies' fell foul of the authorities and found their leaders harassed and arrested. At local level the campaign found some support for not only could it be turned to advantage in pursuit of local rivalries and ancient scores but it played upon both generational and gender conflicts (Brand, 1977-8, pp. 82-7; Elwert, 1984, pp. 289-92). The campaigners sought more to regulate and routinize the cults' activities than to ban them:

permission had to be sought for ceremonies and processions, while uniforms were forbidden and the *couvents* (female societies governing transition to adulthood) replaced by formal initiation centres (Ayo, 1982, p. 358).

Violence and abuse of all forms marked the campaign. Ayo (ibid., pp. 359–75) gives several examples involving the deaths (apparently by suicide) or flight of accused 'witches', and of armed raids by district officials on ceremonies and *couvents*. The variety of permissions required and the dangers consequent on being denounced as a witch made easy both corruption (ibid., p. 360) and the ventilating of family conflicts; it was often a cousin who denounced a *féticheur*. Wong (1977, p. 22) confirms Ayo's judgement, saying that the campaign was used 'to extort money from poor frightened women' in Ayou. She then elaborates this theme, seeing the *féticheurs* as competing with local administrators for peasant surplus cash extracted as fees for ceremonies or in complex transactions with officials (ibid., p. 65). Elwert finally, while showing how witchcraft accusations and their target (poor elderly women) can be understood in terms of the growth of economic differentiation in the locality and the presence of an economic crisis arising from local crop failure, also mentions the routine use of torture by local officials. 'The quarter headman, mayor or policeman would put some of the accused women in the middle of a fire circle, place a heavy stone on the belly of those who were pregnant, leave other "witches" standing upright for days in the sun at noon [sic], or just ask someone who served in the colonial army to beat them "according to military standards"' (Elwert, 1984, p. 291).

The campaign came to an end after 1977 as the regime's assessment of its power and security improved, though the restrictions remained and have caused clashes since (Ayo, 1984, p. 369). Relations with the churches seem to have improved, aided perhaps by the Pope's visit in 1982 and by Archbishop Gantin becoming a Cardinal (and an influential one, heading the Justice and Peace Commission until recently). Relations with Islamic groups, which have always been calm and distant, seem not to have been influenced by Benin's close ties with Libya, although it is significant that attempts were made to convince Benin that Kérékou had converted to Islam during a visit to Libya in 1980. The assertions were false and quickly denied (*WA*, 1980, 2044, 2336) and it has been assumed that the episode was part of factional manoeuvre within the regime (*ACR*, 1981–2, B399).

Gender

Women's lives in Dahomey showed patterns common to West Africa in that period. Rural women tended to play a subordinate domestic and economic role, though one that varied with the precise community and culture involved. Their capacity to achieve a degree of economic independence by for example processing agricultural products and selling their output, or by craft activity, had been seriously undermined at least in the south by the advent of mechanical processing (for example of palm kernels) and of imported goods (see Elwert, 1983; Elwert & Wong, 1978; and Robertson, 1987). In urban areas trading offered a means of subsistence, and petty trade like petty commodity production was dominated by women. Little has changed since 1972, either for rural women (Frey-Nakonz, 1984) or for their urban sisters (Midiohouan, 1987). Thus the 1979 census indicates that about 15 per cent of the population, almost all of them women, are involved in trade. For those involved full time, incomes are comparable to wage labour (ILO, 1984, pp. 166–8). Women's involvement in more lucrative occupations or in wholesale trade is far less common, though as in other West African states there exists a small group of 'Mama-Benzes', illiterate but sophisticated business women with a large turnover. One recent estimate of the annual turnover of the wealthiest of them produced a figure of CFA fr. 3–4 billion ($14–19 million) in the late 1970s when the Nigerian oil boom created very high levels of illegal trade (*EOM*, 1986, p. 22). Occupations needing formal qualifications also have fewer women, owing to male prejudice and to the smaller proportions of girls attending school, a feature of the education system that the 'new school' reforms did little to alter. In 1969 30 per cent of those in school were girls, 28 per cent in 1977 (Min. Coop., 1979, p. 4); and the proportion in secondary and tertiary education or in rural schools was lower still (falling to 18 per cent for the university intake).

Also little changed by the advent of the new regime has been women's political participation. During the late-colonial period when women across Africa, like other socially marginal groups, tended to be involved in radical nationalist activity, Dahomean women seem to have been inactive. As part of its attempt to undermine the old political system especially in rural areas the new regime did attempt to recruit hitherto excluded groups, notably youth and women. Thus the local councils created in 1974 had officially to be one-fifth women, a device used elsewhere with such institutions (for example Guinea-Bissau and Mozambique). Women were also recruited into the army and militia from 1976, and formal equality—with some qualifications—was included in the 1977 constitution, as was the right to maternity leave. While the political status and activity of youths increased, there is no evidence to suggest that women made similar progress, and some evidence that the rules on women's participation were ignored. Above local level there has been very little direct participation by women in formal political structures. Before the last elections there were only twenty-seven women members of the Assembly (implying that almost all of them were representing women's organizations rather than being elected as peasants or in other social economic categories). Three of those were to be found on the Assembly's Permanent Committee; with 'one woman ambassador, two district heads, some members of the national Bureau of the UNSTB, [and] some in senior technical posts in the administration' (Midiohouan, 1987, p. 61), they make up Benin's roster of women in politically significant positions.

No attempts, finally, have been made to encourage women to organize themselves for political action (other than nominating their category of assembly members). A large variety of rural and urban women's organizations exists, organized loosely after 1974 in Comités d'Organisation des Femmes (COF) and now brought together in the OFRB, but it seems unlikely that this has any other goal or effect than of making them a little easier to control. In this objective Benin resembles other African socialist states, but in its failure to mobilize women or to take seriously their lack of political power it is atypical (see for example Urdang, 1984).

Labour

The relationships between labour and the new regime have been made more complicated by the different reactions of rank and file workers and of union leaders. During the 1960s governments had sought to cope with large demands from the small but powerful public-sector unions by alternating episodes of wage increases and austerity plus repression, the latter normally leading to the downfall of the government involved. The rank and file reacted with a growing alienation from governments and the political system on which they relied, while continuing to support individual union leaders as their best hope of increased wages. The leaders by contrast were frequently involved in the clientelist politics of the period, with many supporting Ahomadegbe (although some developed a more radical critique of the political and economic order).

Kérékou benefited·at first from the unpopularity of the old system and from union desires to create a single powerful union centre which would support and influence the new government. Also important was the ending of austerity measures signalled both by the first significant increase in the minimum wage since 1968, and by other measures which increased take-home pay, such as the partial payment in 1973 of salary increases arising from promotion, blocked since 1966. In 1975, however, certain new austerity measures were introduced to pay for the education reforms, and some union leaders were involved in the coup attempts of that year, especially Aikpé's. After Aikpé's death there were large demonstrations, mainly of workers, and a general strike was called. The government attacked both the demonstrations and the union leadership severely. There were dozens of arrests in June and again in October (after discovery of the 'Zinsou' plot), with union members being detained for the rest of the year. By sequestering those in the union leadership hostile to it, the government was able to encourage its own supporters to take power, and then control the single union centre, the Union Nationale des Syndicats Travailleurs du Bénin (UNSTB). To reduce rank-and-file discontent public-sector pay scales (but not the minimum) were raised by 14 per cent.

Since then the regime has followed a strategy with three elements. Tight control over formal trade-union structures has been built up by making the UNSTB the sole legal centre, and by suppressing attempts at formation of rivals to it. Thus in 1980 a group of unionists involved in forming unofficial unions were detained for three months, although their action may have been as much a part of factional manoeuvre within the regime as it was resistance to central control by workers (*ACR*, 1981-2, B399; *Amnesty International Report*, 1982, p. 20). In 1983 there were further detentions 'for suspected membership of an unofficial trade union, the Centrale Syndicale des Travailleurs du Bénin' (*Amnesty International Report*, 1985, p. 20). UNSTB senior officials are appointed by the Central Committee (its secretary general is president of the National Assembly) and since 1979 it has been an official PRPB auxiliary.

The second part of the strategy has been to permit a limited degree of worker participation at plant level, through the formation of Comités de direction, allowing workers some voice in management. That this was successful is attested by Langellier (1976) who wrote 'workers, at least those in the towns, nevertheless appreciate being consulted at their workplace, even if this often means rubberstamping decisions already taken. 'For the first time' one worker told us 'they're interested in us'. The Committees for the Defence of the Revolution although sometimes seen as competing with union branches performed a similar crudely representative function up to 1978 (but compare Godin, 1986, p. 169).

The third and last element has been regulation of pay scales. The minimum wage has been raised twice since 1974, in 1980 and 1983, by which time it was 80 per cent more than its 1974 cash level, but well below its 1974 real value. New entrants into manual labour are thus worse off than in the 1970s, but those who have been in work for several years, especially in the public sector, have benefited from promotion and increases in pay scales that together with housing and other allowances have helped to sustain real wages. Thus unskilled manual workers in 1980 were paid from 1.6 to four times the minimum; and private-sector rates were somewhat higher (PECTA, 1982). Until the economic crisis of 1983 and after, this combination was enough to restrain overt worker discontent. The past history of attempts to create unofficial unions, and the failure to raise both the minimum rate and actual wage packets since 1983 suggest that the government will not succeed in containing labour unrest much longer, and may soon be faced with its first major strike since 1975.

The Armed Forces

By the early 1970s Dahomey's small army, in which a predominantly southern and Fon officer corps commanded a largely northern rank and file, had lost its institutional integrity and internal discipline, and was riven with regional, partisan and rank-related fissures. As Decalo says, 'the armed forces had become a patchwork of competing personalist ethnic allegiance-pyramids centred around popular officers of all ranks in which superior rank or authority was only grudgingly acknowledged' (Decalo, 1979, p. 234). The main cause of this was the officer corps' incorporation into spoils politics from 1965 onwards and ever-growing pressure by the then political leaderships to recruit support among army officers for factional advantage. Like many others in this period in West Africa, the 1972 coup can be seen as a response by junior officers to this loss of integrity and as an attempt to force a restoration of military as much as political order. In this case the process took at first the form of prolonged conflict within the army as the junior officers around Kérékou established their political and military authority against both their seniors (who were retired, jailed or offered safe sinecures) and their co-ranking rivals (Aikpé, Assogba, Badjagoume, Beheton etc.).[7] During this period government remained both insecure and in the hands of the military; only a few civilians participated as members of the CNR or its powerful Political Bureau, and of the Central Committee of the PRPB.

From 1976 onwards, despite the 1977 invasion and the subsequent stress on security, the army gradually withdrew from government, and a process of centralization akin to that in the political system occurred within the military system. Kérékou, who as head of the PRPB was also head of the armed forces, had reinforced his military authority immediately on taking power by becoming Minister of Defence and Chief of Staff. In 1976 and 1977 the army, other services and the militia were reorganized, first into a tripartite structure and then into a single People's Armed Forces. Kérékou assumed overall command, as Commander of the People's Militia, Chief of General Staff and Supreme Chief of the Armed Forces. To restore the lower levels of the command structure, severely depleted by arrests, deaths (including five in the invasion) and other forms of removal, Kérékou promoted junior officers, using the opportunity to enhance northern representation and influence, and thus to maintain ethnic balance and locate his supporters in key positions, especially within the Presidential Guard and the various security organs (on which see *ACR*, 1984–5, B429). Military spending rose very swiftly, more than any other major budgetary element: from CFA fr. 1.75 billion in 1976 to 10.9b francs in 1983, a six-fold cash increase and a near doubling in its toll on the budget (from 11 to 20 per cent). To some degree this reflected both a growth in size as the army expanded in the late 1970s and again in 1981, and an increased flow in weapons, the great majority from the Soviet Union.

These processes, of remilitarization of the army, and of creation of loyalty to the president and presidency, continued after 1983 but were inevitably affected by the economic crisis. On the one hand Kérékou has continued to remove senior officers not only from government but also from command, in favour of those whose careers have been made since 1972 (such as the three chiefs of staff appointed in 1985). On the other hand it has become increasingly difficult to satisfy military demands. Spending fell abruptly in 1985 and is still only at 1983 cash levels, inflation having been 12 per cent a year since then—and part of the wooing of the IMF has been a promise to review military as well as civil service payrolls. To help bolster spending the United States, the Soviet Union and France have been approached for military aid (or credit), with France responding most eagerly, offering a mixture of grants and loans worth up to 750m francs (*QER*, 1986, no. 3). There have been rumours of discontent at poor conditions, low salaries and the sudden promotion blockage (see for example *Africa Now*, April 1986, p. 15) and at least one attempted coup, in March 1988. Despite the regime's current difficulties with sustaining the political system and reproducing its hold on authority and power (see Chapter 6), it does seem premature to predict its overthrow by 'young army officers trained in the Eastern bloc' as does *Africa Confidential* (1987, no. 28, p. 14).

Repression and Human Rights

It is easy to portray the Benin state as repressive. Since it came to power in 1972 the regime has engaged in a series of arrests, trials and detentions of opponents, without a proper basis in due process of law. In addition certain categories have been formally deprived of full political rights; thus the *hommes de main* of former regimes cannot hold office, nor can those described as belonging to the bourgeoisie, although one such was a minister for years. This has helped to make overt opposition sporadic and conducted often from exile in Lomé, Paris or Brussels. Four categories of opponent have suffered particularly: former politicians (and at local level their clients); would-be coupmakers; trade unionists and students. Each has been subject to arbitrary detention and ill-treatment. Thus in the aftermath of the 1972 coup the available former heads of state were placed under house arrest, while former ministers were jailed. Further arrests followed the attempted coups in 1973 and 1975 and the 'Zinsou plot' of 1975, after which large numbers were tried by special courts and condemned to death, normally *in absentia*. None of these death sentences has been carried out, even when it was possible to do so. The ex-ministers were released early, after refunding assets for which they could not account, but the remainder stayed in detention or under house arrest until released under the amnesties of 1981 (when Maga, Ahomadegbe and Apithy were set free) or 1984, when Alphonse Alley and Janvier Assogba among others were released, leaving only those arrested in 1977-8.

This relatively conciliatory treatment contrasts sharply with that accorded many trade unionists or students since 1979. On several occasions, associated either with student protest (1979, 1981, 1985) or with attempts to form independent unions (1980, 1983), large numbers in both categories have been detained without trial. The majority have been released within months, but many have been detained continuously or with only brief periods of freedom; thus several students released in the 1984 amnesty were rearrested soon after as independent student activity revived on campus in the period before the 1985 strike. Conditions for these prisoners have been bad. Amnesty International mentions 'reports of severe overcrowding, poor lighting and ventilation, inadequate sanitary and washing facilities, and grossly deficient medical care; as well as torture' some detainees have died (*Amnesty International Report*, 1985, p. 22; see also reports for 1982-4, 1986). There seems to have been no trend for the better over the 1980s; rather as the economic situation has worsened so recourse to repression and ill-treatment has become somewhat more likely.

The government has also been prone to identify internal dissent[8] with the externally based opposition. In the 1970s it was the 'Zinsouists' who were the source of all political evil, especially the manifestation led by former Ambassador Gratien Pognon and known as the Fronte de Libération et de Réhabilitation du Dahomey (FLRD). This Brussels-based organization was believed, probably rightly, to have been involved in the 1977 invasion, but appears to have been inactive since 1980, perhaps undermined by amnesties.

The other bogey has been the Communist Party of Dahomey (PCD), a *groupuscule* based largely in Paris but with some support in Cotonou and Porto Novo. Kérékou has claimed that several of the leaders of the independent university student cooperative set up in 1985 were PCD members and two university students have been detained on that basis.

Other recent evidence would underline this repressive picture: the introduction of identity cards in 1985, the increased size, complexity and budgets of the different security organs and their closeness to Kérékou (or at least the presidency). Yet to see this regime as merely repressive like its forebears, or as indifferent to human rights in a fashion assumed to be typical of socialist states, would be a mistake. A large volume of dissent and criticism occurs without an automatically repressive response, as in the case of the 1979 'conférence des cadres'[9] or in the 1977 decisions by CRLs to ignore the production campaigns. The response in such cases (the majority) is to ignore the event or more rarely to take it seriously and react constructively, as with the reform process of 1978-82. An alternative perspective is then to view the regime as authoritarian, as seeking to pre-empt and regulate dissent and criticism through its capacity to disorganize opposition and to incorporate potential dissident groupings (students and labour especially) into the centralized political system. The detentions are instances of failure and are atypical actions from this perspective (though not for that reason to be condoned or seen as minor matters); their increasing frequency can then be interpreted as an indicator of the weakening of the political system built since 1974.

There is also some positive evidence for a less dismissive view of political freedom in Benin. Trivially, formal freedoms are guaranteed in the constitution, where they are also qualified by article 140, which baldly states that no one may 'abuse democratic freedoms to threaten the interests of the state, people and revolution'.[10] Actual freedoms as we have seen are harder to come by but are to some degree enjoyed by most of the population. The press and cultural life are now more free, though nothing like Nigeria. Thus the official daily *Ehuzu*, while never pretending to humour or entertainment, carries a column criticizing the failings and abuses of *les cadres*, and a recent local film, *Ironu*, though not overtly set in Benin has drawn large and enthusiastic audiences to its portrayal of incompetence and corruption in the bureaucracy. Identity cards are often not carried out of sheer indifference; discussion of the regime and conditions—even with foreigners—is open and Kérékou shuns motorcades, though not armed guards (see Danielle Weiss in *EOM*, 1986, p. 18-19).

The judiciary has also been less manipulated than in many African states (and in Dahomey in 1970–2).[11] Instead it has been reformed and in certain cases bypassed. The reform, achieved finally in 1981, is intended to bring the court system—though not legislation, which is little changed—into line with other structures. For each level of administration there corresponds a type of court, and each includes lay magistrates nominated by the PRPB. The lowest level is made up of typical 'people's courts', wholly lay, dealing with domestic disputes, drunkenness and other minor social abuses, and using conciliation and arbitration more than formal sanctions. At the same time the government has used a variety of special courts to try political offences. The former CNR became such a court after the 1975 coup attempt, trying Assogba and his codefendants and those accused in the 'Zinsou plot'. The CNR's successor, the National Executive Council, has also functioned in this way as has the Central Committee. Such 'courts' do not obey the rules of due process, nor is appeal allowed. In 1986 a formal special court was established to deal with corruption, major economic crimes and subversion (*QER*, 1986, 1), but no details are yet known of its composition or operation. It appears to have been used first in October 1988, hearing charges arising from the March 1988 attempted coup (*LA*, 1988, 2183).

Colonial rule and colonial development left Dahomey's economy stagnant and highly dependent. The massive oil palm groves of the south had become neglected in the depression and during the Second World War (when peasants were obliged to grow maize for export), and output and exports of oil fell steadily from their peak in the mid-1930s. Other crops were introduced, like cotton, or encouraged (like groundnuts and coffee) but their contribution was not enough, even though they came to make up 20 per cent of all exports. Dahomey, which had contributed revenue to the French treasury before the war had by the 1950s 'a substantial annual fixed deficit' (Manning, 1982, p. 251) as well as a huge deficit in the balance of trade. It had become even more tightly integrated into the French economy after the war as a result of French colonial monetary policy and the creation of the cfa franc zone (G. Martin, 1986). Over 75 per cent of Dahomean trade in 1953 was with France, and almost entirely through French firms. There was very little industry; four oil-extracting mills, two other factories processing raw materials, a brewery (of course) a soft-drinks firm, a small plant producing shredded coconut and another compressed air (Thompson, 1964, p. 188).

The development policies of post-independence governments brought about no fundamental change in this pattern. A few more factories opened—for freezing shrimps, producing pasta and making shoes—and there was a little more processing of local crops. More significantly, the nature and levels of exports remained unchanged, and Amin (1973, p. 114) estimates that the export values rose only one per cent in real terms in 1960-8. The balance of trade became still more unfavourable (see Table 4.1) in large part the result of urban consumption financed by budget deficits. Dahomey's budgets which were largely accounted for by salaries, were in deficit from the late 1950s to 1970 by an average of about 20 per cent; the shortfall was covered by a grant from France. Real incomes, and real consumption, would appear to have fallen in this period, at least for the poor, with subsistence food and fruit (and calorie intake) falling as pressure to maintain exports increased (ILO, 1984, pp. 71-3).

Thus by the 1972 coup the faults of the Dahomean economy were obvious: it was too small and provided too little revenue; it was excessively dependent, and that mainly on France; it failed to provide an adequate standard of living; and it was too reliant on agricultural exports, in particular a single declining crop. In its first two years the Kérékou regime tended to

Table 4.1 Dahomey's trade, 1960–74 (CFA fr. m. francs)

	Imports	Exports	Balance of trade	Exports as % of imports
1960	7,643	4,513	−3,130	59.0
1961	6,275	3,579	−2,696	57.0
1962	6,626	2,699	−3,928	40.6
1963	8,249	3,154	−5,094	38.3
1964	7,762	3,254	−4,508	42.0
1965	8,491	3,367	−5,124	39.8
1966	8,270	2,585	−5,685	31.2
1967	11,983	3,750	−8,233	31.2
1968	11,211	5,505	−6,706	45.0
1969	14,129	6,693	−7,436	47.3
1970	17,660	9,062	−8,598	51.3
1971	21,202	11,648	−9,554	54.9
1972	23,510	9,189	−14,321	39.0
1973	24,859	9,794	−15,065	39.4
1974	35,174	8,815	−26,989	23.3

Source: BCEAO.

continue with past policies while adopting a harsher tone towards foreign companies. The pattern of deficits (and French subsidies), declining agricultural incomes and production and of reliance on France continued until late 1974 (*WA*, 1976, p. 203). The official adoption of a socialist development path led to more coherent and confident economic policies, but these are more readily seen as a simple nationalist response to the faults listed above, than as a socialist strategy.

Thus the regime sought to achieve greater local control over the economy and to reduce the extent to which economic relationships were monopolized by France; to ensure greater accumulation of capital locally; to create growth within the economy both in agriculture and through industrialization (citing the familiar maxim 'agriculture as the base, industry as the motor of development'); to achieve food self-sufficiency and expand food exports to Nigeria and Togo; and to distribute the benefits of development less unfairly. What was put forward was thus a state-led, public-sector-based economic strategy, with goals of growth and egalitarianism rather than of transformation.[1]

The means chosen to achieve these goals were inherently limited: nationalization and the creation of state and mixed companies, or parastatals; diversification of aid, trading partners and production for export; the establishment of industries to supply local and regional markets or to process crops formerly exported in a raw state and thus to obtain a better return; and the promotion of agricultural expansion and rural mobilization through cooperatives and supportive state institutions notably the Centres d'Action Régional pour le Développement Rural (CARDER). The extent to which policies were implemented, the nature of the institution created and the impact of reform are discussed below.

In one area we can point to limited success: diversification. France remained the largest single trading partner, but its percentage was much reduced, falling from 42 per cent of exports and 53 per cent of imports in 1970 to 20 per cent of exports and 29 per cent of imports in 1979. The figures were even less in 1977–8 when economic relations with France were affected by the aftermath of the 1977 invasion. Into the gap created moved Germany, Japan, The Netherlands, Britain, Benin's neighbours—and China, the sole socialist state to trade significantly with Benin. The range of donors also expanded with the largest donor being again France but with significant amounts coming from multilateral agencies, from the new trading partners, even from the United States despite diplomatic coolness. By 1979 France was providing 29 per cent of total aid and 48 per cent of bilateral aid; multilateral sources now made up over a third (38 per cent) of all public aid.

Reliance on France for budget subsidies had also gone: they ceased after 1976, in part because heavier taxes and more efficient collection doubled revenues between 1975 and 1979. Other aspects of the budget were unchanged or worsened. The proportion spent on salaries rose from 60 per cent to 70 per cent, and on defence from 10 per cent to 15 per cent (another response to the invasion). Still more familiar was the deficit on trade which increased sharply as imports, mainly of food and other consumer goods rather than capital goods, doubled between 1974–80, as it had between 1970 and 1974. Since exports did not rise, the imbalance in recorded trade worsened as did the proportion of imports covered by export receipts (51 per cent in 1970, 9 per cent in 1978).

The failure of exports to grow or even to be sustained reflects a major decline in production which occurred in the mid-1970s and which was only partially reversed later in the decade (see Table 4.2). Because world prices rose in this period, export receipts were less affected but they still fell to 67 per cent of their 1972 level by 1978, recovering briefly to peak at 144 per cent in 1980. It was not only production for export that faltered but also output of

Table 4.2 Exports from Benin, 1972/3–1979/80

	72–3	73–4	74–5	75–6	76–7	77–8	78–9	79–80
(A) Volume *('000 tonnes)*								
Groundnuts	3.65	4.73	4.82	7.00	7.89	2.72	1.34	1.13
Cocoa	19.63	4.37	1.75	1.07	2.30	1.37	4.11	6.06
Coffee	0.38	0.11	0.57	0.09	0.80	0.40	0.14	0.48
Cottonseed	50.02	45.08	30.95	20.07	17.50	13.89	18.74	25.77
Karité	6.74	9.63	0.38	12.37	2.95	8.27	0.25	17.70
Palm products	48.83	38.54	46.36	49.79	41.43	11.82	23.43	29.04
Tobacco	0.96	1.15	1.58	0.33	0.40	0.21	0.17	0.18
(B) Value *(m francs)*								
Groundnuts	109	142	195	384	434	149	74	62
Cocoa	1864	545	436	266	576	343	1028	1515
Coffee	37	10	58	10	92	54	19	8
Cottonseed	1800	1622	1237	903	764	875	1031	1417
Karité	67	115	5	186	59	199	6	220
Palm products	1025	848	1437	1543	1284	366	785	1076
Tobacco	—	—	—	—	44	25	21	23

Source: BCEAO.

food, according to official figures (though the decline was considerably less than in the 1960s) (see Table 4.3).

There was some success too in a second goal of policy, the creation of new industries and especially of agro-industries. Apart from increasing oil-milling capacity and building second textile and cement plants, factories were established to produce maize meal, fruit juice and tomato paste—a key ingredient in West African cooking like palm oil, whose smell, taste and colour permeate all too many dishes. Larger, and of greater potential than these were two huge projects undertaken with Nigerian aid, a sugar complex at Savé, and a third cement works, doubling national capacity, at Onigbolo. These two, proposed before 1972 but only realized by the new regime, were intended to supply the Nigerian market as much or more than domestic demand. Their financing relied heavily on private-sector sources and Benin's indebtedness rose very rapidly towards the end of the decade. In 1974 external debt was only $140m, a quarter of it owed to multilateral agencies. By 1978 it was $356m but still mainly inter-governmental (47 per cent) or multilateral (43 per cent). Over the next two years, however, total commitments more than doubled to $811m, and almost all of that increase, some $432m, came from private creditors. Debt service—a mere $8m in 1980—would reach $100m on this basis by 1985, without any further borrowing.[2]

Despite the heavy investment in new industries and the rise in the associated labour force (3,000 in 1974, 6,600 by 1980) the contribution of this sector to GNP actually declined after 1976 (Benin, 1983, p. 64). In many cases production fell and capacity failed to be utilized. Thus the textile factory opened in 1975 was producing only a third of its potential output by 1978; at the same time the oil mills were operating at even less of capacity (Memento, 1980). The cement factories, both old and new, managed to produce just 60 per cent of their capacity in 1979, which—allied to inefficient distribution by

Table 4.3 Food output of Benin, 1973/4–1979/80 (thousand tonnes)

	1973–4	1974–5	1975–6	1976–7	1977–8	1978–9	1979–80
Cassava	589	547	461	350	609	698	735
Yams	500	428	445	500	551	643	699
Maize	238	229	217	181	235	308	307
Sorghum	79	79	52	71	76	65	69
Beans	19	13	11	23	25	n.a.	n.a.

Source: BCEAO.

the relevant parastatal—resulted in 'shortages of cement, hoarding and high prices' (*WA*, 1981, p. 272) which the central government was unable to control.

The new industries became the responsibility of one or another of Benin's parastatals charged with managing the greatly expanded public sector. At first the expansion was slow, occurring through the nationalization of 1974–5 which covered petrol stations, insurance, banks, telecommunications, transport companies, the brewery and one hotel; for all this, total compensation was but $8m. One commentator (Malirot, 1975) has argued that the nationalizations were not even part of policy, and they were by no means a major step in gaining control of the economy. That step was taken by the creation from 1975 onwards of about 125 parastatal bodies, managing agro-industries, agricultural development programmes, purchasing and marketing of crops, external trade (but *not* the very important internal trade sector), and other sectors of the economy. On the capacity of these bodies to direct, develop and mobilize the economy rested many of the regime's hopes of realizing its goals. The hopes proved ill-founded, as I shall show later.

Other than the decision to set up new agro-industries there was little new in agricultural policy, and very little finance allocated to rural development. Only 5 per cent of recurrent spending went to rural development ministries in the late 1970s; only 11 per cent of the 1977–80 plan (Benin, 1977) was assigned to agriculture (and 6 per cent of the abandoned 1980–90 plan), and only 2 per cent of external finance up to 1980 was spent on it (Flesch, 1982). In place of investment the government relied on exhortation through a national production campaign, and on institutional changes. Both were directed at expanding export crop production despite the reassertion of food self-sufficiency as a primary goal (Anson-Meyer, 1983). The campaign echoed similar, failed, campaigns of the 1960s and rested on peasants working harder rather than more efficiently. Every administrative unit from the village to the president's office, each parastatal and every school had special fields to cultivate and production targets (set relatively low). Aided by the better weather of 1977–8 the campaign does appear to have resulted in higher output, although no reliable figures were produced (for a case study see Kora, 1979; and see Lagarde, 1978).

The institutional changes built on existing structures for credit, marketing and extension services while also trying to transform the cooperative movement. Provincial level planning and credit machinery was created, together with a new national agricultural credit agency, the Caisse Nationale du Crédit Agricole. The actual administration of credit at local level, like all the main agricultural services—marketing, extension and development—was in the hands (and still is) of the Centres d'Action Régional pour le Développement Rural (CARDER). CARDERs worked largely through extension agents and the cooperative movement, which came to have three levels. At the base, forming a pre-cooperative level, were the Groupements Villageoises (GVs), above them the GRVCs (Groupements Révolutionnaire à Vocation Coopérative) and the CAETSs (Coopératives Agricoles Experimentales à Type Socialiste). The GVs were originally established in the late 1960s as marketing cooperatives. They were tightly controlled by the administration and linked to private companies purchasing crops, such as the Companie Française pour le Développement du Textiles (CFDT) (Ayo, 1982, pp. 124–6).[3] Once free of at least the latter, and to a lesser degree of central control, the GVs expanded rapidly, especially in the north, helped by their association with literacy programmes and peasant control of weighing (Kora, 1979: 113–14; Auroi, 1977–8). They were however limited to the provision of inputs, sale of production and bargaining on behalf of their members. The newly created GRVCs added production itself to these functions, setting up collective fields while retaining individual plots for their members, who also received preference in the distribution of credits and inputs. By 1979 there were some 363 GRVCs in existence (Rosier, 1982, chap. 2; Ayo 1982, pp. 327–31), though Samson offers a figure of 'more than 500' (1985, p. 45), which seems doubtful in the light of their slow development in the south (Elwert & Wong, 1978: p. 137).

The CAETSs were meant to combine the features of the GRVCs with greater political consciousness and the use of modern techniques of production, as well as a greater degree of democratic participation by members. Some care was taken by CARDER to avoid setting up these cooperatives in villages ill-suited to them, and prior political education for members was provided (Ayo, 1982, pp. 285–7). Few, however, were created— perhaps fifty by 1980—and (like the handful of state farms) they have been supplemented as the favoured institution by the GRVCs (Rosier, 1982, p. 25). Part of the reason for this lies in failings familiar from the experience of such institutions elsewhere in Africa, as Ayo has shown. In the CAETSs he studied, membership fell off rapidly after initial enthusiasm, owing to financial problems; these he attributes to unfamiliarity with management and credit, bureaucratic interference and difficulty in handling new technology (Ayo, 1982, pp. 301–24; 1984, 366–7).

The Sources of Decline

Even the Benin government tends to see policy errors and administrative failings as the causes of post-1974 decline. There are, however, other reasons, important because they lie outside the scope of government influence and have continued to be significant in the 1980s. While the point may seem banal, it should be borne in mind that the new government inherited a peculiarly intractable set of economic problems even by the standards of small, weak African states: extreme dependency, poverty (one of the world's lowest per capita GNPs), endemic budgetary and trade deficits and a very weak revenue base. In addition the rural development policy of the preceeding twenty years, while leading to increased cotton production, had also undermined the viability of palm oil production through neglect of the natural palm groves, leading to a high proportion of aging trees, vulnerability to poor rainfall and low productivity. Further north in Borgou encouragement of cotton and groundnuts was associated (as elsewhere; see Timberlake, 1985) with soil erosion and degradation, loss of tree cover and moisture retention, reduction of fallow periods and use of marginal soils and reduction of grazing areas. Acreage devoted to food declined as did output of food, and by 1972 the area was one of permanent food deficit; indeed there were local famines in 1971, 1974 and 1976 (Kora 1979, pp. 160–7).[4] Thus the decline in cotton production of over 40 per cent in 1975–8 was due not simply to such policy measures as the replacement of the private French purchasing company CFDT by cooperatives and parastatals (a move popular with producers) but also by peasants switching from cotton to food out of sheer need. Producer prices, another factor much cited, were low, but they were increased by 37.5 per cent in this period, a move that should have discouraged a switch towards production of food for sale as opposed to autoconsumption.

Benin also suffered from poor rains in the 1970s and especially in 1975–6 (together with flooding in some southern areas in 1976). The drought seriously affected output of palm products in 1976–8 as well as reducing the future viability of the natural palm groves, which then accounted for 90 per cent of natural production. At least part of the decline in marketed output in the 1970s (from 138,000 tonnes in 1970–1 to 53,000 tonnes in 1977–8) was thus due to drought. Output recovered somewhat in the 1980s though it never matched past levels.

A final factor is Benin's closeness to the large economy and permeable borders of Nigeria. These influence greatly much of Benin's economy, especially its trade which has become an increasingly large part of GDP since

1972. Benin functions as an entrepôt for both Nigeria and Niger, but an unknown and large[5] amount of its trade with Nigeria is illegal: food and imported goods flow into Nigeria, while certain crops (notably cocoa at one point) and petrol flow out. Benin's ability to export cocoa despite producing very little, and the marked variations in the amount involved are both explained by smuggling (Igue, 1976a; 1976b). Both legal and illegal trade are sensitive to the state of the Nigerian economy. The Nigerian boom of 1976-7 is clearly reflected in Benin's import figures: foodstuffs and luxuries increased in value by 70 per cent, and other consumer goods by 80 per cent, while capital goods and oil products rose by no more than prices in general. Trade is also sensitive to border security (which helped reduce the cocoa inflow after 1973) and to import restrictions (as in 1978). Under such conditions regulation of the economy becomes even more difficult. Pricing policies—an essential element of rural development planning—can easily be undermined by smuggling, and local consumers including agro-industries can be deprived of food. Revenue is affected, especially as the key source for Benin of taxes on trade. Benin's government is however unable to influence Nigerian decisions and hesitates itself to reduce the trade since that lies in the hands of the other politically powerful groups in the country, the merchants—who are mainly Yoruba, and whose interests were represented in government by the surprisingly wealthy Barthélemy Ohouens, a minister until 1984.

Matters more under the control of the central government include economic administration, the content and quality of planning and the goals and impact of policy. None have been satisfactory. The first of these factors has been the most criticized in Benin, especially in 1979-81. A series of enquiries into rural development administration and into the parastatal sector produced a very similar set of reports. The institutions were found to be hierarchical, authoritarian and highly bureaucratic, leading to failure to perform essential tasks, to waste and inefficiency. The personnel, apart from being in many cases unqualified or ill-qualified, tended to be idle, undisciplined, arrogant and above all corrupt, so that fraud as well as inefficiency abounded within the parastatal (and cooperative) sector. Instead of contributing to national revenue and growth, they battened on one and reduced the other.[6] There can be no doubt that the transfer of responsibilities to parastatals (as with cotton purchasing in 1975), the multiplication of parastatals after 1976 and the incompetence with which they were run were important causes of Benin's decline.

Incompetence also affected planning, for even in technical assistance Benin possessed neither adequate planning institutions nor enough able planners (Benin, 1983, p. 28). Planning machinery, set out like so many of

Beninois institutions in elaborate organization charts, existed in practice only at national level, and planning activity was both highly centralized and sectorally oriented. Accurate data was not available and regional variations tended to be ignored. In Lachenmann's charitable words 'the planning system is still very much in its infancy' (1980, p. 121; see also pp. 122–30). The content of plans reflects this, marked as they often are by wholly unrealistic or impractical targets either for mobilizing or for investing capital. Perhaps the worst was the 1980–90 plan which not only failed to specify how 60 per cent of planned investment would be allocated but also proposed to double the GDP by investing no less than four times GDP in infrastructure, an extraordinarily low rate of return. One result was that plans could not be implemented fully. The 1977–80 plan was only half fulfilled by the end of its period, and a large proportion of what was achieved was represented by just two projects, the Savé and Onigbolo complexes. The 1977–80 plan had to be both scaled down and extended a further year, while the 1980–90 plan was abandoned soon after publication, and replaced by a series of shorter, *ad hoc* and more modest plans.

Partial implementation further biased the plans' pattern of investment towards large projects in agro-industry and especially in infrastructure. As Lachenmann (1980, p. 134) says, 'a particularly striking feature of the [1977–80] development plan is the discrepancy between the objectives and priorities it sets and the resources actually allocated to projects actually planned': 46 per cent for industry (of which 38 per cent was for but four projects), 23 per cent for infrastructure, but only 11 per cent for agriculture. This lack of investment in agriculture reflects donor preferences in a development strategy that relied very heavily on external funding (only 2 per cent of which was assigned to agriculture) and a domestic economy that was itself lacking in capacity to accumulate. Not only were peasants themselves too poor to invest (except their labour) but the state managed to overspend on salaries (including the army) while paying salaries that except for a very few did not permit significant saving. State revenues were dissipated through waste, inefficiency and corruption, and the private sector, dominated by trade, not only did not pay taxes on much of its activity and earnings but also did not invest in productive sectors especially agriculture (Lachenmann, 1980, pp. 124–5), though speculative land purchasing did occur.

Despite the lack of direct investment in agriculture, the effects of investment in other sectors and of production campaigns was to increase the pressure on peasants to expand crop production for sale and export. Even allowing for unrecorded trade with Nigeria it is clear that this expansion did not occur. Without investment in agriculture, increased output implied the cultivation of larger areas using the same technology. Government favoured this solution as can be seen from the content of the production campaigns and its frequent use of the statistic that only 15 per cent of suitable land was being cultivated in the 1970s: (a figure which ignores large regional variations: the heavily populated south is far more intensively cultivated than the north). Cultivation of larger areas implied more work and more competition with local food production where technologies are simple and yields stagnant (Rosier, 1982, ch. 1). Furthermore, the labour requirements of export crops are often far greater than those for food crops. Cotton growing in Borgou, for example, has been calculated to require 200 days' work per hectare as against ninety days for the local staple, sorghum (Kora, 1979, p. 132). It is not surprising that one peasant interviewed soon after the 1977 production campaign should have commented. 'I no longer get back from the fields before sunset, nor can I visit farmers in nearby fields, I no longer go to the market in Kandi to drink beer with my friends, indeed I hardly even manage to chat with them' (Kora, 1979, p. 183).

The prices peasants received for their output after independence was inadequate to ensure that they could feed themselves without extensive recourse to subsistence production. As Elwert has argued (1983; more briefly 1980), high levels of subsistence production permit low prices to be offered and a greater surplus to be earned by the trading companies, and more recently by the purchasing parastatals. Prices were raised by the new government after 1974 in some cases by considerable amounts: 44 per cent for palm kernels in 1974, 37.5 per cent for cotton from 1974 to 1977, 36 per cent for groundnuts in 1975. Producers had suffered from a decade of static prices before then and (apart from cotton) there were no significant price increases for the rest of the 1970s. The prices of imported goods like food, fuel, salt, simple tools and so on rose considerably during the 1970s, however. Lachenmann (1980, p. 126) estimates that 'the cost of living rose by 30% in the case of domestically grown foodstuffs, and by 50% in the case of imported goods between 1975 and 1980' and her conclusion is supported by Modiano (1982) and by price data on individual commodities (see Table 4.4). Real incomes of peasants thus fell during the 1970s, by 2.6 per cent a year according to official sources (for example Benin, 1983, p. 47).

Peasant responses, as elsewhere (for example Hyden, 1980) were to resist administrative pressures for increased production or for sale at fixed prices. They turned to smuggling (Ayo, 1982, p. 237) and to migration, both internal and external (Lachenmann, 1980. pp. 126, 128). In some cases they switched to food production (Kora, 1979, pp. 177–8), in others to simple evasion and avoidance. The long history of administrative pressures for more production

Table 4.4 Commodity prices in Benin, 1972–80 (CFA fr.)

	1972	1973	1974	1975	1976	1977	1978	1979	1980
Sugar (kilo)	105	130	190	250	241	200	200	225	315
Rice (imported) (kilo)	70	86	150	125	130	100	150	150	225
Maize (adjandjan)*	–	85	125	175	221	225	450	450	500
Gari (adjandjan)	–	125	125	175	298	400	400	400	700
Palm oil (litre)	–	–	100	165	143	225	250	240	200

* One adjandjan – about 4 kilogrammes.
Source: BCEAO.

and for tax revenues, accompanied by force and by corruption (see especially Wong, 1977) and by authoritarian and elitist attitudes of extension agents and other officials,[7] combined to stimulate such reactions, although at their root is the competition between production for self-consumption and production for trade, and the failure to raise peasant incomes.

The 1980s: Reform and Retreat

The response of government to growing criticism of the policies and structural changes of the 1970s was first to gather evidence. This process covered two years from late 1979 and while largely confined to the party and administration did involve some public discussion, especially over education (see Chapter 5). It led in turn to distinct changes in policy, especially towards the public sector, rural development and education. At the same time the process was slow, in part because it threatened the interests of administrators (nearly two-thirds of whom worked in parastatals). The pace was influenced also by a sense of optimism, of time and space within which reform could be achieved—and limited. This had two sources: an expectation of economic growth, and the attitudes of donors and investors.

Despite its economic problems, Benin's GDP had risen in real terms in the 1970s; the World Bank has estimated the absolute increase at 4.3 per cent a year, against the IMF's 3.3 per cent, but both exceed the population growth rate (3.0 per cent per annum). This trend continued in the early 1980s and was expected to continue as the large projects of the late 1970s began producing (see for example Benin, 1983). These hopes were bolstered by the agreement in 1980 by Saga Petroleum of Norway to take on oil production.[8] Although the investment needed was high ($100m at 1980 prices), potential income should also have been high ($150m) at the promised rate of output of fifteen to twenty thousand barrels a day, to be achieved soon after 1982. Such factors weighed with the donor community. Thus a 1979 World Bank report was 'relatively optimistic' about Benin's prospects despite its growing indebtedness (*ACR*, 1979–80, B479) and a United States' Department of Commerce report written late in 1982 and directed at American investors makes similar judgements, albeit with reservations (US, 1983). The Benin government was therefore confident that it would obtain funding for its 1983–7 plan, which embodied some of the new policies; of the $900m in external support required, however, only $250m was pledged at the 1983 donor conference, indicating growing doubts of the impact of reform and viability of the economy.

The main changes in economic policy were a reorganization of the parastatal sector, and a greater stress on rural development (and less on industry). The first, agreed in April 1982 at a joint meeting of the Central Committee and the National Executive Council, involved reducing the numbers of parastatals by half, especially in the agricultural sector and at provincial level (where thirty agencies were cut to six) (Jouffrey, 1983, pp. 39–40). This process has continued since 1982 and has been combined with gradual privatization, not in the sense of the transfer of public agencies to private management but by permitting the entry of private capital into areas hitherto exclusively public. By late 1984 the Central Committee had decided to consider further closures of major reorganizations of parastatals and four mergers. It also confirmed a new policy: that private capital should be allowed access to all but 'strategic' sectors (energy, agriculture, communications, banking); significantly industry, once the 'motor of development', was not considered strategic (*EOM*, 1986, pp. 27–8). Combined with this downgrading of the public sector have been attempts to upgrade its personnel through retraining. Dismissal or other sanctions for the gross misconduct which Kérékou had often denounced in 1980–1 did not occur. It is perhaps no surprise to learn that a Central Committee report late in 1986 should once again have seen corruption as a major factor in economic decline (*African Business*, November 1986, p. 31; see *QER* 1988/1 for further evidence of corruption).

Rural development was allocated 29 per cent of funding in the 1983–7 plan. This plan was never likely to be implemented fully: by October 1985 for example only 42 per cent of planned spending for that year had been achieved, and most of that was accounted for by the few large projects remaining (*EOM*, 1986, p. 22). Among those projects, however, were two major integrated rural development schemes undertaken with World Bank support in Zou and Ouémé. Another—the Borgou Project—had been started earlier, in 1979, and was thus completed. What they had in common was a stress on direct investment and technical improvement to achieve increased exports, notably of cotton and of food crops (by trickle-down, spin-off and demonstration effects). Behind this lay the notion of Benin's comparative advantage in agricultural production for world and regional consumption (and in transit trade). This highly orthodox analysis has not entirely displaced older notions of the key role of agro-industry, but the plan did show a distinct shift in emphasis towards small and import-substitution industries,[9] and the only large agro-industrial project mentioned was the maize mill at Bohicon, an inheritance from earlier plans. Also surviving from earlier policy was the special position of cooperatives, especially the GRVCs, and the state farms.

While both have increased in numbers—the former to 1,050 by the end of 1985—there are no plans to expand further, and their function would seem to be to act as demonstration farms for modern techniques. They account for only 5 per cent of production (*EOM*, 1986, pp. 25–6).

The change in agricultural policy would seem to have helped raise output,[10] or at least sales, to the extent that a National Cereals Office was created in 1985 to handle storage of surplus and export sales. Several export crops and especially cotton show significant increases in production and yields in the 1980s, while food output rose to levels at which claims of self-sufficiency seem justified. Table 4.5 shows clearly the good season of 1984–5 when rains—unlike the rest of the 1980s—were excellent.

One effect of this, and of the ability to export oil, was that the balance of trade improved. In 1982 it reached a peak deficit of CFA fr. 145 billion (about $460m) and official exports then covered only 5 per cent of imports (even the largest estimates of unofficial trade, at CFA fr. 50 billion, would only indicate a coverage of 35 per cent). Thereafter, however, the deficit fell despite declining world prices for cotton, until 1986 when oil joined cotton in decline and export volumes probably fell also. Imports also fell as projects came to an end, entrepôt trade declined (the Nigerian border closure) and

Table 4.5 Agricultural output in Benin, 1981–7

	1981–2	1982–3	1983–4	1984–5	1985–6	1986–7
Export crops (tonnes)						
Groundnuts	40	86	46	—	—	1,492
Cocoa	402	2,928	6,015	1,299	54	1,045
Coffee	399	486	32	3	16	918
Cotton (seed)	14,470	31,576	44,912	87,827	89,325	107,209
Karité	3,374	1,760	25,506		22,921	12,800
Palm products	23,866	24.006	18,194	24,697	7,755	7,065
Food crops ('000 tonnes)						
Maize	287.9	272.9	281.9	373.5	425.1	375.6
Millet, etc.	63.6	68.6	62.6	92.9	90.9	106.3
Rice	8.5	8.8	5.3	7.7	6.3	8.5
Beans	28.0	29.0	28.6	47.5	39.1	40.3
Yams	665.9	671.9	620.2	769.9	776.6	874.5
Cassava	575.2	609.9	580.2	685.7	708.0	725.3

Source: BCEAO

internal purchasing power decreased. By 1984, with imports at less than 60 per cent of their 1982 level, the deficit was down to CFA fr. 68 billion (*EOM*, 1986, p. 34), though it has probably risen since.

Other indicators however suggest a far grimmer picture—'the worst economic crisis in the country's 25 year history' according to the American Embassy (*QER*, 1986/2). Since 1983 especially several factors have severely undermined the economy and the government's capacity to influence it.[11] The international recession has reduced demand and prices, and made aid and capital harder to obtain. Even had aid been available it would have been required in grant form, since Benin has lost the capacity to service its large external debt, mainly built up in the 1979–82 period as the major agro-industrial projects and the oil refinery were financed. By 1984 debts had reached two-thirds of GNP, while servicing them was made more difficult by the falling value against the dollar of the French franc (to which the CFA franc is tied) and by the declining proportion of total disbursed debt that was at concessional rates of interest (from 71.5 per cent in 1979 to 49 per cent in 1983). Annual debt service has exceeded $100 million since 1984, but actual payments in 1983–6 were little better than 35 per cent of the amounts due. Arrears have increased rapidly and will continue to do so in the absence of rescheduling (*QER*, 1986/4, 1987/1, 1988/1).

The state's capacity to raise revenue has fallen, producing smaller recurrent budgets in 1985 and 1986 than in previous years, and still smaller out-turns since revenue failed to match estimates (*EOM*, 1986, p. 20). In 1984 a budget subsidy from France was necessary, while in 1986 the budget had to be reduced—to three-quarters of its original level—in September. The planned expenditure for 1987, though more than 1986, was still well below that of 1983, and allowing for inflation at about 12 per cent per annum, public spending overall had more than halved in five years. GDP, which increased continually in the 1970s and early 1980s fell in real terms in 1985 by 5 per cent and in 1986 by $6\frac{1}{2}$ per cent; it had already been falling in per capita terms ever since 1981.

Part of the reason for this decline in GDP lies in the poor performance of industry and more recently of trade; and the reason for these illustrate and symbolize Benin's problems, both self-inflicted and external in origin. Trade was greatly affected by Nigeria's decision to close the border in April 1984 (for two years as it turned out) and to police the border more effectively. Most estimates agree that at least half of cross-border trade was lost (*Courrier*, May–June 1987, p. 19; Newnham, 1985). Even when the border reopened in 1986 the initial effect was to export Nigeria's high prices to Benin. Another feature of relations with Nigeria has been the fate of the costly (CFA fr. 106 billion) joint sugar and cement projects. These were based on the assumption that Nigeria would import part of their output—80 per cent of it in the case of the Savé sugar plant. The cement plant, however, produces at above world prices and the Nigerians buy elsewhere. The plant thus operates at 25 per cent of capacity. The sugar factory has barely functioned since it was completed in 1983. Nigeria has again found alternative suppliers, in some cases bartering its oil for sugar as the oil market has become depressed. Even the local market for sugar has not been supplied, for bad planning and inadequate local funding have led to excessively late harvesting and poor yields. The plant, with a capacity of 50,000 tonnes, produced no sugar in 1983 or 1984, 2,000 tonnes in 1985 and 7,000 in 1986. It was hoped to satisfy local demand (20,000 tonnes) in 1987, but at this level the plant cannot cover operating costs and debt service. Kérékou has recently suggested privatizing it.

Oil, which should have contributed so much, has in the end been of little help, in part because of falling prices.[12] Actual revenues are not published and have passed directly to the president's office, allowing much scope for rumour on their size and use. Kérékou's own comment on this is 'most earnings from Sémé . . . have been used to pay for the running and development of the project, and, most important to pay back the debts we contracted to finance it. This is why Sémé has not had any noticeable effect on the economy so far.' Production first began in 1982 and reached 400,000 tonnes (0.17 per cent of African output) in 1984, but stagnated thereafter. Earnings would also seem to have been small: one French source asserted that only $11m had been paid by Saga up to August 1985, and Saga's own declared profits from the Benin operation were but $0.24m for 1984. For these reasons, apparently, Benin suddenly revoked Saga's contract in August 1985 and a Swiss-based company, Pan Ocean, announced it had taken over—promising a more than three-fold increase in output, sales of $250m a year, and $2b of new investment in major projects. Few even in Benin can have believed all this, though Pan Ocean did apparently make some cash payments in early 1986, by which time the oil price had collapsed. The Norwegian government tried to rescue the contract for Saga, offering $2m in grants should it be restored, and Saga rather belatedly offered to raise Benin's earnings from 2 per cent of income to 25 per cent. The World Bank investigated and let its dissatisfaction with Pan Ocean and the terms of the new contract be known; it also froze its assistance towards the second phase of development of the oil industry. Kérékou, who claims not to have been consulted about the details of the contract, set up an enquiry in November 1985, and in mid-1986 Pan Ocean withdrew. Until April 1988, when Ashland Exploration agreed a two-year contract, no company could be found to take over management of the field, and Benin has discontinued payments on the over $100m of private loans incurred in developing the field and refinery.

The Pan Ocean affair was only one of many reverses in 1985-6, and Kérékou's speech to the PRPB congress in November 1985 was particularly sombre. Benin was forced to reduce the levels of government spending, and was unable to pay salaries for several months in 1986. A job freeze and early retirement were introduced to the public sector, and civil service and Army staffing levels and payrolls were reviewed during 1987, though no reduction announced. Approaches were made to the IMF in 1984 and talks on standby credits were announced in November 1985. They have still to reach agreement (*Courrier*, May-June 1986, pp. 17-18; *IMF Survey*, 1988, p. 32). Benin fears that conditions for a loan will prove too severe (as they did for Zambia), and the IMF remains unimpressed by Benin's shift towards the private sector and spending cuts. Donors, despite personal pleas from the president, will not move until the IMF shows signs of approval, and Benin seems to have little option but to accept IMF terms even though these will create problems with urban groups whose incomes and jobs will be threatened. By early 1988 Kérékou was referring to an agreement with the Fund as an 'absolute necessity' (*WA*, 1988, p. 1157), and housing allowances—10 per cent of salary—were abolished.

Society

The nature of Benin's economy and of its recent history has two obvious implications for its social structure. Firstly, the process of transformation from a rural, subsistence-based society into a developed, urbanized society is little advanced. Benin is still a largely rural country, in which only 29 per cent of the population live in towns of over 10,000 inhabitants. The size of the formal sector within towns is small, confined by the lack of industrialization and the limited extent of public spending; thus the working class is small even by African standards. Secondly, the main social processes since independence have not been fundamentally different from those before, in character or pace: the creation of a peasantry reliant on income from sale of crops rather than solely or primarily on subsistence; the growth of a stratum of urban poor, mainly reliant on petty trade and petty commodity production; and the expansion of a petty bourgeois stratum including those associated with the state, those involved in commerce and those with landed property or capital.

There is unusually little information available on Benin's main social groups.[13] Even the 1979 census, the only one ever taken, is not fully published, and there are very few regular statistical series on wage employment etc. Where rural society or communities have been studied recently, it has been their role in and response to rural development activity that has preoccupied authors rather than social differentiation and political sociology.[14] I am therefore obliged to be brief and to rely on case studies together with a narrow range of quantitative data.

Rural Strata

The main forces which promoted differentiation and class formation within rural society are the commoditization of crops, the integration of rural production into urban and international markets, land purchases and the growth of locally owned crop processing and freight operations. While all of these are found in the south (and to a much more limited degree in most of the north) the extent to which they have promoted social change is significantly less than in, say, Ghana or Nigeria. There is a very small rural elite, those with large land-holdings[15] and who have invested their earnings (or sometimes salaries) in setting up crop-processing operations or small transport businesses, as well as being involved in produce trading. This group, which overlaps with the old ruling families and former chiefs, was closely associated with the political leaderships of the 1960s. It has lost part of its power, and its access to those in power, since 1972 (Ayo, 1984; Wong, 1977), but not its capacity to acquire wealth since with a few exceptions the government has not attempted to intervene in this process (for one, see Wong, 1977, p. 24). Where it has—in, for example, forbidding speculative land purchases—it has not been successful (Elwert & Wong, 1978, p. 50).

Below this group (on all indicators) are a mass of rural producers, all of whom rely to some degree on subsistence production as well as on sale of crops, all of whom have access to land (though not in large amounts) and all of whom are involved in hiring or providing limited inputs of wage labour. The outcome is a pattern of differentiation familiar elsewhere in Africa (see for example Hill, 1972) and which Elwert & Wong (1978, pp. 16–42) describe for a district in Atlantique. Like Hill (whom they do not cite) they asked their informants to identify appropriate categories and assign fellow-villagers to them. The results are intuitively pleasing while also linked to important economic processes that underlie differentiation. Three categories of household were identified: the poor, who work for others, have few possessions of any sort and are short of food: middle peasant households, which produce enough for their needs and do not sell their labour except for immediate cash needs (that is for the costs of a ceremony, rather than food); and the rich, who have surplus land, can accumulate and invest (and lend) money and who habitually hire labour. The cash incomes associated with the categories were small: CFA fr. 20,000 for the poor households, 40,000 for the middle, and 130,000 for the rich (that is $90, $180 and $590). The minimum wage in 1978 was 93,600 francs.[16]

The rich (if one should call them that) were few in number, 6 per cent of the sample, and no more than 16 per cent in any of the villages surveyed. They owe their position to four things: inheritance and/or purchase of land; use of paid labour or the labour-power of clients who had, for example, borrowed land; money-lending; and involvement in cash-cropping, oil-pressing or trade. The poor did not trade, did not cultivate palms or process palm kernels (though they did harvest wild palm) and had to obtain paid work—on average twenty days a season. While these processes and relationships can lead to a permanent pattern of stratification, Elwert and Wong found as did Hill that the pattern was not stable over generations: one could fairly easily become rich (or more easily become poor). With such a pattern, social conflict may express social differentiation but is far more likely to be rooted in conflict between generations or the sexes (see Chapter 3; Brand 1977–8; Elwert 1983, 1984), or that between communities and the state, discussed below.

The Urban Poor

Benin has few large towns, and only Cotonou is substantial (see Table 4.6). The growth rate is not high (6.5 per cent per annum) partly because urban migration rates within Benin are a little lower than usual: about one-third of adult townspeople in 1979 had arrived in the previous ten years, rather than the half one might have expected.Migration rates appeared to increase, however, in the late 1970s, from 10,000 a year to 28,000 (Hadjadj, 1982, pp. 10–11). Like the rural population, nearly half of this urban mass is less than fifteen years old. The adults make their livings mainly from artisan occupations and trade, the latter especially for women. Few are wage earners: the entire modern sector employed only 28,500 in 1967 and 71,000 in 1980. In both years it was the public sector and the service sector that dominated—industry employing only 2,150 in 1967 and 6,450 in 1979, compared to 19,000 and 50,000 in the non-industrial public sector (see Table 4.7).

Though small the urban labour force was an important political force in the 1960s, capable of ending a government's life though not of installing a

Table 4.6 Urban population of Benin, 1961–79

	1961	1979
Cotonou	78,300	327,600
Porto Novo	64,000	132,000
Abomey-Bohicon	26,400	72,900
Ouidah	17,200	25,300
Parakou	14,000	60,800
Djougou	9,500	28,800
Total	209,400	647,500

Source: 1979 Census (total urban population, 1979 – 1.314m).

Table 4.7 Wage and salary earners in Benin, by sector, 1980

	Public sector	Private sector	Other	Total
Agriculture etc.	4,792	86	134	5,012
Primary extractive	96			96
Manufacturing	4,608	1,842		6,450
inc food	1,279	825		2,104
textiles	1,945			1,945
Electricity etc	700	17		717
Construction	1,756	6,555		8,311
Commerce, hotels etc	3,494	4,376		7,870
Transport	11,946	723		12,669
Banks etc.	2,271	274	188	2,733
Services	25,511	1,473	153	27,135
inc public admin	11,380			11,380
education	9,758	326		10,084
health	3,442	244		3,686
	55,189	15,329	473	70,993

Source: ILO, 1984, pp. 364–7.

new one. Since 1975, however, there has been no major confrontation between labour and the state, and this despite the minimum wage being low. Thus from 1974 to 1980 it was 93,600 francs a year, rising to 107,600 in 1980 and 167,500 in 1983, amounts less than or comparable to earnings from trade or even agriculture, and considerably less than the minimum in Burkina Faso (1978 — 150,000; 1982 — 237,000) or the Ivory Coast (1978 — 300,000; 1982 — 400,000), though not (since 1983) in Togo. One reason for this dearth of confrontation is control of union organization and activity (see Chapter 3) and the decline in militancy of the public-sector unions, led largely by civil servants from the more senior ranks who are now closely integrated within the political system. Another is the fact that relatively few workers, in either sector, are paid the minimum wage. Wages for public-sector manual workers range from 1.5 to seven times the minimum, and few families would rely wholly on the earnings of such a worker for household income. Since work ends at 2 p.m. it is also possible for formal-sector employees to be active in trade or other parts of the informal sector (see Table 4.8).

The rest of the adult urban poor are busy in trade or a range of artisan activities—furniture-making, repair work, tailoring etc. Data on this group are very deficient, although there are some short dissertations by University of Benin students (see Lachaud, 1987, pp. 6–23). It is difficult even to estimate their total numbers, though the category is probably as large as the wage labour force (ILO, 1984, pp. 111–18). Their incomes vary considerably and have not been surveyed; an ILO team estimate that they ranged (in 1980) from 192,000 to 420,000 francs a year, making them a relatively poorly paid group, though Lachaud (1987, p. 27) offers a much wider range of figures resulting from 'some visits to workshops in Contonou' in 1985 (180,000 francs up to 1.8 million). Traders, by contrast, do better (so long as we exclude those who for example sell cigarettes individually from the single packet they can afford to invest in, or who collect and sell empty bottles). A variety of surveys, none comprehensive, of this huge group—some 480,000 in Benin in 1980, perhaps 150,000 of whom were town-based (ILO, 1984, pp. 165–6)— show that for full-time traders in staple goods (maize, gari, cloth etc.) the return equals or exceeds the pay of manual workers (ibid., 167–76).

The Petty Bourgeoisie

Benin cannot be said to have an indigenous capitalist class. The private sector is small—22 per cent of formal-sector employment—and the largest enterprises within it, like the recently closed Bata shoe factory, are foreign owned.

Table 4.8 Distribution of salaries to employees in Benin, by sector, 1982

Monthly salary (francs)	Public sector					Private sector
	Civil service	Parastatal	Other nat'l	Local parastatal	Local gov't	
<10,000	2.4	3.0	0.5	6.3	9.9	7.1
10–15,000	8.6	19.4	13.2	36.0	24.4	11.4
15–20,000	22.3	17.9	16.3	21.3	37.6	17.3
20–30,000	19.5	26.5	39.6	22.5	20.4	24.6
30–40,000	14.7	10.5	12.0	5.6	3.4	13.4
40–80,000	20.3	14.9	8.6	4.1	2.8	19.6
80–125,000	4.6	4.0	7.3	1.0	0.5	1.1
>125,000	1.4	2.6	1.0	0.6	0.5	2.2
not known	6.2	1.2	1.5	2.6	0.5	3.4

Source: Lachaud, 1987, 116; figures exclude 10 per cent housing allowance for public sector (national).

Of the 167 private enterprises identified by the 1982 ILO team, 120 were small bakeries; of the forty-seven only four were large (more than 100 employees) and twenty-one medium (twenty-five-ninety-nine employees), and many of these smaller firms would not have been owned by Beninois nationals. Similarly the Chamber of Commerce identified only 220 of its members as 'merchants, importers and traders' in 1980 (and eighty-six in 1972). Little is known of the income or capital of these groups, although returns to the ministry of commerce for 1980–1 by licensed cloth sellers suggested that at least 500 of them had a turnover about CFA fr. 50 million ($160,000) (ILO, 1984, p. 294). The largest traders are far wealthier. One, thought to be among the 'five richest business women in Benin' claimed an annual turnover of CFA fr. 3–4 billion in 1977–80 (*Courrier*, May–June 1986, p. 22). Thus, while there are a handful of individuals with considerable wealth, they are probably best thought of as the richest members of a broad stratum of small indigenous capitalists, especially as they do not appear to invest much in Benin. This characteristic they share with non-Beninois local capital, which is largely Lebanese or Indian and concentrated in the import-ing of consumer durables, fabrics, rice, salt and sugar, and in flour milling.

The rest, and the majority, of the petty bourgeoisie are the senior officials and army officers associated with the state. At most about $2\frac{1}{2}$ per cent of public-sector employment can be placed in this category, some 1,400 people. Their salaries are ten to twenty times larger than manual workers, but form only part and perhaps only a minor part of their total incomes. Other sources include theft and corruption—serious enough for Kérékou to devote a series of speeches in 1980–1 to denouncing such activity—and trade and ownership of urban property and farming land. It is impossible to etimate the net 'worth' of senior figures in government, the parastatal sector or the armed forces, and one cannot assume they are all equally wealthy; but one can guess that their incomes and accumulated wealth will prove to be of the same order as the traders and businessmen and women referred to earlier.[17]

Class, Stratum and Conflict

Benin has an 'official' class analysis that echoes the categories of Marxist analysis. In early speeches (1973–6) Kérékou and others identified 'feudal' elements in the countryside, and foreign and domestic bourgeoisies (which include merchants, senior bureaucrats and the liberal professions). Against these stood the mass of the people—workers and peasants in alliance—and a small 'patriotic petty bourgeoisie' of intellectuals and the military (see for example Paraiso, 1980, p. 410; *ACR*, 1976-7, B550). This is no more than the recasting in class language of an important political division, that between strata directly involved in the old regime, and those exploited by it or which felt excluded from power within it. The categories excluded from membership of the PRPB (*ACR*, 1974-5, B625) are very similar to the first half of the dichotomy above, while those whom the new regime sought to involve in the new political institutions were essentially drawn from the second and from women. In later statements the same fundamentally political categories are used, though attempts have been made to achieve more precise definitions. Thus according to *Ehuzu* (29 September 1979) the 'industrial bourgeoisie' comprises those employing more than ten persons and the 'commercial bourgeosie' those who own 'means of trade', transport (five light or two heavy vehicles) or fixed property (more than two houses). Though curiously exact these categories do not reflect political divisions in the way earlier ones did.

Neither set of categories is of much value in understanding the social basis of power in the present political system. For that task it may be useful to turn to analysis of roughly comparable systems such as those in Tanzania (Shivji, 1976) or Mali (Meillassoux, 1970) as well as to the work of Elwert and Wong. All stress the concept of a 'bureaucratic bourgeoisie' as a component of a petty bourgeoisie, using its command of state power to accumulate, to expand its size and control of resources and to struggle against its rivals within the petty bourgeoisie or against antagonistic classes (workers, peasants). There are major problems inherent in treating the petty bourgeoisie (or the bureaucratic bourgeoisie) as a class in marxist terms, as Shivji's attempts to define it indicate (1976, pp. 48-50). But the notion of the (senior) bureaucracy as a distinct social category with distinct interests which political power makes it possible to defend and realize is readily applicable to Benin.

Under the former regime the operations of clientelism and spoils allowed the direction of state resources to fall into the hands of politicians and their regional backers, a few army officers, and some senior officials; but the bureaucracy as a whole, like the officer corps, was kept at arms' length from power and from spoils. Since 1972 the bureaucracy and the officer corps have largely monopolized power, and pursued policies that enlarged the public sector and greatly expanded the size of the bureaucracy, now nearly three times larger than in 1970.[18] The proliferation of parastatals in 1974-8 provided a large number of new senior positions for both officers and bureaucrats. It also provided opportunities for corruption and the allocation of contracts to relatives. Under such conditions it is not surprising that the parastatals proved inefficient, wasteful and unprofitable. That is precisely what one would expect if their perceived function was to satisfy the interests of the bureaucracy rather than to increase revenue, or the capacity to control the economy or public welfare. The post-1981 reforms of the parastatals entailed reorganization and the ending of the state monopolies, but not dismissal of the corrupt nor privatization; and it has been ineffective in making the sector efficient. The political system under such conditions will be one that reproduces the bureaucracy's hold on power, only allowing changes in policy or in which individual holds a particular office.

Both Shivji (for example) and Elwert go beyond this simple notion to argue that the realization of the interests of the bureaucracy is necessarily in conflict with other 'class' interests, notably those of domestic capital (merchants, owners of property, small businessmen and manufacturers etc.) and those of the subordinate classes: workers and peasants. This analysis implies a form of class struggle, but if such a struggle is being pursued in Benin then it is peculiarly muted. Kérékou, for example, has frequently attacked domestic capital for its failure to invest, its parasitism etc., but no attempts have been made to undermine or even regulate domestic capital. There have been no expropriations of land, or nationalizations of rented property or formation of parastatals to monopolize domestic trade.[19] Even Ghana under Nkrumah or Mali under Modibo Keita did more to confine domestic capital than has Benin under Kérékou.

Two reasons suggest themselves: that it is not in the interests of the bureaucracy to do so, and that it is not within their power. The former is suggested by the (limited) evidence that the bureaucracy is itself deeply involved in the operations of domestic capital, investing in land, property and trade. The latter arises from two linked factors: the heavy financial reliance of the Benin state on taxes on trade and the importance of illicit trade with Nigeria. Between 55 per cent and 75 per cent of revenue since 1974 has been raised through indirect taxes, of which the bulk are taxes on imports, up to 80 per cent of which are destined for Nigeria. Thus not only does the bureaucracy depend for its salaries on the trade with Nigeria (70 per cent of state recurrent spending is on salaries), but that trade is by its nature difficult to nationalize. It cannot even be taxed (except as imports), and no attempt has been made to police or reduce it, even when the result has been diversion of food from Beninois consumers. Thus the state has established an accommodation with domestic capital: no encroachment by the state on capital in return for no attempt by capital to exercise political power directly.

Relations with the peasantry are less obviously amicable, and there can be less interlocking of interests between peasants and bureaucrats. Yet it is hard to agree without qualification with the bald assertion that 'the relation between agricultural producers and bureaucracy is the dominant (exploitative) relation' (Elwert, 1980, p. 62), still less that the basic political contradiction is 'that between the peasants and the state' (Wong, 1977, p. 68; see also Wong 1979). Elwert bases his assertion on three features of the mid-1970s. First, he argues that the state attempted to increase output of export crops rather than food, and intervened in production more directly through expansion of state oil palm cultivation and through the imposition of cultivation of collective fields. Second, the peasants were forced to sell through state monopolies and 'the bureaucratic class appropriates these with monopoly profits to itself at the rural producer's expense' (ibid., p. 57). It is able to do so in large part because the majority of peasant consumption needs are provided by subsistence production rather than by cash earnings. Surplus is extracted by the state paying fixed prices that are well below national or international market prices. Third, the state raised a large part of its revenue from taxes on imports purchased with foreign exchange acquired from export crops but did not allocate this revenue to rural areas, favouring bureaucratic and urban consumption instead.

This account, though weak in its final argument, is confirmed by the evidence of the 1972-7 period, much of it covered in Chapter 4. For this period it is possible to argue that there was an aggressive attempt at realization of bureaucratic interests through extraction of rural surplus and rapid expansion of the state sector. Over a longer period however it is necessary to qualify the account and especially the implication of peasant/ state antagonism. This qualification arises from evidence on peasant incomes, the pattern of production and the nature of marketing. In their report on urban–rural income disparities, the 1981 ILO team concluded that 'in Benin the gap between incomes in town and country is modest and not systematically to the detriment of the country' (PECTA, 1982, p. 23). Their argument undermines notions of a general bias towards urban consumption in policy, and it is strengthened by the calculations of a later ILO team, who concluded that while there are marked regional variations, returns to peasant labour more than doubled in the 1970s, producing incomes comparable to the minimum wage by 1980 (ILO, 1984, pp. 101-8).[20] Even allowing for the urban bias in welfare spending (see Chapter 5), this trend in the 1970s and its outcome do not suggest an increasing intensity of peasant exploitation but rather its opposite.

Peasant incomes rose not because they were forced to cultivate larger areas of export crops. If anything the absolute areas so cultivated fell from the mid-1970s (or fell per capita, as with cotton); and as we already know output at best stagnated during the 1970s. Nor can higher income be attributed mainly to higher official prices, although there were increases which may—together

Table 4.9 Produce prices and price index for Benin, 1974–87

Crop	1974–5 price francs/kilo	Relative price (1974–5 = 100)						
		1976–7	1978–9	1980–1	1982–3	1984–5	1986–7
Groundnuts	40.5	136	136	123	160	198	235
Cocoa	250	100	100	100	–	–	140
Coffee	103	117	131	194	209	228	272
Karité	15	133	233	233	267	367	400
Palm kernels	31	100	108	121	135	194	65
Tobacco	105	105	114	133	152	219	228
Cottonseed	40	125	138	138	200	250	275

Source: BCEAO.

with increasing yields and labour inputs—have influenced cotton output (see Table 4.9). The main factor would appear to be the ability of peasants to produce food crops rather than export crops alone, and to sell them outside the official marketing channels, at prices which were higher (and increased faster) than official prices (ILO, 1984, p. 96). The main beneficiaries apart from peasants were of course traders, since it was to Nigeria (and other neighbours), and to the large urban markets, that the produce went. And just as the state cannot, or will not, control illicit trade, so it does not control food production or sale, other than to encourage it. Thus the state lacks the capacity, and the bureaucracy and power, to carry out the realization of bureaucratic interests to more than a limited extent. As with domestic capital, the bureaucracy has been obliged to reach an accommodation with the peasantry.

This pattern of failure to secure bureaucratic interests and abandonment of aggressive attempts to do so has two implications. It helps to explain why Benin's politics are marked not only by stability (since 1976) but also by an absence of social conflict, as opposed to factional manoeuvre, clashes over particular interests (as in 1985) or externally originating crises. The Beninois state is weak, kept in place by a political system carefully adapted to that purpose (see Chapters 3 and 6) and by compromises between major social forces. All this depends on Benin continuing to act as an entrepôt and the base for one of the world's larger smuggling enterprises, and thus on the state being able to rely on raising revenue other than by heavy direct or indirect taxation. Economic conditions since 1983, and the likelihood that a structural adjustment programme will soon be introduced fully (rather than cautiously and piecemeal as at present) make the present system less and less possible. The political future for Benin would appear to be one of increasingly sharp social conflict.

5 Domestic and Foreign Policy

Introduction

The essential criticisms of the pre-1972 regimes that were made by the more radical officers and by civilian opponents amounted to three: that all post-independence governments had been dependent on and subordinate to France, that they had been elitist, and that they had lacked a popular base. Previous chapters have shown how the Kérékou regime attempted to devise a political system that was more participatory, and an economic system that was less dependent. In this chapter I discuss attempts to devise less elitist policies in two key areas, education and health, and a foreign policy that was less aligned with French interests. In none of these policy areas were reforms fully successful, and in no case can one describe the outcome as a socialist policy, though the changes in education and health did make those services more accessible to the bulk of the population.

The reasons for failure were similar in each case. Lack of resources in particular made it impossible to carry out the reforms in education and health swiftly or fully, so that economic decline in the 1980s forced the regime to abandon either the policy (education) or its continued implementation (health). Similarly, while reliance on France and the West was lessened in the 1970s there was a distinct return to closer relations with and reliance on aid from the West as the economy began to stagnate and then shrink after 1980. Less important but still significant were other factors: lack of sufficient skilled personnel (forcing the use of the untrained teachers, for example) and inertia in the system arising from professional interests resisting change, and from growing opposition to the effects of the reforms, notably those in education, from the intelligentsia and especially the civil service. Thus by 1987 Benin's policies in these three areas were, like its economic policies, closer to those of the pre-coup regimes than those of the 1970s.

Education

The first policy area to be tackled by the new government, long before significant changes were made in the economy or health, was education. Dahomey, like other African countries, had a high proportion of its population below the age of fifteen (45 per cent) and demand for education as the main means of personal advancement has always been strong at all levels of the population. The educational system of the 1960s was a direct inheritance from the colonial period, with teaching in French, a feature which automatically ensured that most rural students would be disadvantaged and alienated. Intake at primary level covered about 27 per cent of potential pupils, with numbers falling off rapidly as the six-year course cycle proceeded (and with high percentages of pupils repeating years). Only 6.5 per cent of those who began primary education qualified for entry into secondary school, while tertiary education for which just one in a thousand of the original intake would qualify (Ronen, 1975, p. 143) was carried out abroad, in France and Senegal. The system was effectively biased towards selection for higher education, and discriminated heavily in favour of urban children, especially those with educated parents, thereby reducing enrolment rates in the essentially rural north to half their level in the south. It was also expensive, even though Dahomey spent less per child than its neighbours ($19 in 1960; Kitchen, 1962, p. 476). During the 1960s, about a quarter of the budget was devoted to education, mostly to salaries, with the proportion falling in the early 1970s.

Among the more vehement critics of the post-independence political system were teachers, and especially those active in the teachers' unions, which tended to be radical. It is hardly surprising that the 1972 *Discours-programme* should have paid specific attention to education, or that discussion of needed reform should have begun quickly. The *programme* argued that education had served foreign economic and cultural interests and needed to be replaced by a democratic system serving national and developmental needs. In May 1973 a national commission on education was convened and set out basic principles: education was to avoid elitism and the pursuit of certifications (the 'diploma disease'; see PECTA, 1982) in favour of the integration of schooling into development, especially rural development; it should be free and universal; and it should be in national languages. Subsequent discussions elaborated these goals, making it clear that education should 'not impart merely abstract and theoretical knowledge, but rather practical training adapted to the environment and its productive occupation' (Pliya, 1979, pp. 190–1). Teachers in turn should become social and developmental leaders, and formal examinations (at least at primary level) should be replaced by continuous assessment and student profiles. Although described by Kérékou as 'revolutionary' these were commonplace ideas among teaching professionals in the 1960s and early 1970s, and have been embodied in several national educational systems, including Scotland's.

Two practical decisions were also taken early, in 1974: nationalization of the private primary schools (largely Catholic) which taught about half the pupils; and major changes in the syllabus and in school activity. Only 40 per cent of the new syllabus was to be traditional subjects, the rest being split between production and moral and political training, culture and sport. Each school was to become a production unit, pupils and teachers forming cooperatives which would farm, produce craft goods and trade. These units would encourage self-reliance, give students experience of production and management, and by providing topics and themes for study would allow teachers to 'make the environment become the source, object and end of knowledge' (Houeto, 1981, p. 196). They were the crucial institutions in the reform.

Equally crucial, however, was money. The government's aim was to increase enrolment rates from 40 per cent to 61 per cent by 1983. They were to do this while transforming the syllabus and schools (and the school year, changed to fit the farming cycle). And they were to do it with an inadequately staffed ministry of education, a teaching body only half of whom were qualified, teacher-training facilities starved of funds,[1] and in the absence of any appropriate teaching materials. Pliya rather drily comments that 'the first attempts to estimate the cost of the new education produced such enormous figures that the reformers took fright' (1979, p. 193).

Costly it certainly was, and the education budget rose rapidly year upon year from 1974–5 when the reform began to 1981–2 when it was reconsidered. By this stage it consumed over a third of recurrent spending. It was essential for the state to find means of containing costs, and various short-cuts and expedients were adopted, with marked effects on the reception and outcome of the reform.[2] Resources for training, for equipping schools to become production units and for the rest of the necessary support were not available or inadequate; indeed the division of the ministry of education into three distinct ministries at this time absorbed still further resources on central administration (Hadjadj, 1982, p. 20). Salaries for teachers were kept low, so much lower than nearby francophone states that migration was stimulated and the quality (and morale) of the teaching staff fell. As pupil intake rose, more teachers had to be found; to reduce costs untrained teachers were used. Thus from 1974–5 those who had first completed lower secondary education (three years) had to do two years teaching as 'Young Revolutionary Primary Teachers' (JIRs); and by 1978 they made up a sixth of all primary teachers. University students had to do one year's teaching at the end of their second year of study. Both groups received only two months' training, half in the field, and were paid less than qualified teachers—55 per cent for JIRs, 80 per cent for the university students. In 1979 recruitment of university students ceased, and instead those who had just passed their *baccalaureat* were used, as Young Revolutionary Teachers (JBRs). The quality of such 'teachers' was low: 'their knowledge of education is rather rudimentary and their knowledge of production techniques pitiful' commented the then director of the national teacher training facility (Houeto, 1981, p. 196).

Costs affected also the productive functions of the schools. Not only were the start-up costs left to local communities to find, but the profits from production became an important source of school funds. A survey in May 1978 cited by Houeto (1981, p. 196) claimed that 60 per cent of running costs (CFA fr. 70,000) were provided by the profits. This seems high compared to official norms (20 per cent) and to earlier statistics suggesting sums closer to 25,000 francs (Guezodje, 1977, pp. 466–7). It is also high compared to the earlier but voluntary 'ruralization' experiment involving production units in 1966–72, studied by Sims (1974). She reports (p. 162) that incomes above 15,000 francs were achieved by only 3.5 per cent of her sample, although administrative estimates were higher—5 per cent over 25,000 (ibid., p. 163). None the less it is clear that production was being valued more as a source of cash than for its pedagogic benefits, a change made easier by the great difficulty in finding teachers able to teach according to the new principles (Houeto, 1981). From the perspective of the community the school was becoming a burden, even an obstacle to their own activity, for local traders complained of unfair competition.

A second major obstacle to the success of the reform was the speed and level of preparation with which it was introduced. No pilot study was done, even though the 1966–72 scheme had failed and should have served as a warning. Instead the new ministry of primary education saw it in glowing terms and as an example of what could be achieved (Guezodje, 1977, pp. 456–8; compare Sims, 1974). There was also no time to prepare new teaching materials and no resources to produce enough copies of what was prepared; those that were available went mainly to urban schools (PECTA, 1982; pp. 35–6). New syllabuses were not ready in 1975 and were only fully introduced in 1980. Teacher training had to be in-service and done by older teachers often out of sympathy with the reforms (Houeto, 1981, p. 194).

One reform was not made at all, that in methods of assessment. The old certificates remained, as they had during the 1966–72 experiment; so also did the criteria for university entry. This had two effects, providing a measure of the reform's impact on 'standards' for those who preferred the old system, and reproducing pre-reform professional norms. Other factors had similar effects: teachers were still inspected and assessed according to old criteria, and saw their promotions as depending on exam results.

By 1979 strong criticism had begun. A warning had already been given by an early field test of the reforms in Paouignan commune in 1976, where despite intensive specialist inputs observation of actual teaching practice showed 'no real links between the production effort and the intellectual work ... [and] ... hardly any change in classroom methods and behaviour'. The schools were not, of course, functioning as local centres of development (Guezodje, 1977, p. 465). Houeto writing four years later reaches very similar conclusions: 'the various measures adopted ... are still not producing the new type of teacher' she says; and 'educational supervision, the presentation and use made of lessons, teacher assessment and teachers' personal training are still ill-adapted to the aim of the school cooperative, which leads to very little interest on the part of the teacher in whatever is not conventional teaching' (1981, p. 197).

Thus the reform failed in its pedagogic and political goals. It did succeed in raising enrolment, remarkably—from 210,000 at primary schools in 1972–3 to 357,000 in 1979, a 70 per cent increase. Secondary intake doubled in the same period, and regional but not urban–rural or gender disparities were reduced (Hadjadj, 1982, p. 21). Agricultural activity has also been introduced to rural schools (and some urban), though this could be seen as doing no more than echoing the colonial call for rural education (Ronen, 1975, p. 69) or the 'back to the land' campaigns of the 1960s (ibid., p. 148; Costa, 1966). But the costs were high; fewer qualified teachers, larger classes (fifty-five pupils in primary schools, forty-six in secondary) and worse results. In 1980 the first group to have completed their secondary education in the 'new school' took the *baccalaureat*: the pass rate was half that achieved in the mid-1970s (Benin, 1983, p. 122); PECTA, 1982, p. 36). Parents and the bureaucracy protested, and the issue was among those raised at the 1979 *conférence des cadres* (ACR, 1979–80, pp. 474–5).

The ministry's initial response to its own realization of failure was to confirm that failure in a series of commune-level studies, and then to attempt to refloat the reforms by an intense publicity campaign whose terms were a tacit recognition of just how little had been achieved to change the principles, contents and methods of education (Houeto, 1981, p. 201). All this was however overtaken by the intensity of public discontent, and in 1981 the government launched a more politic response. Led by the president a vast national debate on education occurred, stimulated by the media and then with the local revolutionary committees prominent in the process as spokesmen for criticism (Jouffrey, 1983; Soudan, 1983). The school year was reintroduced as were the former structure and length of the primary and secondary cycles, but relatively little else could be done before the post-1982 economic crisis had begun. Spending on education has stagnated since, though it was still 32 per cent of the planned budget in 1987. Class sizes have been reduced steadily, stabilizing at around thirty-three in 1984, as have total student numbers. In the end the main achievement of educational reform has been its impact on enrolment rates: 64 per cent of children of primary age and 19 per cent of secondary (1984 figures). For a small, very poor African country this is remarkable, but it is not socialism.[3]

Health Policy[4]

In the immediate post-independence era Dahomey's health situation and medical system was typical of small, underdeveloped states. Medical care was concentrated in the coastal areas, especially Atlantique region and was particularly poor in the north. Doctors, and indeed all qualified medical staff were found mostly in the towns (including Paris: Decalo (1975, p. 43) claims there were more Dahomean doctors there in the early 1970s than in Dahomey). Their philosophy and treatments were curative rather than preventive and focused largely upon urban populations, especially the elite. Professional norms prevailed, as did a very hierarchical system (racially as well as qualification based). The health of the general population, weakened as it was by endemic diseases such as malaria and by decreasing nutritional standards, was poor. In the early 1960s 22 per cent of children died before their fourth birthday, giving an average life expectancy of thirty-seven years.

Kérékou's *Discours-Programme* of 1972 referred in passing to health, saying that preventive medicine should take priority over curative, and that traditional medicine and healers should not be neglected, forming as they did part of Dahomey's national culture and resources. These principles reappeared in the 1977–80 Plan (Benin, 1977), which marked the first formal presentation of the new health policy. As with other policy areas the development of policy was slow, even after 1974, and required considerable consultation. At the root of the new policy, then, were: equal access to health care, which should eventually be free; preventive medicine as the main elements of basic health care, aided by clean water supplies and health education; and the integration of traditional with 'modern' medicine. Rural areas in particular were to receive priority, and villagers were to be directly involved in health care, on the principle of self-reliance.

The key institution to be created, for which there already existed a pilot scheme in Atlantique (Berthet 1978), was the village health unit (Unité Villageoise de Santé, UVS). Each unit was to be staffed with three part-time local volunteers, trained by the state but maintained and housed by the village, and consisting of a midwife, a nursing auxiliary and a dispenser. The unit would be responsible to an elected village committee including women and traditional healers among its members. Above this would stretch the formal, state-run, health service with health complexes at commune level (three nurses and sixteen beds), district health centres (a fifty-bed hospital and appropriate general medical staff), provincial hospitals and at the apex the existing university hospital at Cotonou able to cope with specialized problems and research. Private medicine was to be left untouched, and has been. Each level of this structure would refer cases, where necessary, to the level above, but it was assumed that the village units, with their staff drawn from the village itself, and cooperating with traditional midwives and healers, would be able to cope with the great majority of patients.

Even if the villagers did sustain their units, this conception was expensive and would take time to build, at least a decade. By 1982 the targets had been reduced somewhat and the degrees of attainment achieved as shown in Table 5.1.

Progress has slowed: in 1979 there had already been thirty-seven village units in Atacora alone. It was also uneven, as the final column in Table 5.1 shows, in part because when external aid has been offered for health care, it has been mainly for training or hospitals (especially that from China and North Korea). Standards of health have risen (as they have elsewhere in West Africa), and only 13 per cent of children now die before their fourth birthday, life expectancy has increased to forty-nine years and the number of

Table 5.1 Public health aims and achievements in Benin, 1977 and 1982

Level	1977 target	1982 target	Attained	%
University hospital	1	1	1*	100
Provincial hospital	6	6	4†	67
District centre	84	79	47‡	60
Committee complex	510	426	72§	17
Village units	3,400	2,500	292	12

Source: Benin, 1983, p. 140.
* Did not accept referrals.
† All below standard.
‡ 42 below standard
§ 43 below standard, 5 not operational.

inhabitants per doctor (or nurse) has halved. The distribution of curative health care is less uneven, although Atlantique is still relatively overendowed, and Mono poorly staffed.[5]

Three main problems appear to have influenced the implementation of the new health policy both in its extent and its content: resources, bureaucratic and professional values and interests and state–society relationships. Their overall effect has been to strip the policy of its political content, reducing the element of preventive activity and collaboration with traditional healers and undermine the self-reliance of the village units. What was a new approach to health care has become merely a new structure for a health service.

Resources were always going to be a problem, whether human, infrastructural or cash. There was never enough money to ensure rapid growth, for while in cash terms the health budget rose by 84 per cent from 1974 to 1983, the proportion of the national budget this represented fell from 10 per cent to 7 per cent. In real terms health spending fell by at least 25 per cent, and since recent budgets have been lower than 1983, real health spending will have declined further, perhaps to half of its 1974 level.

Bureaucratic and health professional norms stress hierarchy, centralization, and qualifications; and they favour technical conceptions and solutions over political and popular ones. The philosophy of the village health units was opposed to these norms, but Lachenmann's (1980) case study of the application of the new policy in a district on the southern border of Atacora makes it clear that these norms came swiftly to predominate. This could be seen both in the absence of the necessary coordination between health and other sectors, especially rural development and education, and in the conception of the village units. The criteria chosen for village health workers, which included literacy in French, showed that they 'were regarded as an additional auxiliary labour force, which is subject to professional norms'. Lachenmann goes on to say 'the people have not been mobilised to help themselves autonomously. Instead a new category of health personnel has been created and now forms the lowest level of the existing structure' (Lachenmann, 1982, pp. 261, 262).

State–society relationships affected both the village units and traditional healers. As I argue elsewhere, the impact of the Dahomean and to a lesser degree the Beninois state on rural society has been perceived by it as damaging and exploitative (see for example Kora, 1979: Elwert & Wong, 1978). The village units' policy required that the village supplied the three (sometimes four) volunteers with housing, produce and cash, although each also helped support herself (or himself) with work in the fields or other occupations. In practice housing was supplied, but other support was at best 'sporadic' (Lachenmann, 1980, p. 130).[6] Villagers saw no good reason to make yet further contributions to a state service, and indeed Lachenmann elsewhere suggests that the main attraction to the ministry of the village units may have been their cheapness (1982, p. 258). Some of the volunteers reacted by making charges for their services, but since this can most readily be done for curative care, they abandoned their preventive duties. Others worked less or moved into the formal sector.

Traditional healers are an important part of basic health care, whether they use local herbal or other remedies or rely on psycho-social techniques. The healers were, however, suspicious of the administration's motives in trying to integrate them into the health service, fearing that their professional secrets would be stolen (Lachenmann, 1980, pp. 111–14). The prolonged anti-witchcraft campaign in the 1970s, which I discuss elsewhere, also made many traditional healers reluctant to have anything to do with the state, as have clashes between local administrators and healers (Ayo, 1982, pp. 383–4; Ayo, 1984, pp. 368–9).

Foreign Policy and External Relations[7]

Dahomey's economic and political subordination to France in the immediate post-independence period was mirrored in its external relations, tightly confined as these were to France and the organizations of francophone states including OCAM and the smaller Conseil d'Entente, both dominated by conservative positions and by relationships between heads of states rather than between states themselves. Although some discussion of more than formal links with Nigeria had occurred before 1972, it was not until 1971 that an ambassador to Lagos was accredited, and 1972 that economic assistance from Nigeria began (Ronen, 1975, pp. 177–86). The impact of the 1972 coup and of the adoption of the socialist path has, however, been more an expansion of external relations and the principles underlying them than the substitution of one polarization or set of principles for another. Like many other small states, including radical states, Benin has sought to achieve at least good relations with all states including France and the great powers.

The principles set out or implied in the 1972 *Discours-Programme* have been elaborated but not altered in subsequent policy statements (for example Benin, 1976; PRPB, 1979; see also Houndjahoue, 1984b). They remain nationalism, anti-imperialism, non-alignment and 'good neighbourliness'. These have dictated less a questioning of the existence of links with France or francophone organizations as an attempt to revise the terms of these links. Similarly, while in pursuit of non-alignment (and anti-imperialism) Benin has increased contact with the Soviet Union and created and built on contacts with China, North Korea and other socialist Third World states (Cuba, Nicaragua, Afghanistan etc.), but it has also tried to achieve good relationships with the United States and West European powers, including West Germany, Norway and the United Kingdom. The need to reconstruct and develop the economy has led (in addition to a constant search for aid) to closer ties with the regional economic power, Nigeria, and to economic cooperation with Niger, Burkina Faso and Libya.

Where there have been changes in relationships they have either been temporary, or the product of the changed circumstances of the 1980s and the impact of world recession. Conflicts over the violation or delimitation of boundaries have occurred with each of Benin's neighbours (Nigeria, Togo, Niger, Burkina Faso). None has reached the stage of potential conflict and all have been resolved through negotiation, aided by the creation of permanent joint commissions. Less easy to conciliate have been the tensions arising from domestic political factors. Thus the 1975–7 period with its coup attempts and invasion undermined relationships with several African states. Morocco (already alienated by Benin's support for Polisario in Western Sahara) and Gabon were implicated in the preparation of the invasion, and relationships remained hostile for several years thereafter. Other conservative states such as Senegal and the Ivory Cost which had little sympathy for Benin's radical stand, became more distant as did Togo. Togo's location makes it the closest base for Benin's political exiles, and Benin frequently accused Togo of conniving at or supporting conspiracies and attempts against it by exile groups during 1975–8. The border was closed several times, most notably after the 'Zinsou plot' of October 1975 when it remained shut for six months. Once the effects of the 1977 invasion had waned however, relationships with Togo improved—though the bombings and apparent coup attempt in Lomé in 1986 evoked Togolese suspicions of Beninois complicity and a cooling of relations.

Given Nigeria's wealth and the regional ambitions of its military governments (see Nwokedi, 1985; Shaw, 1987) it has had to be a key state in Benin's external relations. During the 1970s both diplomatic and cooperation ties were strengthened. Benin, as a member of ECOWAS (the Nigerian-founded regional association) and of the wholly francophone regional bodies, has tried to mediate between Nigeria and the francophone states, notably the Ivory Coast. It has also signed a variety of cultural, scientific and economic agreements with Nigeria, two of which covered major development projects—the Onigbolo cement factory and the Savé sugar complex. Both had Nigerian capital and were intended to supply the Nigerian market. As Nigeria's economy declined in the 1980s, its conduct towards Benin altered, becoming less considerate of the effects of its essentially domestic actions on the Benin economy. In 1983, 224,000 Beninois were expelled from Nigeria (Aluko, 1985) as were a great many more Ghanaians, and while both states received aid to cope with the influx, the expulsions are one cause of the rapid erosion of the economy after 1983. The expulsions were repeated on a smaller scale in 1985, by which time Nigeria had also closed its border with Benin. This action, taken to reduce smuggling and other forms of cross-border exchanges (such as migration) lasted two years and had serious economic effects (see Chapter 4). Nigeria has also refused to buy the output of the cement and sugar projects, arguing that the prices are too high (as they are, by international standards), thus making the projects unviable and serving only to increase Benin's debts. The tone of Nigerian comments on its relationships with Benin became harsh in the mid-1980s, less neighbourly and more arrogant. Benin perforce cannot respond other than by pleading for more consideration and better relations, without success until 1989 (*WA*, 1989, p. 307).

Another victim of recession has been Libya, though to a lesser degree than Nigeria. As part of its assertion of non-alignment and anti-imperialism Benin established diplomatic ties with Libya early in 1973, following these with the creation a Libya–Benin commission and the financing by Libya of three joint companies. Benin has supported Libya diplomatically (notably in its conflicts with the United States), and more than merely diplomatically in its activities in Chad. Here Benin has provided training and transit camps for supporters of Libya's Chadian clients, especially Goukouni, leading to worsened relations with Niger from 1983 on. A growing appreciation of the cost of Libyan alignment and distaste for the heavy pressure for it from Libya has coincided with a decline in Libya's economic aid and the failure of the three joint companies to make a profit. Like Ghana and Burkina Faso, Benin has tended to retreat somewhat from close ties with Libya, aided in her case by pressures from France. The United States forced Benin to expel the long-standing Libyan ambassador, Mustapha Abu Setta, in 1988. It accused him of coordinating regional destabilization (though producing no evidence), and threatened to prevent Benin obtaining World Bank loans (*QER*, 1988/2, 1988/3).

Greater continuity is visible in relations with socialist states and major powers, and to the extent that there has been change it has not been at Benin's initiative. Over the years since 1972 there has been an increasingly high-level exchange of visits with China and North Korea, together with a flow of technical assistance and even project aid; China for example has built a sports stadium and a cigarette factory. The Soviet Union by contrast has provided very little beyond military assistance, and even that is linked to hard-currency arms sales. It provided 90 per cent of arms purchases in 1979–83 (*QER*, 1986 no. 1) and the most recent high-level contact was a military delegation (*QER*, 1987 no. 2).

During the 1980s the Soviet Union's ties with Benin have become looser, perhaps more the result of its indifference than of active choice. The other great power has shown no greater interest (Houndjahoue, 1984a). The United States provided some food and medical assistance in the 1960s as well as technical assistance and a little project aid. Its reactions to the coup and the adoption of a socialist path were cautious, but after troops forced their way into the American ambassador's residence in search, they said, of a suspected arms cache, the United States suspended aid and withdrew its ambassador. Houndjahoue says it also tried to influence international agencies to deny Benin funding (ibid., p. 28). Another breach of diplomatic norms occurred in 1977 after the invasion police and troops harassed foreigners, including American diplomats. Other minor incidents served to sustain American suspicions, but by 1982 both governments were ready to restore relations; an ambassador was finally appointed in November 1983. American aid, which had in practice resumed before then, has not been particularly generous since.

Far more important to Benin than either great power has been the former colonial power, which pursues a very active African policy (see for example Bayart, 1985). France dominated Dahomey's economy, budgeting, policy and external relations until 1972, and even then despite anti-French sentiment released by the coup, Kérékou was anxious to maintain the link with France. Sustained it has been though not without modification[8] and an occasional hiccup—as with the withdrawal of the ambassador for most of 1975 after accusations of French complicity in the 1977 invasion and a virtual boycott of the ambassador later in that year. Relations and the flow of aid improved after Mitterrand became president of France, and Kérékou and he exchanged visits in 1981 and 1983. France remains Benin's major donor ($23 million in 1985), although Benin has successfully diversified both trade and aid, and a broad spectrum of states including West Germany, Norway, Japan as well as Arab agencies have provided loans and grants in the 1980s.

Benin's conduct of its external relations has been governed much more by principles common to many small Third World states—non-alignment, nationalism and collective action—as well as a pragmatic judgement of what is possible for small, weak states (Calvert, 1986) than it has been by socialist ideology. Yet it would be wrong to see the ideology as mere rhetoric. Benin has shown a commitment to non-alignment, to supporting radical international causes (see for example Natchaba 1985-6) and to maintaining relationships with socialist states, despite the costs that this has at time involved. That it is now being drawn more tightly into relationships with Western powers and institutions is more the result of the underlying weakness of its economy than a fundamental change of position or abandonment of principle.

6 Conclusion: Stability and Socialism

Remarkably little analytical material has been produced on contemporary Beninois politics. The work of the late 1970s (Ronen, 1979; Decalo, 1979, 1982) where it is not simply descriptive tends to contrast the regime's practice with its claims, especially that of its adherence to Marxism. It thereby replaces the question of what is Benin's political system and by an often sour discussion of what it is not. More recent work (Medeiros, 1981; M. L. Martin, 1984, 1985; Ronen, 1987) focuses on only part of the question in that it sees Benin as a military regime to be understood in the context of comparative studies and theories of military rule. Thus M. L. Martin (1985) sees Benin as an example of an inevitable deradicalization ('thermidorianization') of military rule, itself seen in terms of three phases: a moderate technocratic and apolitical phase (1960s African coups in general; Benin 1972-4), a politicized, radical phase (some 1970s coups; Benin 1974-9) and a phase of demilitarization and lessened radicalism (Benin, 1980-). This produces a tidy descriptive framework for Beninois politics but in the absence of a convincing account of why military intervention and rule should follow such a pattern (if indeed it does), and of why military rule should be treated as an analytically distinct category, it fails to provide an analysis of Benin's political history or political system. In this chapter I shall attempt both, though to a limited degree, by identifying Benin not as an instance of military rule but as one example of a common African political system, to be found among both civil and military regimes, and which arises from a common post-independence African problem: instability.

In Chapter 2 I argued that Dahomey's instability in 1960-72 could be traced in large measure to the reliance of the party leaderships on clientelism (patronage) as their means of attracting electoral support and of creating a cohesive party network. Since clientelism is a swift and efficient means to such an end, it was the means adopted by party leaderships in all cases in which decolonization came about through an electorally mediated transfer of power (the vast majority of cases). Yet clientelism is also profoundly destabilizing. Because it is based upon competition for access to or control of state resources, but lacks any means for containing or mediating such competition, it inevitably creates or enhances various forms of conflict (communal, intra-elite, local-central), promotes corruption and political violence and erodes regime legitimacy. Soon after independence, political crises arise from the contradictions of clientelism; if unresolved a further development occurs, into what Richard Joseph (1983) has called 'prebendal politics', involving endemic corruption, violence and instability. The regime will fall, normally to a coup.

In a large number of regimes, however, this sequence has not occurred or has been prevented from recurring. In such regimes there have been, to varying degrees and with varying timing, a set of institutional and political reforms, notably:

— the creation of a strong executive presidency;
— bureaucratization of the party;
— control of national representative institutions; and
— control of local and sectional representative institutions.

These authoritarian and centralizing reforms reduce the scale and scope of clientelist competition and make it more possible to contain its destabilizing effects while retaining its representative and legitimizing roles. There are of course limitations to this process. It appears impossible to introduce and sustain such reforms in every state, and perhaps Ghana under Nkrumah was an instance of an unsuccessful attempt. The reforms do not, furthermore, eliminate conflict nor guarantee stability; containment of class and stratum conflict lie outside their scope. Yet they do appear to be closely associated with stability, the creation of legitimacy and authority and the institutional-ization of political systems, shown in the growing frequency with which peaceful, constitutional presidential succession can occur.

What I describe was not necessarily done as a carefully designed strategy, nor uniformly. The extent to which the political system changed in each state, and thus the extent to which the old system may be seen within the new, varies in each state over time, and between states. In part, the reason lies in the gradual building up of reforms in response to particular political crises arising from the general crisis of clientelist politics, in states with different degrees of political development and extents of class formation. I have attempted to abstract from a large number of case histories what appear to be the essential elements of a general trend towards centralization and bureaucratization, arising like spoils politics (see Chapter 2) from the breakdown of clientelism, but without leading to instability. Rather they are associated with the absence of coups, or the endings of a sequence of coups. Regimes in many African states have carried out such reforms, among them Tunisia, Kenya, Tanzania, Malawi, Zambia, Botswana, Senegal, the Ivory Coast, Guinea-Conakry, Togo, Benin, Cameroon and Zaïre.[1] Of these, only one—Guinea—has fallen to a successful coup. Several others have weathered economic or political crises of the same scale and intensity as those which preceded coups or other violent changes in government elsewhere. By contrast Ghana, Nigeria, Sudan, Uganda and Chad have suffered repetitive political crises and breakdown, and in three cases the collapse of government itself, as opposed to a particular regime. Below I set out this argument in more detail and link it to the case of Benin.[2]

The Dynamics of Clientelist Collapse

Three broad consequences flow from the growing crisis of clientelist politics, and create conditions under which the regime becomes subject to military intervention.

The prime need for retaining, or gaining, power affects both the leading/ ruling party and the opposition. The former attempts to secure itself against defeat by three techniques—harassment of the opposition, or its cooptation; followed by manipulation of the democratic process, through more or less extensive (and successful) election rigging; and abandonment of the democratic process, in whole or part, through banning the opposition, cancelling the elections etc. Gradually all the institutions that are part of political participation fall into disuse or are transformed into means of control (Nelson Kasfir's 'departicipation'). The process is habitually accompanied by the erosion of civil liberties and growing political violence. The opposition, faced with such activity and itself desperate to gain power, at the very least at some significant local level, will itself respond with violence.

Equally the opposition will use the most effective techniques it can find for creating support. At root there are two. It can play upon local rivalries and recruit those who are opposed to the ruling parties' local notables, thus intensifying local divisions and conflicts. Or it can play upon larger, communal divisions, in an attempt to transform itself into a communal party with enough support to force the ruling party to come to terms with it and share power, or even to displace that party. In the process communal conflict is intensified and politicized, transformed into regionalism and 'tribalism'. Clientelism also makes the likelihood of economic crisis grater, and its impact worse, through encouraging the inefficient use of resources, and through corruption, which not only withdraws resources from development activity, but also alienates whole sections of the population. Equally important is the conflict between the use of state resources to reproduce support and their use to increase accumulation by that part of the elite aligned with the governing party, which is resolved in almost every case in favour of the elite, by raising taxes and cutting the incomes of the poor. Such 'austerity programmes' alienate further support, including in some cases that of the officer corps.

Thus clientelism encourages competition for resources as the main means of creating support for local and national politicians. Yet it provides no means for regulating and controlling competition, whether between individuals, factions, communal groupings or strata. As competition intensifies, it is transformed into political and often communal conflict, in a context of growing violence. The political system becomes dominated by intense, violent and exclusive competition for control of state resources between rival factions of the elite, in which the political base of the regime undergoes sharp contraction, owing to alienation of mass support and the exclusion of sections of the elite from political participation and a share in the spoils. The normal outcome of this process is a military coup, and a regime which itself falls victim to the development of spoils politics, ushering in an apparently endless series of unstable regimes.

Achieving Stabilization

There appears then to be a dilemma: with clientelism, no stability; without it, no support. It is, however, possible to resolve the clientelist dilemma, at least in the medium term, by a series of political reforms, which have three basic effects:

- containment and downgrading of the role of clientelism within the political system (and thus also the role of the key clientelist institution, the party, where it still exists);
- centralization of power, combined with the decentralization of competition;
- substitution of a largely bureaucratic structure for the former party-based structures, with consequent effects on elections, the party and the legislature.

Executive control/presidentialism

An almost universal reform is to combine the positions of president and prime minister into an executive presidency. This is followed by:

- the granting/taking of additional powers by the president:
- the transfer to the office of the president of all or part of the powers of various ministries;

— the transfer of resources to the office of the president, allowing the president, as opposed to the cabinet, increased control over the budget, and over the utilization of external funds, notably aid; and
— the creation of new institutions, again coming under the president.

One consequence of these changes is the declining importance of individual ministries, and of the cabinet as a collective body. This is reflected in the growing tendency to appoint non-politicians to cabinet posts (for example, bureaucrats, army officers) or to replace full ministerial positions with ministers of state, who then become part of the president's office. Politically, what has been achieved includes:

— centralization of authority;
— an increase in political capacity and sometimes in administrative efficiency;
— the elevation of the party leader from being only the leader of the dominant faction in the party, fighting it out with other faction leaders (who will normally be ministers), to a position with the potential to be above factional conflict, and to regulate it.

This process I have described in some detail in Chapter 3, though in the case of Benin it is the gradual replacement of officers, especially those associated with the 1972-5 period, by civilian ministers that occurs rather than that of civilian politicians by bureaucrats and officers. It is also the case that in Benin Kérékou has not marginalized the National Executive Council (the cabinet) in the way that for example was done in Senegal or Malawi, though he was clearly able to dominate it after 1975-6.

Bureaucratization of the party

Under the impact of clientelism the ruling party (or parties) becomes transformed into a cornucopia for (at least part of) the elite, and into a repressive institution for the electorate. Rather than this, the party is here transformed into (or in some cases displaced by) an administrative hierarchy linked to the president. In some cases (as in Tanzania from the late 1960s) administrative and party posts are merged, especially at regional and district level where the party tends to be weak, and the new post becomes part of the local administration. In others—as in Ghana during what I see as an unsuccessful attempt by Nkrumah to bring about bureaucratic-centralizing reforms—party positions are given additional, administrative functions; and in others still, like Kenya and the Ivory Coast, the party was simply allowed to atrophy as a distinct institution, leaving only local politicians and parliamentarians without much party machinery. Apart from strengthening the administration, its political effect is to help shift allocation of a great deal of local spending from the hands of local political leaders into the hands of administrators, and ultimately the president: that is it creates one means of controlling the extent, spread and costs of clientelist competition over resources at local level.

In the case of Benin the old party machinery was as far as possible eradicated and its protagonists forced into inactivity. What replaced it was the complex sytem of local councils and committees described in Chapter 3 which combine limited local representation with the transformation and exercise of central authority. The PRPB does not perform a general representative (or mobilizing) function being—like the single party in Kenya—a club for the powerful, and thus being small, with a narrow social base, poor linkages with the grassroots and little activity outside its leading organs (which are essentially parts of government) and on ritual occasions such as conferences.

Control of national representative institutions

The principal representative institutions at national level are parliaments and parties. Where there has been no coup and the reform process occurs under civilian leadership then it is common to find that a formal one-party state is declared, allowing for rival parties to be made illegal while at the same time the leadership of such parties is incorporated into the new single party (as in Senegal or Cameroon). This allows the leader of the single party (the president) to achieve greater control over political competition thereby containing conflict. Those leaders that cannot be incorporated are dealt with brutally: exile, detention or death is their fate.

Where, as in Benin, a military regime has already banned the old parties these 'processes' are unnecessary, though the banning of political organizations other than those created by the new state is common to both cases. So also is the downgrading of parliament by the erosion of its powers and significance. It will usually remain in existence, or a new one be created; and it may play the part of loyal critic. At the same time:

— it loses its legislative initiative, *de facto* or *de jure*;
— its membership is vetted by the government and part of it may not be elected but appointed;
— it may not provide the sole route into the cabinet, or even the majority of ministers;

— and where there are (semi-) competitive elections, members will be far more electorally insecure than before. It is common to find half of an assembly or parliament losing their seats at an election (as in Benin 1984).

Control of local or sectional representative institutions

These institutions are the means of representing and mobilizing parts of the population, and are the scene of a great deal of clientelist activity in the unreformed system (until it begins to decay) as can be seen from Ahomadegbe's careful cultivation of union leaderships in Porto Novo. In both cases the impact of the reform adopted is to reduce the potential for competition, and thus conflict, and at the same time to integrate the institutions more firmly within the centralized administrative machinery. Their representative function is not eliminated, however, though it is circumscribed and controlled; and conflict likewise is not eliminated so much as contained.

Local government institutions, where these have been elected bodies, are usually replaced by appointed counterparts, or by a structure reminiscent of the colonial local administration: a commissioner assisted by a group of administrators and party bureaucrats. Not all locally elected bodies may be eliminated, however, for it is often true that local party elections, or those for the offices and committees of local sectional organizations (such as cooperatives) will continue. Indeed it appears to be more effective, from the regime's standpoint, if they do, as they allow a means of representing local demands and opinions (as may parliamentary elections) without threatening overall control of the state. Thus Bayart points out in an article on Cameroon how keenly contested elections are for positions in local and municipal councils (Hermet *et al.*, 1978, p. 80), and discussion in Chapter 3 of local councils indicates that the same holds for Benin.

Sectional organizations such as trade unions are linked to, and controlled by, the administration in several ways. The formal structure becomes legally defined, the government creating a single national centre (for example for workers or students) to which all unions/student bodies must belong. Often it is also obligatory for individuals to belong as well. This eliminates competition between rival organizations, and helps to reduce the officers' reliance on reproducing support from their members or on external sources of cash (for example the international trade union movement). This in turn reduces the need for clientelist recruitment. The leadership is bureaucratized, as with the party. The officials may all be appointed, as in Tanzania; the union general secretaryship may be combined with the post of Minister of Labour;

or the elected secretary may be transformed into an administrator, while the other leaders, national and even local, are drawn into a set of committees which turn out to be largely concerned with the execution of government policy. Alternatively the organization may become (or continue to be) a section of the single party, as in Benin, with candidates for office drawn from among party members only, and vetted or selected by the party leadership at national level or the administration at local level. The administration will also intervene (as it does for party elections) in the local union elections, to ensure the 'right' result, as far as possible. Links with outside bodies (for example the international student or union federations) may be forbidden or strictly controlled, and resources available to the organization are strictly regulated especially those from abroad; but they are not necessarily reduced. Thus the introduction of payment of union dues by 'check-off' (that is directly by the employer deducting it from members' pay) combined with compulsory union membership will automatically increase union revenue dramatically. It also makes it difficult for members to control the officials. A set of rules, restrictions and structures governing activity is established by government. They include formal industrial relations' machinery, which forbids strikes, makes 'arbitration' by the administration obligatory, creates official bargaining and regulatory machinery, regulates union structures and elections, etc. Finally repression of dissident or unofficial activity will continue, usually in an institutionalized form, and sometimes violently.

The Impact of Reform

The inevitable crisis of clientelist politics thus gives rise to two distinct forms of politics: spoils politics, and centralized-bureaucratic politics. The former, which has also been called 'prebendal' or 'neopatrimonial' politics, has at its core uncontrolled and exclusive competition for state resources ('winner takes all'), principally in order to maximize individual accumulation. The latter attempts to contain clientelist competition within a centralized and bureaucratized political system focused on the presidency, with twin goals of ensuring political order and promoting class formation. That these goals can be achieved, albeit to varying degrees, can be attributed to the contrasting role within the latter of clientelism and resource allocation, participation and communal and class conflict. The root difference between the two forms of politics lies in the partial displacement of clientelist networks by centralized, bureaucratic structures. Clientelism may then be controlled essentially by two techniques: reducing the resources available for clientelist competition;

and reducing the scope of the political arena within which clientelism is significant.

The first of these involves channelling much of state spending, provision of licences etc. directly through the bureaucracy to recipients. This allows for clientelist networks to continue to operate, but only to compete for a limited proportion of the spoils, and in the presence of a more powerful competitor, the administration. The presidency can then permit, or encourage, clientelist competition, as a political technique. When more active or visible support is required (as in Senegal during 1968 following student and worker activity, or in the late 1970s during peasant discontent) more resources can be channelled temporarily into clientelist networks. The second technique, which is that found in Benin, involves an attempt to confine clientelist politics to the local level, eliminating it as far as possible from national politics. Resources are channelled to the local level, and made available for local competition, through the administration (or as in the case of Tanzania, through the bureaucratized party). In that competition, the local party organization or elected local councils may very well be only one of many important distinct and competing clientelist networks: Bayart mentions several in his work on Cameroon.

Thus the allocation of resources is no longer wholly determined by the outcome of clientelist conflict and individual greed; and thereby conflict at the centre is reduced and with that the likelihood of political crisis. Instead allocation is determined by the presidency and the national/provincial administration at the centre, and is influenced locally by the administration, which has several implications. The capacity of politicians to influence national allocation by mobilizing ethnic support may be reduced, making tribalism less a source of conflict and instability. Thus in Dahomey political life seemed at times to consist solely of regionalism—Decalo's 'tripartite struggle for ultimate hegemony' (1976, p. 51) between 'remarkably stable and cohesive political camps ... divided sharply along ethnic-regional lines' (1979, p. 233). Benin by contrast has shown little sign that regionalism or 'tribalism' remains important political forces, although there is some anecdotal evidence that Kérékou has both sustained northern influence within the army and government, and has engaged in ethnic balancing in selection of candidates and making of appointments. That regionalism should have been so subdued indicates both that it was a product of the old system and that the new one provides effective means of control.

A further implication is that allocation to the base can occur both through local politicians as before, and through state machinery, which allows for local competition while also creating some regime support. Allocation to the residue of the clientelist network is smaller, and more subject to regulation than before, though there must always be some resources available for local competition. Finally corruption will still occur, but may be easier to regulate, and be subject to regulation. Wong, for example, who provides a vivid and telling account of local corruption in the 1960s (1977, pp. 20–9) also suggests that after 1972 it became less overt and more risky because of official campaigns against it. Clearly corruption still exists, particularly among bureaucrats and probably some ministers; at the same time (as in Zambia; see Szeftel, 1983) more than merely rhetorical attempts are being made to control it and to prevent it becoming a threat to regime legitimacy.

Participation is also contained, essentially with the (s)election of local or sectional representatives whose activity and often whose elegibility is determined to a large extent by the centre. Participation is not excluded—as it is with spoils politics—but regulated. The reforms involve a concerted downgrading of the machinery of a democratic state: the legislature, local government, voluntary organizations, elections. None the less, any stable government must be able to rule without constant recourse to coercion; there must be some basis for legitimacy and some means of representation within the political system. In most cases this is achieved by retaining aspects of the old system, but confining their scope. Thus the retention of clientelism allows a means of representing demands at local level to continue to exist; it was in this function that clientelism had its origins.

Another and linked mechanism through which representation can be ensured but also controlled is electoral activity at local and national level. Elections for local councils (where these exist), administrative posts or party branch offices allow for local competition and acknowledge that the locality should preserve some autonomy. Thus in Cameroon, where most elections are formal affairs, those for the lowest levels have been heavily contested and show all the features of factionalism and clientelism of the old system. Those who are elected both articulate local demands and are responsible to the centre for political order in their locality. If they fail in the first function they will (probably) lose office at the next election; if they fail in the second, the centre can intervene, either by manipulating local competition or by more repressive techniques.

Where (as in the case of Kenya, Senegal or Zambia for example) national elections are based on local constituencies, those elected perform related functions to those of local councillors. They too are judged on their capacity to ensure central resources are allocated to the locality, and on their capacity to ensure political order. They use clientelist methods to create a network of supporters, and obtain resources for the network and the individuals within it by bargaining with the presidency and with the administration, rather as in the late-colonial period. More broadly, the retention of such parliamentary elections and of a working parliament brings additional functions into play. A relatively minor one is the role of parliamentary debate and criticism as a safety valve for opposition, or warning mechanism. More significantly, election to parliament can be a means of recruiting local politicians not so much into a national clientelist network, but into the centralized, bureaucratic system. An MP who successfully contests repeated elections clearly has a secure local base and can be recruited into the 'real' regime; a local political boss, able to influence the outcome in several constituencies, will become part of the group at the very centre of the regime (though he—and it always is he—is far more likely to be such a member already). Benin's Revolutionary National Assembly, with its corporatist basis and lack of real powers, does not (yet) form part of a representative system and hence it and its members cannot perform such functions.

The Limitations of Reform

The forms of conflict which were most readily exacerbated by clientelism were also those more readily controlled by the reforms outlined earlier, especially communal conflict and those local factional conflicts which in spoils regimes tend to escalate to the centre. Equally, intra-elite conflict can be reduced and elite cohesion increased, allowing for the development of an increasingly established (petty) bourgeoise. It is not however possible to eliminate conflict, and the reforms do not guarantee stability. Quite apart from external intervention and economic crisis, centralized-bureaucratic systems are prone to conflict arising from the competing objectives of the reforms, for while these are not necessarily at odds with each other, it is all too easy for a regime to seek to secure one at the expense of another.

The main objectives have been the securing of political order together with legitimacy and support, the creation of a cohesive (petty) bourgeoise and retention of power by the ruling clique headed by the president. The reforms adopted are highly authoritarian involving the exclusion of most of the population from national political influence, centralized political control over the party and other means of representation and elimination of political opposition organized outside the party. At the same time, authoritarianism must not become mere repression; the goal is to limit the use of force by using institutions such as the party, unions, etc as a means of control as well as means for the population to make limited demands. Permanent political exclusion of minorities, or the elimination or nullifying of participation at the local level, or a failure of political order reflected in increasing reliance on force and repression—as in Guinea-Conakry in the late 1970s and early 1980s—will destabilize a regime.

So also will attempts by the elite, or worse still a section of it, to monopolize resources. This becomes visible in growing corruption and theft, and sharply increasing differentiation between elite and poor—all of which occurred in Kenya in the last years of Kenyatta and the earlier Moi period, up to the attempted coup of August 1982. The ease with which the coup was put down and with which Moi strengthened his own authority suggests that such 'system failures' produce crisis rather than an inevitable breakdown.

It is not enough therefore to carry out the reforms; they have to be kept working, something which may require further changes in political structure, as with the reintroduction of local representative institutions and reform of the constitution in Tanzania since 1983, following growing complaints of excessive centralization of power (Shivji, 1985).

The goal of creation of a more cohesive petty bourgeoisie, and its transformation into a local bourgeoisie aided by control of economic policy and by external resources, can encounter two problems, depending on the level of development attained. In a few cases adequate domestic and foreign resources have been mobilized to permit the beginnings of such a transformation, as in Kenya and the Ivory Coast. Its counterpart is however the creation of an urban working class, an enlarged and impoverished urban poor and dispossesion or pauperization of sections of the peasantry: in other words the creation of the potential for class conflict. Successful control of class conflict requires more sophisticated institutions and political machinery than such regimes possess.

In most cases, however, the transformation of the petty bourgoisie does not happen. The economy remains essentially unchanged as does the petty bourgeoisie though it can acquire greater social and political cohesion. The main source for the consumption of this stratum is peasant production, through direct and indirect taxation, and through policies determining the prices of foreign exchange and rural produce. Faced with the growth of the petty bourgoisie, and the strength of its demands for more wealth, the tendency is for regimes to attempt to extract more from peasants, and for conflict to arise between peasant producers and the state, as in Tanzania, reducing the regime's popularity and—to a lesser degree—its legitimacy. This question was touched on in Chapter 4.

Benin as a 'Marxist Regime'

The analysis above places Benin firmly within a large group of African states, very few of which claim to be Marxist regimes and many of which do not even claim the empty title of 'African socialism'. Seen as a political system (and in other ways) Benin resembles Botswana, the Ivory Coast or Togo more than it does Mozambique, Ethiopia or Even Ghana in 1983–4. Is there any point in describing it as a 'Marxist regime'? In the earlier volumes which were the precursor to this series (Szajkowski, 1982), the editor argued for the principle of self-ascription: those states that announce themselves as Marxist should be studied as a distinct category and should be expected to show resemblances arising from a common rhetoric and a common view of the relationship between party and state. If however the rhetoric is no more than that, mere rhetoric—as it certainly has become in Benin and perhaps always was—and if further the relationship between state and party exists only in the guise of formal structures and documents and not in reality, then the basis for acceptance of self-ascription breaks down.[3]

Young (1982: pp. 27–32) also accepts self-ascription, but argues that in the African case there are certain common features of 'Afro-Marxist' states which 'demarcate these regimes from most others in Africa'. There are six such features listed: 'the application of Leninist theory to the organisation of state and party'; the dominance of '"revolutionary democrats"—political figures, intellectuals, teachers'; 'a consistent thrust to gain control of the "commanding heights" of the economy'; extreme caution in promoting socialist agriculture; 'no taste for mortal combat with religion'; and 'extensive ties with the Communist states'. But for the negative criteria, it is not easy to recognize Benin from this list. The application of Leninist theory is both purely formal and has been married at points to quite different theories (as with sub-national administration). The revolutionary democrats were defeated in 1973–5, and cannot be deemed to have surfaced again in the *Ligeurs*. What has been nationalized excludes the commanding heights (trade and land). And while there are ties with Communist states, those with the Soviet Union are weak and even those with China or North Korea have none of the significance of ties with France.

To categorize a regime as 'Marxist' is analytically useful only if it helps us understand that regime, or to understand Marxism and its realization in political action. Calling Benin a Marxist regime does neither and hampers recognition that what we do encounter in its case is a common African political system—with socialist gilding, there because Marxist analysis and policy prescriptions were compatible with the nationalism that informed much of what was done after 1972, appeared also to cast light on Benin's development predicament and provided a helpful cover for the pursuit of bureaucratic self-interest.

Notes on Benin

Chapter 1

1. Even now, after more than a decade of stability it ranks third on McGowan's and Johnson's somewhat mechanical 'total military involvement score', after Ghana and Sudan (McGowan & Johnson, 1986).
2. On the various ethnic groups see Argyle (1966), Mercier (1969), Lombard (1965), Mulira (1984) and Medeiros (1984).
3. For summary treatments see Asiwaja & Law (1985) and Crowder (1973, ch. 1); and for more detail, Akinjogbin (1967), Cornevin (1981) and Lombard (1965). Manning (1982) is the best economic history; see also Polanyi (1966).
4. See Spiegler (1968), Ballard (1965), Garcia (1970); and Manning's summary (1982, ch. 11).

Chapter 2

1. There were also representatives in the Council of the Republic and the Assembly of the French Union.
2. On the UPD see Glélé (1969) and Staniland (1973).
3. Through this alliance Maga increased his vote from 2 per cent in 1951 to 30 per cent in 1956.
4. Regionalism and localism are discussed at length by Glélé (1969, part 3); Ronen (1975; chs 3, 4) and Staniland (1973). The last of these is most helpful.
5. Staniland (1973, p. 306) comments that Apithy's PRD 'effectively disappeared between elections' and 'did not have any permanent organisation until 1957'.
6. See for example the excellent studies of Nigeria by Luckham (1971) and of Sierra Leone by Cox (1976).
7. On divisions in the army see Decalo (1976, especially pp. 53–7; and Lemarchand (1968: p. 53). On radicalism, see Ronen (1987, pp. 114–17).
8. Thus Decalo (1973, pp. 453; 471) indicates that those at the bottom of the clientelist network in Atacora 'has not benefited from their activites on behalf of Maga' and that villagers did not now expect any benefits to flow from supporting him.
9. This failure was epitomized by the governments' incapacity to resolve conflict with the unions. Spoils politics provides only two techniques to deal with workers' demands: concession or coercion. The first was used to gain union support, usually by governments that had just come to power (as in 1970) or were desperate to retain it (1969). Concessions however only increased the drain

on public resources—threatening elite consumption—and were always followed by attempts to reduce wages either through a wage freeze (as in 1963-5) or by cuts and taxes (as under Zinsou). These in turn forced unions into direct conflict with successive governments, providing in most cases the context or occasion for their collapse. As Chapter 4 shows, neither concessions nor coercion were effective in controlling Dahomey's overspending in any but the short term.

10. Judging from Kérékou's first broadcast the coupmakers shared these views. It referred to the tripartite presidential system as 'truly a monster' and having produced 'inertia . . . congenital deficiency . . . notorious inefficiency . . . [and] unpardonable incompetence' as well as threatening national unity (*ACR*, 1972-3, B580). For discussion of a similar process of alienation in Ghana see Azarya & Chazan (1987).

11. It was Ahomadegbe's inability to dismiss Chabi Kao in the face of Maga's opposition that symbolized the incompetence of his government for the coupmakers.

12. *ACR*, 1973-4, B631. Beheton was dismissed for encouraging dockers to strike against the 'favouritism and nepotism' of the port authorities. His removal and that of Badjogoume was one reason for student discontent in 1973.

13. One consequence of changes in the officer corps and in government was to make both visibly more northern: the bulk of the senior officers sent to sinecures were, like Beheton and Badjogoume, southerners.

14. On these groups see Godin (1986, pp. 274-8) and Ronen (1987, pp. 114-17); FACEEN is discussed in the context of its organizational and literacy work in the north in Benini (1980).

15. Reflected in their eyes in Kérékou's apologies to the French for the February 1973 riots, or the dismissals of Beheton and Badjogoume from the cabinet. The *Ligeurs* had by this point, however, decided to support Kérékou (Godin, 1986, p. 275).

16. Even though several authors give that impression, notably Decalo (1979) and Michael Wolfers, who summarizes 1972-4 as 'months of speeches' (*WA*, 1974, 1514).

17. A report in *Jeune Afrique* (see *WA*, 1975; 879) claimed that Aikpé was planning a coup but that the arrest of a co-conspirator, the union leader Mito Baba, led to its discovery. Mito Baba was a former student leader and had been active in the FUD in 1973-4.

18. The CNR was also swamped with Kérékou appointees, in the shape of the thirty-nine executive secretaries of the newly created District Revolutionary Committees.

19. Details of these can be found in Auroi (1977-8); Benini (1980) and Giesecke & Elwert (1983).

20. The raid is discussed in the United Nations Security Council (1977); Péan (1981) and Herzog (1979); summaries in *ACR*, 1977-8, B616-17 and *Afrique-Asie*, 13-26 June 1977, pp. 31-82.

21. References to these 'class allies' had been quite common in speeches and other official statements since 1975; see *ACR*, 1976-7, B549-50; 1978-9, B594).

22. They included the formal decision to create single organizations for youth and for women, as auxiliaries to the party. The unions, although within a single national centre from 1976, did not become a party auxiliary until 1979.

23. See for example, *Africa Confidential*, 1984-6, or *ACR* for the 1980s.

24. The best source of material on detentions etc. are the publications of Amnesty International, especially its annual *Report*.

25. Also dropped from the Bureau were Gratien Capo-Chichi (Minister of Literacy and Popular Culture 1980-4) and Armand Monteiro (higher education, 1980-4); Jean-Didier Alavo had already been removed before the congress. Three new members were 'elected' by the new Central Committee: Joseph Degla (a *Ligeur*), Justin Gnidehou and Idi Abdoulaye Malam. They joined Kérékou, Azonhiho, Giriguissou Gado and Simon Ogouma (both *Ligeurs*), Vincent Guezodje and Ramon Vilon Guezo (both Fon) and Roger Garba and Sanni Mama Gomina (both associated with FACEEN). Of the eleven members of the Bureau, only three were ministers (Kérékou, Guezodje and Gado), and one a prefect (Azonhiho).

Chapter 3

1. Effectively, 'class enemies' of the revolution were excluded, these being defined as the bourgeoisie and those associated with it such as members of the liberal professions, and leading members of former regimes and parties.

2. This article also has details of the political criteria on which election is supposed to be based.

3. De Gaudusson, 1981, pp. 81-2; corresponding figures for CRLs were 2,542 and 3,375.

4. Similar events had occurred in 1972-3, this time led by chiefs (169), who may again have played some part, for Lachenmann (1980, p. 78) points out that in her area (Bassila, in southern Atacora) elected village heads 'often found a basis for agreement with the representatives, now dismissed, of traditional leadership . . . who had not lost all their power in the social life of many communities'.

5. For an attempt to provide a Marxist pedigree for the constitution, see Paraiso (1980).

6. He might also have said that it was consistent with the self interest of the bureaucracy; see Chapter 4: 'society'.

7. While Aikpe and Assogba suffered severely, Badjagoume and Beheton simply resumed their military careers, on being dropped as ministers, eventually becoming respectively commander of the paracommando barracks and of the gendarmerie. *Africa Confidential* (not a very reliable source) claims they were both arrested in 1984 after a coup attempt (1984, no. 17, p. 5).

8. There is also dissent within government, expressed in factional activity of longstanding, in turn linked to the original small left–nationalist groups that supported the 1972 coup, like the northern student grouping FACEEN (Front d'Action Commune des Elèves et des Etudiants du Nord), the Jeunesse Universitaire du Dahomey (JUD; largely southern) or the more overtly and officiously Marxist *Ligeurs*. These groups do have genuine differences of analysis and policy, but are primarily vehicles for intrigue. Somewhat fanciful accounts of their activities can be found in *ACR* and in *Africa Confidential* (especially in 1984).

9. It should be said, however, that the leading cadre at the conference (and its organizer), Bruno Amoussou, was jailed in November 1984 for four months, for no revealed reason. He had been director of the Banque Commerciale du Bénin and had remained a spokesman for the senior civil service in the interim; 123 cadres and intellectuals signed a protest at his jailing (*Jeune Afrique*, 20 February 1985).

10. For an apparent instance of its use, see *Amnesty International Report*, 1982, p. 19.

11. For an apparent instance, see *ACR*, 1975–6, B673.

Chapter 4

1. Kérékou is said to have argued that the nationalizations of 1974 'did not have particularly revolutionary motives'. Instead the government 'wanted to ensure that the most profitable sectors of the economy contributed to national development' (*ACR*, 1974–5, B631).

2. See *BAN* 17 May 1985, 1272; and Flesch (1982) debt tables.

3. One other type of cooperative predated 1972, those attached to the state oil palm plantations and the parastatal, Sonader. These compulsory organizations were hardly cooperative, and formed instead part of the machinery that made the peasants involved into a variety of wage labourer. For details see Gosselin (1978).

4. One estimate (ILO, 1984, p. 72) suggests a 40 per cent fall in available calories from stable foods in Borgou during the 1960s and a further 18 per cent decline, to 2,300 calories a day per head, in the 1970s.

5. One estimate of the size of illegal trade can be made by comparing the official trade figures, produced by Customs, with the national accounts' calculations available from the late 1970s. While Customs gave a figure of CFA fr. 6 billion francs for exports in 1978, the national accounts claim nearly 40b worth of goods were exported (*WA*, 1982, 1379), implying a trade deficit of 20b rather than 54b. The United States Department of Commerce makes similar estimates for 1982–4, suggesting that up to 90 per cent of trade is unofficial. One implication of this is that Benin's apparently appalling trade balance is an artefact and does not represent either reality or even a trend (though on 'true' figures it is still negative).

6. The reports are summarized in *ACR*, 1979–80; *WA*, 1980, 1818; *ACR*, 1980–1, B464; see also speeches by the president in *WA*, 1980, 2201; *WA*, 1981, 659 and the general critique in the early chapters of Benin, 1983.
7. See Kora, 1979, pp. 187–90; Ayo (1982, pp. 325–6) remarks that 'many peasants wonder what justifies the existence of the local authorities and especially the extension agents who do not "work" with them in the fields but simply give "orders"'.
8. Oil has been discovered in 1965 but exploitation was hindered by the American concession holder (Union Oil) deciding that production would not be sufficiently profitable. The concession lapsed in 1974 (*WA*, 1979, 788).
9. Projects under way in 1985 included yet another brewery, a sweet factory, two bakeries, and plants to make batteries, paper bags, glass products from waste glass and brake shoes (*BAN*, 1985, 1283, p. 13).
10. Other factors include a small increase (around 5 per cent) in areas cultivated (*EOM*, 1986, p. 23) and increases in producer prices that came close to matching inflation (12 per cent per annum).
11. One indicator of decline is the fall in new vehicle registrations, from 2,191 in 1981 to 635 in 1985 and 194 for the first half of 1986 (*QER*, 1987/1). A similar trend occurs in vehicle imports, down from 2,500 in 1982 to 559 in 1986 (*World Automotive Market*, 1987).
12. This section is based largely on reports in *QER*, 1985/4 to 1987/2; see also *Petroleum Economist* (1985).
13. I was unable to obtain either Francine Godin's thesis (1984) or the book derived from it (1986) before writing this section; readers should also consult the latter. I have relied for quantitative data to a considerable degree on the very useful compilation undertaken as part of a recent report on employment and employment generation (ILO, 1984) and on the 1979 census.
14. See, for example, Ayo (1982), Gosselin (1978), Houdete (1980), Kpodjedo-Sossou (1977), Ladjouaz (1980), Lissanou (1981), Mensah (1980), Mondjannagni (1984), Quénum (1980), Segbénou (1982), Tomanaga (1982).
15. Much land purchasing in the south has been done not by farmers wishing to expand but by civil servants, army officers etc. for speculative purposes.
16. These incomes, to which should be added the value of subsistence production (see PECTA, 1982, pp. 11–12) reflect the low level of technology in peasant agriculture, in which the majority of households rely on hoes, machetes and an axe or two (ILO, 1984, p. 52). They are consistent with other estimates based on production. An ILO team for example concluded that rural incomes in 1976–7 varied considerably by district (even in the north), ranging for the less well-off from 95,000 to 224,000 francs per household (PECTA, 1982, pp. 22–3). A large and later ILO survey (ILO, 1984, pp. 86–110) estimated incomes of CFA fr. 115,000 for each person involved in farming in 1979, over twice the level of 1970.
17. Thus in 1980, 45 per cent of central government employees earned between

300,000 and 400,000 francs; 36 per cent earned from 150,000 to 300,000 (ILO, 1984, p. 371).

18. Growth was particularly rapid in 1977–80, when the public sector grew at 17 per cent per annum, and the A and B grades (requiring university education) rose from 3,300 to 6,300 (ILO, 1984, pp. 368–70).

19. Some erosion of the monopolies in external trade enjoyed by non-Beninois domestic capital has occurred.

20. This contrasts sharply with the 1960s, for which the same team concluded there had been falling output, food consumption and calorie intake (ibid., p. 74).

Chapter 5

1. The proportion of the budget spent on teacher training fell from 4 per cent in 1969 to 2 per cent in 1972.

2. Here I have used mainly Houeto (1981), Benin (1983), Waldmeir (1981) and Hadjadj (1982).

3. It may not be education either: data on the proportion of children repeating years show a considerable rise since the mid-1970s. Thus in primary schools the average rate has risen from 21 per cent (1975) to 29 per cent (1983), while in secondary schools the rate has gone from 14 per cent to 35 per cent (UNESCO, *Statistical Yearbook*, 1986).

4. I have relied heavily in this section on the work of Gudrun Lachenmann (1980; 1982).

5. Sources: World Bank *Development Report* (1987), Benin (1983), Mission (1982).

6. Ayo (1982, p. 391) reports that voluntary labour to the value of CFA fr. 50 million was provided in Zou for the building of ten health centres, only for the peasants to find that there was no money to equip them.

7. In addition to journalistic sources I have used the work of Ronen (1975), Houndjahoue (1984a, 1984b, 1987) and Nwokedi (1982, 1985). There are some dissertations on the subject—for example Yaba (1978), Sekpon (1980), Codo (1984)—though it is regrettable that Guy Hazoume, once foreign minister, has not completed his thesis on diplomacy in the 1970s.

8. A similar pattern marks Benin's participation in francophone regional organization. It remained in OCAM, seeking to depoliticize it, and returned to the Conseil d'Entente, having walked out soon after the coup. Kérékou was chairman of OCAM in 1979 and of the Conseil in 1983.

Chapter 6

1. It is not possible fully to reference such a statement. Useful accounts of the processes I describe can however be found in Gertzel *et al*. (1984), Shivji (1985),

Schumacher (1975), Kabwit (1979), Hermet *et al.* (1978); and related accounts in the discussion of 'princely' roles in Jackson & Rosberg (1982), and in Callaghy (1984) on Zaïre.

2. Benin differs from most of the cases mentioned in that it was a military regime that carried out the reforms long after the full flower of the clientelist crisis, rather than a civilian regime encountering that crisis for the first time. In the latter case the attempt to halt the development of political crisis occurs mainly by adding institutions to those already there or adapting them, and thus changing the role of the older institutions. In Benin the older institutions were largely removed at national level in 1972–5, and even at local level were quite severely damaged, allowing a wholly new set of institutions to take their place. Thus in Benin not only were the reforms more coherent and simultaneous than was usually the case elsewhere, but they operated far more directly and required less compromise through cohabitation with the residue of the former system. The dramatic contrasts since 1975—Africa's least stable state becomes one of its most stable, and a country ravaged by regionalization becomes seemingly united—are perhaps one consequence of this lack of compromise.

3. White (1983) provides a general critique of self-ascription of which this argument is a particular and highly simplified version. See also Harding in Szajkowski (1982).

Bibliography

Akinjogbin, I. A. 1967. *Dahomey and its neighbours 1708-1818*. Cambridge, Cambridge University Press.

Anson-Meyer, M. 1983. Les illusions de l'autosuffisance alimentaire: exemple du Ghana, Togo, Bénin et Nigéria. *Mondes en Développement*, vol. 41, no. 2, pp. 51-79.

Argyle, W. J. 1966. *The Fon of Dahomey*. Oxford, Clarendon Press.

Asiwaju, A. I. & Law, R. 1985. From the Volta to the Niger 1600-1800. *History of West Africa*, ed. J. F. Ajayi and M. Crowder, 3rd edn. London, Longman, pp. 412-64.

Auroi, C. 1977/78. L'alphabétisation rurale au Nord Bénin: la fin de l'exploitation commerciale des paysans. *Geneva-Africa*, vol. 16, no. 1, pp. 89-108.

Ayo, S. B. 1982. L'administration locale et le développement rurale en République Populaire du Bénin 1960-81. Thèse 3ème cycle, Bordeaux 1.

—— 1984. Ideology, local administration and problems of rural development in the Republic of Benin. *Public Administration and Development*, vol. 4, no. 4, pp. 361-72.

—— 1986. Traditional rulers and the operation of local administration in the Republic of Benin. *Verfassung und Recht in Ubersee*, vol. 19, no. 2, pp. 139-47.

Azarya, V. & Chazan, N. 1987. Disengagement from the state in Africa: reflections on the experience of Ghana and Guinea. *Comparative Studies in Society and History*, vol. 29, no. 1, pp. 106-31.

Baker, P. H. 1984. Nigeria as an emerging regional power. *African Security Issues*, ed. B. E. Arlinghaus. Boulder, Westview.

Ballard, J. A. 1965. The Porto-Novo incidents of 1923. *Odu*, vol. 2, no. 1, pp. 52-75.

Bayart, J. E. 1979. *L'état au Caméroun*. Paris, Presse de la FNSP.

—— 1985. *La politique africaine du Président Mitterrand*. Paris, Karthala.

Benin 1976. *Charte portant fondéments, principes directeurs et implications de la diplomatie nouvelle a l'usage des représentations extérieurs du Bénin*. Cotonou, ONEPI.

—— 1977. *Plan d'état de développement économique et social 1977-80. Rapport de synthèse*. Cotonou, ONEPI.

—— 1983. *Le développement économique du Bénin. Table ronde des partenaires au développement économique et social de la République Populaire du Bénin. Rapport de présentation*. Cotonou, Ministère du Plan.

Benini, A. A. 1980. *Community Development in a Multi-ethnic Society*. Saarbrucken, Breitenbach.

Berthet, E. 1978. Recherche d'une promotion sanitaire et sociale en milieu rural africaine. *Revue internationale d'éducation pour la santé*, vol. 21, no. 3, pp. 189-93.

Brand, R. 1977. Structures révolutionnaires au Bénin: impact sur une société paysanne. *Geneva-Africa*, vol. 16, no. 1, pp. 67-88.

Callaghy, T. M. 1984. *The State-Society Struggle: Zaïre in Comparative Perspective*. New York, Columbia University Press.

Calvert, P. 1986. *The Foreign Policy of New States*. Brighton, Wheatsheaf.

Codo, L. 1984. *L'insertion politico-diplomatique du Bénin dans l'espace ouest-africain*. Mémoire, Centre d'études africains, Bordeaux.

Cornevin, R. 1981. *La République Populaire du Bénin. Des origines dahoméenes à nos jours*. Paris, Maisoneuve Larose.

Costa, E. 1966. Back to the land: the campaign against unemployment in Dahomey. *International Labour Review*, vol. 93, pp. 29–45.

Cox, T. S. 1976. *Civil-Military Relations in Sierra Leone*. Cambridge, Mass., Harvard University Press.

Crowder, M. 1973. *Revolt in Bussa*. London, Faber.

Decalo, S. 1970. Full circle in Dahomey. *African Studies Review*, vol. 13, no. 3, pp. 445–58.

— 1971. Dahomey 1968–71: return to origins. *Geneva-Africa*, vol. 10, no. 1, pp. 76–91

— 1973. Regionalism, politics and the military in Dahomey. *Journal of Developing Areas*, vol. 7, no. 3, pp. 449–78.

— 1976. *Coups and Army Rule in Africa*. New Haven, Yale University Press, pp. 39–86.

— 1979. Ideological rhetoric and scientific socialism in Benin and Congo Brazzaville. *Socialism in Subsaharan Africa*, ed. C. G. Rosberg and T. Callaghy. Berkeley, University of California Centre for International Studies, pp. 231–64.

— 1982. People's Republic of Benin. *Marxist Governments*, ed. B. Szajkowski, vol. 1, London, Macmillan, 87–115.

De Gaudusson, J. de Bois de. 1980. Chronique de réformes administratives. *Année Africaine*, pp. 374–8, 455–92.

— 1981. La nouvelle administration territoriale de Bénin. *Année Africaine*, pp. 79–93.

Desjeux, D. 1984. Les religions agraires en Afrique noire: la lutte de l'ordre et du désordre. *Le Mois en Afrique*, nos. 223/4, pp. 134–45; and nos. 225/6, pp. 120–31.

Egero, B. 1987. *Moçambique: A Dream Undone*. Uppsala, Scandinavian Institute of African Studies.

Elwert, G. 1980. From subsistence economy to state capitalism—agrarian structures in Benin. *Vierteljahresberichte*, vol. 79, pp. 57–64.

— 1983. *Bauern und Staat in Westafrika: die Verflechtung socio-economischer Sektoren am Beispiel Benin*. Frankfurt: Campus Verlag.

— 1984. Conflicts inside and outside the household—a West African case study. *Households and the World Economy*, ed. J. Smith, I. Wallerstein and H. D. Evers. Beverley Hills, Sage, pp. 272–96.

Elwert, G. & Wong, D. 1978. *Structures agraires et procès de développement dans la province de l'Atlantique*. Universitat Bielefeld.

EOM 1986. Bénin 1986. *Europe Outremer*, vol. 62, no. 669/70, pp. 5–45.

Flesch 1982. *Situation financière de la République Populaire du Bénin*. Annex to Mission, 1982.

Frey-Nakonz, R. 1984. *Vom Prestige zum Profit: zweifallstudien am sudbenin zur Integration der Frauen in die Markwirtschaft*. Saarbrucken, Breitenbach.

Garcia, L. 1970. Les mouvements de résistance au Dahomey (1914–17). *Cahiers d'études africains*, vol. 37, pp. 144–75.

Gertzel, C. *et al*. 1984. *The Dynamics of the One-Party State in Zambia*. Manchester, Manchester University Press.

` Giesecke, M. and Elwert, G. 1983. Literacy and emancipation. *Development and Change*, vol. 14, no. 2, pp. 255–76.

Glélé, M. A. 1969. *Naissance d'un état noire*. Paris, Libraire générale de droit et de jurisprudence.

—— 1981. *Religion, culture et politique en Afrique noire*. Paris, Economica/Presence Africaine.

GMR 1972. *Discours-programme du Col. Mathieu Kérékou, le 30 Novembre 1972*. Cotonou: ONEPI.

Godin, F. 1984. État, accumulation de capital et luttes de classes au Bénin 1972–82. Thèse, Montreal.

—— 1986. *Bénin 1972–82: logique de l'état africain*. Paris, Harmattan.

Gosselin, G. 1978. Réforme agraire et coopération dans la palmerie dahoméene. *L'Afrique désenchantée*. Paris, Anthropos, pp. 265–342.

Grossenbacher, P. J. 1976. Alphabétisation fonctionelle des membres des groupements villageois du Borgou. *Die Dritte Welt*, vol. 4, nos. 3/4, pp. 391–404.

Guezodje, V. 1977. Educational reform in Benin. *Prospects*, vol. 7,no. 4, pp. 455–71.

Hadjadj 1982. *Donnés économiques et sociales*. Annex to Mission, 1982.

Hermet, G. *et al*. (eds) 1978. *Elections Without Choice*. London: Macmillan.

Herzog, C. 1977/78. UN at work: the Benin affair. *Foreign Policy*, vol. 29, pp. 140–59.

Hill, P. 1972. *Rural Hausa*. Cambridge, Cambridge University Press.

Houdete, T. 1980. Emploi rural et exode rural . . . en République Populaire du Bénin. Thèse 3ème cycle, Grenoble 2.

Houeto, C. Senami. 1981. Benin: training teachers to implement the reform. *Prospects*, vol. 11, no. 2, pp. 193–203.

Houndjahoue, M. 1984a. Bénin: révolution socialiste et politique étrangere. *Le Mois en Afrique*, nos. 225/6, pp. 31–6.

—— 1984b. Le différend americano-béninois de 1976 a 1983. *Le Mois en Afrique*, nos. 219/20, pp. 25–31.

—— 1987a. Le Bénin socialiste et le bon voisinage: 1972–86. *Le Mois en Afrique*, nos. 253/54, pp. 28–41.

—— 1987b. Notes sur les relations internationales du Bénin socialiste 1972–86. *Études internationales*, vol. 18, no. 2, pp. 371–88.

Hyden, G. 1980. *Beyond Ujamaa in Tanzania*. London, Heinemann.

Igue, O. J. 1976a. Evolution du commerce clandestin entre le Dahomey et le Nigeria. *Canadian Journal of African Studies*, vol. 10, no. 2, pp. 235–57.

—— 1976b. Un aspect des échanges entre le Dahomey et le Nigeria: le commerce de cacao. *Bulletin de l'IFAN*, vol. B38, no. 3, pp. 636–69.

ILO 1982. *Disparités de revenus entre les villes et le campagnes au Bénin*. Addis Ababa, ILO.

—— 1984. *Emploi d'abord: éléments des strategies pour la priorité a l'emploi*. Addis Ababa, ILO.

Jackson, R. H. & Rosberg, C. G. 1982. *Personal Rule in Black Africa*. Berkeley, University of California Press.

Joseph, R. 1983. Class, state and prebendal politics in Nigeria. *Journal of Commonwealth and Comparative Politics*, vol. 21, no. 3, pp. 21–38.

Jouffrey, R. 1983. Le Bénin depuis 1981. *Afrique contemporaine*, no. 127, pp. 34–43.

Kabwit, G. C. 1979. Zaïre: the roots of the continuing crisis. *Journal of Modern African Studies*, vol. 17, no. 3, pp. 381–407.

Kitchen, H. (ed.) 1962. *The Educated African*. London, Heinemann.

Kora, G. 1979. Contribution a l'économie rurale: la politique de développement agricole au Bénin, étude de cas, le Borgou. Diplome, Paris 7 (EHESS).

Kpodjedo Sossou, M. 1977. Traditions villageoises et changement social au Bénin. Étude comparative de trois micro-regions. Thèse 3ème cycle, Paris 10 (EHESS).

Lachaud, J. P. 1987. *Urbanisation, secteur informel et emploi: les activités informelles et l'emploi au Bénin*. Geneva, ILO (World Development Programme).

Lachenmann, G. 1980. *Soins de santé primaire et développement*. Berlin, Deutsches Institut fur Entwicklungspolitik, 1980 (shortened and reworked as: 'Elements and requirements of primary health care policy in . . . Benin', *Health and Development in Africa*, ed. P. Oberender, H. J. Diesfeld & W. Gitter, Frankfurt, Peter Lang, 1982, pp. 249–69).

—— 1982. People's Republic of Benin: difficulties on the path to independent development. *Poor Countries of Africa*. Berlin, German Development Institute, pp. 111–41.

Ladjouan, M. 1980. Intervention de l'état dans l'agriculture béninoise (zone de palmeraie): analyse d'une action de développement rural: les coopératives d'aménagement rural du Grand-Hinvi. Thèse 3ème cycle, Paris 10.

Lagarde, D. 1978. Benin's push for prosperity. *West Africa*, 15 May 1978, pp. 921–2.

Langellier, J. P. 1976. Deux ans de 'marxisme-leninisme' au Bénin. *Le Monde*, 30 November and 1 December.

Lavroff, D. G. 1978. L'évolution constitutionelle de la République Popularie du Bénin: la constitution de 1977. *Année africaine 1977*, pp. 128–59.

—— (ed.) 1980. *La politique africaine du Général de Gaulle*. Paris, Pedone.

Lemarchand, R. 1968. Dahomey: coup within a coup. *Africa Report*, June, pp. 46–54.

Leymarie, P. 1978. Bénin: une démocratie populaire qui s'estime constamment menacé. *Revue français d'études politiques africaines*, no. 135, pp. 52–8.

Lissanou, I. 1981. Les problèmes de production agricole et de développement rural du Bénin. Thèse 3ème cycle, Paris-EHESS.

Lombard, J. 1965. *Structures du type 'féodal' en Afrique noire*. Paris/Hague, Mouton.

Luckham, R. 1971. *The Nigerian Military*. Cambridge, Cambridge University Press.

McGowan, P. and Johnson, T. H. 1986. Sixty coups in thirty years. *Journal of Modern African Studies*, vol. 24, no. 3, pp. 539–46.

Malirot, G. 1975. Le Dahomey sortira-t-il un jour du marasme actuel? *Eurafrica*, July–August, pp. 19–22.

Manning, P. 1982. *Slavery, Colonialism and Economic Growth in Dahomey 1640–1960*. Cambridge, Cambridge University Press.

Martin, G. 1986. The franc zone, underdevelopment and dependency in francophone in Africa. *Third World Quarterly*, vol. 8, no. 1, pp. 205–35.

Martin, M. L. 1984. Note sur le changement politique et constitutionel en République Populaire du Bénin depuis l'indépendance, *Année Africaine 1982*, pp. 91–127.

— 1985. The rise and 'thermidorianisation' of radical praetorianism in Benin. *Journal of Communist Studies*, vol. 1, nos. 3/4, pp. 58–81.

Medeiros, F. de 1981. Armée et instabilité politique béninois. *La politique du Mars. Les processus politiques dans le partis militaires*, ed. A. Roquié. Paris, FNSP.

— 1984. *Peuples du golfe du Bénin*. Paris, Karthala.

Meillassoux, C. 1970. A class analysis of the bureaucratic process in Mali. *Journal of Development Studies*, vol. 6, no. 2, pp. 91–110.

Memento 1980. Bénin. *Memento de l'économie africaine*. Paris, Ediafric, pp. 1–18.

Mensah, E. 1980. Les paysan de la province populaire du Zou. Leurs conditions de vie et de travail, à travers l'impact des rendements et de la commercialisation de leurs produits agricoles. Thèse 3ème cycle, Paris-EHESS.

Mercier, P. 1968. *Tradition, changement, histoire: les Somba du Dahomey septentrionale*. Paris, Anthropos.

Midiohouan, T. 1987. La femme dans la vie politique, économique et social du Bénin. *Présence Africaine*, no. 141, pp. 59–70.

Ministère de la Coopération 1979. *Bénin: donnés sur l'éducation*. Paris, Ministère de la Coopération (Services des études et questions internationales).

Mission 1982. *Mission de diagnostique et d'orientation de l'aide française en République Populaire du Bénin*. Paris, Ministère de la Coopération.

Modiano, P. 1982. Better times for Benin? *West Africa*, pp. 156–7, 230–1, 307–8.

Mondjannagni, A. C. 1984. Participation paysanne dans le cadre de la réstructuration des campagnes du Sud-Bénin. *La participation populaire au développement en Afrique noire*, ed. A. C. Mondjannagni. Paris, Karthala, pp. 281–98.

Morgan, S. 1977. Will Kérékou return to the barracks? *Africa*, no. 73 (September).

Mulira, J. G. 1984. A history of the Mahi peoples from 1874 to 1920. Doctoral dissertation, UCLA.

Munslow, B. 1983. *Mozambique: the revolution and its origins*. London, Longman.

Natchaba, O. F. 1985/86. Analyse et réflexions sur les votes émis par les états du Conseil de l'Entente a l'Assemblé Générale des Nations Unis. *Penant*, nos. 788/89, pp. 310–46, and nos. 790/91, pp. 13–47.

Newham, M. 1985. Everyday is a slow day at the market. *African Business*, May, pp. 22–3.

Nwokedi, E. O. C. 1982. Le Nigéria et ses voisins francophones: contribution a l'étude de la politique regionale du Nigeria de 1970 a 1981. Thèse, Bordeaux 1.

—— 1985. Strands and strains of 'good neighbourliness': Nigeria and its francophone neighbours. *Geneva-Africa*, vol. 23, no. 1, pp. 39–60.

Obukhov, L. A. 1979. The ideological and political platform of the revolutionary democracy of Benin. *The Most Recent Tendencies of the Socialist Orientation of Various African and Arab Countries*. Prague, Academica, pp. 134–45.

Olodo, A. K. 1978. Les institutions de la République Populaire du Bénin. *Revue juridique et politique*, vol. 32, no. 2, pp. 759–92.

Paraiso, A. 1980. La loi fondamentale et les nouvelles institutions de la République Populaire du Bénin. *Penant*, no. 769, pp. 288–306; no. 770, pp. 403–40.

Péan, P. 1983. *Affaires africaines*. Paris, Fayard, pp. 172–81.

PECTA 1982. *Le syndrome du diplome et le chomage des diplomés: le cas du Bénin*. Addis Ababa, ILO.

Pliya, J. 1979. Educational reform and available resources: an example from the Peoples Republic of Benin. *Educational Reforms: Experiences and Prospects*. Paris, UNESCO, pp. 188–200.

Polanyi, K. 1966. *Dahomey and the Slave Trade*. Seattle, University of Washington Press.

PRPB 1979. *Sur les relations extérieurs*. Cotonou, First National Congress.

Quénum, F. J. 1980. Milieu naturel et mise en valeur agricole entre Sahete et Poba dans le sud-est du Bénin: essai de géographie appliqué. Thèse 3ème cycle, Strasbourg 2.

Robertson, C. 1987. Developing economic awareness: changing perspectives in studies of African women 1976–85. *Feminist Studies*, vol. 13, no. 1, pp. 97–135.

Ronen, D. 1975. *Dahomey*. Ithaca, Cornell University Press.

—— 1980. Benin: the role of the uniformed leaders. *The Performance of Soldiers as Governors*, ed. I. J. Mowoe. University Press of America, pp. 101–50.

—— 1987. People's Republic of Benin: the military, marxist ideology, and the politics of ethnicity. *The Military in African Politics*, ed. J. Harbeson. New York, Praeger, pp. 93–122.

Rosier 1982. *L'économie agricole et agro-alimentaire et le développement rural au Bénin*. Annex to Mission, 1982.

Samson, D. 1985. L'agriculture au Benin. *Afrique contemporaine*, no. 134, pp. 44–9.

Schumacher, E. J. 1975. *Politics, Bureaucracy and Rural Development in Senegal*. Berkeley, University of California Press.

Segbenou, R. M. 1982. Monographie d'une économie rurale en transformation: le cas des Tolinu du district rural d'Avrankou au Sudest de la République Populaire du Bénin. Thesis, Bielefeld.

Sekpon, A. P. 1980. La politique extérieure du Bénin. Memoire DEA, Bordeaux 1.

Shivji, I. 1976. *Class struggle in Tanzania*. London, Heinemann.

—— (ed.) 1985. *The State and Working People in Tanzania*. Dakar, Codesria.

Sims, B. J. 1974. The ruralisation of primary school education in Dahomey. Doctoral dissertation, Columbia.

Somerville, K. 1986. *Angola*. London, Frances Pinter.

Soudan, F. 1983. Bénin: un nouvel ordre et arrivé. *Jeune Afrique*, 23 March, pp. 44–5.

Spiegler, J. S. 1968. Aspects of nationalist thought among French-speaking West Africans 1921–39. Doctoral dissertation, Oxford.

Staniland, M. 1973. The three-party system in Dahomey. *Journal of African History*, vol. 14, no. 2, pp. 291–312 and vol. 14, no. 3, pp. 491–504.

Szajkowski, B. (ed.) 1982. *Marxist Governments*. London, Macmillan.

Szeftel, M. 1982. Political graft and the spoils system in Zambia. *Review of African Political Economy*, no. 24, pp. 4–21.

Thompson, V. 1964. Dahomey. *Five African States*, ed. G. M. Carter. London, Pall Mall, 161–262.

Timberlake, L. 1985. *Africa in Crisis*. London, Earthscan.

Tomanaga, P. 1982. Coopératives agricoles de production et de développement rural en République Populaire du Bénin. Thèse 3ème cycle, Paris-EHESS.

United Nations Security Council 1977. *Report of the UN Security Council Special Mission to the Peoples Republic of Benin, established under Resolution 404 (1977)*. New York, UN.

United States Embassy (Cotonou) 1983. *Benin*. Foreign Economic Trends, FET 83–041, Washington, US Dept. of Commerce.

Urdang, S. 1984. The last transition: women and development in Mozambique. *Review of African Political Economy*, nos. 27/28, pp. 8–32.

Waldmeir, P. 1981. Education in Benin. *West Africa*, 20 April, pp. 872–3.

White, S. 1983. What is a communist system? *Studies in Comparative Communism*, vol. 16, no. 4, pp. 247–63.

Wong, D. 1977. State and peasant in Benin. University of Bielefeld, mimeo.

—— 1982. Bauern, Burokratie und Korruption: ein Beitrag zur Analyse des burokratischen Staates im Fall Benin. *Afrika zwischen Subsistenzokonomie und Imperialismus*, ed. G. Elwert and R. Fett. Frankfurt, Campus Verlag, pp. 235–55.

World Bank 1979. *The Economy of Benin*. Washington, World Bank.

Yaba, B. 1978. La République Populaire du Bénin dans les relations internationales. Mémoire DEA, Paris 1.

Young, C. 1982. Benin: stability under scientific socialism. *Ideology and Development in Africa*. New Haven, Yale University Press, pp. 43–50.

Periodicals Frequently Consulted

ACR	*Africa Contemporary Record* (London)
ARB	*Africa Research Bulletin* (Exeter)
BAN	*Bulletin d'Afrique Noire* (Paris)
EOM	*Europe Outremer* (Paris)
MTM	*Marches tropicaux et méditerranéenes* (Paris)
QER	*Quarterly Economic Review: Togo, Benin, Niger, Burkina* (London: Economist Intelligence Unit); now named *Country Report: Togo, Benin, Niger, Burkina*
WA	*West Africa* (London)

Part II
People's Republic of Congo

Michael S. Radu and
Keith Somerville

Contents of Part II:
People's Republic of Congo

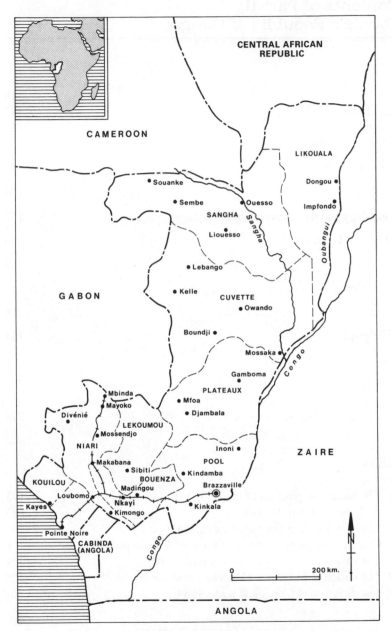

People's Republic of The Congo

Basic Data

Official name	People's Republic of Congo (Republique Populaire du Congo)
Population	2,082,154 (July 1987)
Population density	5.26 inhabitants per sq. km.
Population growth % p.a.	2.59
Urban population (%)	40
Life expectancy at birth (1984)	57 years
Infant death rate (per 1,000)	82
Distribution of the population by age	0–14 years, 43.6%; 15–64, 53%; over 65, 3.4%
Ethnic groups	Kongo; Lari; Vili; Teke; Mbochi; Sanga
Capital	Brazzaville
Land area	342,000 sq. km. (132,047 sq. m.)
Official language	French
Administrative divisions	13 regions (Kouilou, Niari, Lekoumou, Bouenza, Pool, Cuvette, Plateaux, Sangha, Likouala, Brazzaville, Pointe-Noire, Nkayi and Loubomo
Membership of international organizations	UN, OAU, IBRD, IMF, UDEAC, The Lomé Convention, OCAMM
Political structure	
Constitutional structure	Single party, Marxist–Leninist
Highest legislative body	National Assembly
Highest executive body	The Presidency
Prime Minister	Ange Edouard Poungui
Head of State	President Denis Sassou-Nguesso
Ruling Party	Parti Congolais du Travail (PCT)
Economic indicators	
GDP	US$2,010 million (1984)
GNP per capita	US$1,140 (1984)
Annual growth rates (%)	
GNP per capita (%)	3.7 (1965–84)
GDP (%)	8.1 (1973–84) (decline of10% in 1985)
Agricultural production (%)	0.4 (1973–84)
Industry (%)	12.7 (1973–84)

Services (%)	6.9 (1973–84)
Average annual rate of inflation (%)	12.3 (1973–84)

Distribution of GDP by sector (%)

Sector	1965	1984
Agriculture	19	7
Industry	19	60
Manufacturing		6
Services	62	33

Food self-sufficiency	Cereal imports: 1974, 34,000 tonnes; 1984, 113,000 tonnes; index of food production per capita: 1974/6 — 100; 1984 — 96
Foreign debt (total)	US$1,573 millions (1984)
As % of GNP	76.2 (1984)
Long-term debt-service as % of exports of goods and services	20.5 (1984)
Foreign assistance receipts	US$98 millions (1984)
Per capita	US$53.9 (1984)
As % of GNP	5.3 (1984)
Education	
Literacy rate (%)	62.3

Population Forecasting

The following data are projections produced by Poptran, University College Cardiff Population Centre, from United Nations Assessment Data published in 1980, and are reproduced here to provide some basis of comparison with other countries covered by the Marxist Regimes Series.

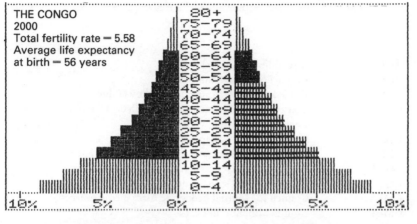

MALES   FEMALES

Projected Data for Congo 2000

Total population ('000)	2,718
Males ('000)	1,348
Females ('000)	1,370
Total fertility rate	5.58
Life expectancy (male)	54.4 years
Life expectancy (female)	57.6 years
Crude birth rate	41.3
Crude death rate	12.2
Annual growth rate	2.91%
Under 15s	44.40%
Over 65s	3.45%
Women aged 15–49	22.68%
Doubling time	24 years
Population density	8 per sq. km.
Urban population	49.5%

List of Abbreviations

ANP	Assemblíe Nationale Populaire
APN	Armée Populaire Nationale
CASL	Confédération Africaine des Syndicats Libres
CATC	Confédération Africaine des Travailleurs Chrétiens
CC	Central Committee
CFCO	Chemin de Fer Congo-Ocean Railway
CFTC	Confédération Française de Travailleurs Chrétiens
CGAT	Confédération Générale Africaine du Travail
CGT	Confédération Générale du Travail
CMEA	Council for Mutual Economic Assistance (Comecon)
CMPT	Comité Militaire du PCT
CNR	Conseil Nationale de la Révolution
CPSU	Communist Party of the Soviet Union
CSC	Confédération Syndicale Congolaise
EMSR	État Majeur Spécial Révolutionnaire
FLEC	Front pour la Libération de l'Enclave Cabinda
FO	Fédération Ouvrière
FPO-PT	Front Patriotique d'Oubangui-Parti du Travail
IBRD	International Bank for Reconstruction and Development
IMF	International Monetary Fund
JMNR	Jeunesse MNR
M-22	Mouvement du 22 février
MNR	Mouvement National de la Révolution
MPLA	Movimento Popular de Libertaçao de Angola
MSA	Mouvement Socialiste Africain
OAU	Organization of African Unity
PCT	Parti Congolais du Travail
PPC	Parti Progressiste Congolais
SIAN	Société Industrielle et Agricole du Congo
SUCO	Sucre du Congo
UDDIA	Union Democratique pour la Défense des Intérêts Africains
UGEEC	Union Générale des Étudiants et Élèves Congolais
UJC	Union de la Jeunesse Congolaise
UJSC	Union de la Jeunesse Socialiste Congolaise
UPC	Union des Populations du Cameroun
URFC	Union Révolutionnaire des Femmes Congolaises

Acknowledgements

Michael S. Radu wishes to acknowledge the support provided by the Foreign Policy Research Institute, which gave him the necessary logistical and editorial support, and to accord special thanks to his research assistant.

1 Introduction

The People's Republic of Congo is the oldest self-proclaimed Marxist-Leninist state in Africa. Having gained independence from France in 1960 as Congo-Brazzaville, the country was proclaimed a People's Republic in 1969, following a radical military coup. Ever since, the regime has claimed allegiance to 'scientific socialism' and has moved increasingly closer to the Soviet bloc in its ideological, political and military relations. Nonetheless, it continues to depend on trade with the West and to receive foreign aid from France.

Geographical Setting

The People's Republic of Congo is located in central-equatorial Africa, with a short (169 km.) but economically important shoreline to the Atlantic Ocean to the south-east. To the north and north-west the country borders Gabon, Cameroon and the Central African Republic; and to the south-west is situated the Angolan enclave of Cabinda. Congo is dwarfed by neighbouring Zaïre.

Most of the northernmost and north-eastern area of the country, along the Oubangui and Zaïre Rivers, and along the border with Zaïre, is a low, alluvial swamp, practically uninhabitable and rarely visited. Both the Oubangui and the Zaïre, as well as some of their major tributaries like the Sangha and Likouala, are partly navigable in that region. The Chaillu massif, a heavily-wooded highland area, is the western watershed of the Zaïre river. The Bateke Plateau south of the swamps, and on a higher elevation, is drier but still sparsely populated. South-west of it, in the Congo Cuvette, the climate is humid but more favourable to human habitation, which explains the urban concentration between Brazzaville and Loubomo. As one moves west from Brazzaville, towards Pointe Noire and the coast, the climate becomes steadily drier and cooler, largely the result of the cold Benguela Current washing the Namibian, Angolan and Congolese coasts. A narrow coastal plain on the Atlantic littoral merges into sandy beaches and towards the Cabinda border in heavily eroded cliffs.

Rainfall, while satisfactory throughout the country, is lowest and least reliable on the extreme north-east, on the Central African border, and on the coast; the former experiences a three-month dry season. The Mayombe range, which rises dramatically from the coastal plain, receives high rainfall and provides hydro-electric (as well as valuable timber) resources in the form of rivers which cut gorges through the hills.

Population

Almost 80 per cent of the total population lives in the south-eastern part of the country, between Brazzaville and the Atlantic port of Pointe Noire, while the north-western two-thirds of the country are sparsely inhabited and include some of the least explored areas of the world. Congo is one of the most urbanized countries on the African continent, with over 65 per cent of the total population living in urban centres.[1] There are four major cities in the country—Brazzaville, Pointe Noire, Loubomo and Kayes. They lie along the southern corridor adjacent to the Congo–Ocean Railway (CFCO). The Vili people live chiefly along the coast, the Kongo in the Brazzaville area and the Teke, Mbochi and Sanga in the centre and north.

Natural Resources

Considering its area and small population Congo is a relatively wealthy African state in terms of natural resources. It has some 80 million hectares of forests, among the most extensive in the continent, of which almost two-thirds are commercially viable at current world market prices. Despite this, timber exports have grown very slowly from 192,000 cu.m. in 1978 to 201,065 cu.m. in 1982. (*QER*, 1983, Annual Supplement, p. 20.) The reliability of the country's rainfall and temperature changes, and sufficient fertile land to allow a rational soil use, give Congo the capacity to satisfy most domestic food requirements.[2]

There are also modest deposits of copper and iron, while potash has for years been a significant national resource. Copper was exported in small quantities until 1979, as were lead and zinc. Substantial iron deposits (estimated at 1 billion tons of 50 per cent metal content) are so far unexploited. These ores are to be found in the Zanaga and Banbamba regions. The potash mine at Holle, near Pointe Noire, was one of the largest in the world but ceased production in 1977 following serious flooding. Gold is also produced in small quantities. Bauxite has been discovered but not exploited.

 • The most significant natural resource of the country and the mainstay of the entire economy is oil. Ranking fifth as a producer and exporter in sub-

Saharan Africa (after Nigeria, Angola, Gabon and Cameroon), Congo's oil fields are concentrated in off-shore areas close to Pointe Noire. Total production reached 5.7 million tons in 1984, but untapped reserves are small and new techniques of exploitation are not commercially profitable given the present depressed world prices. Natural gas deposits at Pointe-Indienne are a source of energy and earnings. The gas was heavily exploited in the 1970s (15,000,000 cu.m. was produced in 1977) and reserves were almost depleted by 1980. But in the following year, with existing deposits producing only 500,000 cu.m. major reserves were discovered off Pointe Noire. These have been exploited by Gaz-Congo—owned by the government, Elf and Agip—but production is still only 750,000 cu.m.

2 Politics

To gain a full understanding of current political developments it is necessary to consider the role played by Congo within France's colonial empire in Africa. While not all recent problems can be traced to the colonial inheritance, Congo's colonial experience has forged the political destiny of this country in an almost deterministic manner. For example, its unusually high rate of urbanization was due directly to French policies. Brazzaville, by its very location, was intended by the colonial power to be a major administrative centre. This intention led to the development of Brazzaville as the capital of French Equatorial Africa (this region comprised the independent states of Gabon, the Central African Republic, Cameroon, Chad and Congo). In addition, the French transformed the Congo, originally an undeveloped and sparsely populated region, into a vital support area for France's equatorial possessions, stretching from Libya's southern border to the Cabinda enclave in the Portuguese colony of Angola.

The French found the local population of the area, the Bakongo, Lari and Vili, particularly open to Western ideas. The result was that these ethnic groups provided a disproportionate share of bureaucrats for the colonial administration in French Equatorial Africa. At independence in 1960, the Congo had an unusually large urban population of intellectuals and bureaucrats. It was this educated, urbanized elite group, combined with dissatisfied intellectuals, radical students, militant workers and progressive army officers, that led the pro-socialist demonstrations in 1963 that, in conjunction with strikes by workers, led to the downfall of the basically conservative and 'neo-colonial' government of President Fulbert Youlou.

There are great similarities between Congo and Benin in their colonial heritage, level of urbanization and comparatively large educated elite of public servants, students and intellectuals.[1] Many Congolese bureaucrats had wide experience in other parts of French Equatorial Africa. This gave them a broader outlook than their counterparts in other newly independent African states. It also had an effect on Congo's policy towards neighbouring states. Many of those who had received education abroad, particularly in France, had come into contact with French communists and socialists. Many were attracted by the analysis of colonialism provided by Marxism–Leninism, notably Lenin's *Imperialism: The Highest Stage of Capitalism* , a pamphlet widely available in French, through the French Communist Party and the Communist CGT trade union.

While the number and influence of bureaucrats have certainly been important factors in Congolese politics since before independence, the country's unusually high degree of urbanization has been another. Unionized workers form a large and militant sector of the urban population often acting jointly with the burgeoning educated or semi-educated but unemployed or underemployed youth and radical students. Between 1960 and 1972, from independence through the Massemba-Debat and Ngouabi regimes (from 'neo-colonial exploitation' to 'scientific socialism') the Congolese bureaucracy grew by 636 per cent from 3,300 to 21,000;[2] The trend has continued and been accelerated under the present regime, with Prime Minister Ange Edouard Poungui complaining in October 1987 that the civil service grew from 54,000 in 1979 to 73,000 in 1986.[3] The most highly politicized and militant elements of the population are concentrated in Brazzaville. Finally, from an ideological viewpoint, the relatively large proportion of non-agricultural workers, most of them unionized, is not only highly unusual in Africa (outside South Africa), but tends to lend credibility to Marxist ideologues' appeals for a socialist state based on the working class; although the actual 'proletariat', in a classical Marxist sense, is still small.

As in many African countries the peasantry in the Congo is part of what one may legitimately call the 'politically irrelevant classes'. As elsewhere in Africa, the peasantry is ethnically and geographically fragmented, isolated from and suspicious of politics and remote from the centre of political action. The Congolese peasantry makes up over half the population but is politically peripheral.

That Congo has consistently been one of the leaders in Africa in educational terms (literacy, school attendance, number of university and high school graduates)[4] is also explained by the country's unusually high rate of urbanization and Brazzaville's importance to the French. This has magnified the effect of the traditional contempt of the educated and urbanized population for the peasants. As has been aptly noted: 'Socialism has made little difference to the rural people, living on subsistence agriculture in the country and largely unaware of the political leaders in towns' (Legum, 1970-1, p. B305). The fact that the Congolese peasants are seen by urban dwellers as incapable of meeting the food needs of the country further weakens their ability to influence government policies or protect their interests. Through their ethnic allegiance, elements of the Congolese population indirectly have a political voice; and in this respect some rural groups are clearly more influential than others.

Politics and Ethnicity

Ethnic cleavages are both obvious and important in Congolese politics. Any serious analysis must examine the effects of inter-ethnic competition for scarce resources within largely artificial state boundaries. Congo inherited from the French colonial empire borders that do not account for ethnic groupings or compatibility of diverse communities. The borders were created during political bargaining by competing European powers in the late nineteenth century and frequently ran along lines of longitude or latitude rather than along meaningful ethnic, geographic or political frontiers. In Congo, the term 'tribe' is not particularly suited to the general picture of Congolese ethnic rivalries. Regional, linguistic and other factors are often as important as narrow tribal ones. Once again, some analogies, imperfect as they admittedly are, are useful: to speak of 'northerners' in the Congolese context (usually meaning the Mbochi) is not far removed from speaking of 'southerners' in the United States.[5]

The Immediate Pre-Independence Period

In Congo, as in most of Africa, pre- and post-independence politics were to a great extent the result of geography and colonial convenience. As elsewhere on the continent, European colonization started from the coast and spread inland, with the result that coastal peoples, owing to longer contact with the Europeans, were more amenable to European influences. They often played a greater role in the colonial structure, received better access to education and assimilated broader influences. This was the case of the Lari and Vili, both Kongo sub-ethnic groups in Congo. Interior populations, on the other hand, were frequently recruited for the colonial police and army, on the assumption that they were more 'warrior-like'. Less accustomed to European ways and less educated, interior populations also tended to see the military or the police as their only means of social mobility. Hence, a vicious circle was created, in which the colonial administration came to see the inland peoples such as the Mbochis and Kouyous as warlike because of their backwardness, while the latter perceived army service as their only path to good education and influence. Thus, while Lari and Vili youths studied at the French lycées in Brazzaville, Dakar and France, ambitious young Mbochis and Kouyous ended up as the dominant majority in the colonial army and at military academies. This pattern became dangerous in a country without a national consciousness or traditions of inter-group solidarity or cooperation.

One peculiar characteristic of pre-independence Congo was the massive rural exodus to the city during the three decades prior to 1960. During the 1930s, the construction of the Congo–Ocean railroad brought many northerners to the Brazzaville area as unskilled labourers; and during World War II the short-lived prominence of Brazzaville attracted additional northerners to the city. The result was that by the 1950s Brazzaville became a microcosm of the colony, with the northern neighbourhoods, including Poto Poto, dominated by northeners, and the southern ones inhabited by Laris and Vilis. Ethnic clashes occurred periodically and resulted in Kongos fleeing Poto Poto to the southern neighbourhoods, and northerners moving to Poto Poto where the Mbochi were in ascendancy (Desjeux, 1980, p. 19).

The politics of pre-1960 Congo were dominated by such realities. The two major politicians in the country during the mid-1950s were both ethnically based: Félix Tchikaya, a Vili, led the Parti Progressiste Congolais (PPC), based among his own people and the Teke, but which claimed to be the first truly national Congolese party; Jacques Opangault, a Mbochi, led the Mouvement Socialiste Africain (MSA), which had been the earliest organized political group in Congo. The PPC represented principally the coastal peoples, the MSA the northerners. Both had to fight against a powerful ghost—the reputation and religious following of André Matsoua, a charismatic former clerk of Lari origin. Initially intending to form an African self-help organiza-tion, Matsoua was victimized by inept and suspicious French administrators and became the centre of a powerful Kongo-based (particularly Lari) evangelical cult (see Sinda, 1972; also a brief and well-informed analysis of the phenomenon in Decalo, 1976, pp. 128–37; and Desjeux, 1980, pp. 17–20). His death did not limit his appeal to Kongo adherents. In elections in 1945 and again in 1951, the dead Matsoua was overwhelmingly elected as Congo's representative to the French Assembly.[6] Naturally, the French authorities declared the runner-up, Tchikaya, the winner, and he installed himself in Paris to lead a comfortable life. Tchikaya's absence and the hostility of many of the Lari to any non-Matsoua follower, resulted in the meteoric rise of a former Catholic priest, Fulbert Youlou as the 'legitimate' heir to Matsoua and through him Lari aspirations. Elected mayor of Brazzaville in 1956, Youlou had to break with his own bishop, largely because his political interests required support for the Matsouanists and he came into conflict with the Catholic Church's interests and doctrine. The bishop to whom he was responsible prohibited Catholics from voting for Youlou. French ineptitude manifested itself once again, as the colonial administration and the Catholic

Church openly opposed Youlou and his Union Démocratique pour la Défense des Intérêts Africains (UDDIA). But the Lari achieved political dominance to the chagrin of Tchikaya, Opangault and the French. The Laris and other Kongos managed to maintain a dominant position in democratic elections. For the latter, Youlou was seen as the heir of Matsoua and French animosity only strenghtened his position. The net result was that by 1960 Fulbert Youlou, representing the central region and peoples of Congo, had become the country's most influential politician against his western (Vili-based and Tchikaya-led) and northern (Mbochi and Opangault-led) rivals. As it soon turned out, Youlou was an independent operator whose links with the Matsoua cult were largely opportunistic, a fact soon discovered by the educated and politically-shrewd Laris. But Youlou and the UDDIA were a major force after the 1956 legislative elections and the granting of domestic autonomy in November 1958. In the March 1957 territorial assembly elections, the UDDIA won twenty-two seats and dominated the south but the MSA took the north and had twenty-three seats. With a single seat majority Opangault became president of Moyen-Congo's internal government. But on 28 November 1958, an MSA deputy defected to Youlou giving him a majority; rioting followed.

Independence and the First Republic (1960–3)

On 28 November 1960 the former French colony of Moyen-Congo achieved independence and became the Republic of Congo (Brazzaville). As in most of French Africa at that time, the process of independence had more to do with decisions made in Paris and with French interests than with strong local action for independence. Simply put, independence for Congo was *la chose à faire* at the time, with no significant traumatic political, economic or social changes expected by most of those involved in Paris or in Brazzaville. France remained dominant economically and highly influential politically. Fulbert Youlou and his UDDIA seemed to be in firm control. Furthermore, Youlou came to an arrangement with the Mbochis, and Opangault became vice-president. Internal government tensions led him to resign the following year, but he returned again to government in 1962. By 1961 Youlou's relations with his erstwhile supporters, the Matsouanists, had deteriorated to such an extent that the army was used against the cult's followers. The main reason was the Matsouanists' rejection of modernity in any form—whether in politics, economics, education or anything else. The cult's followers refused to allow a census, to carry identity cards or pay taxes. Violence between

Matsouanists and Youlou's supporters started before independence. The Youlou regime's base of support further deteriorated as a result of the consistent animosity between the government and the Congolese trade unions. The three trade union federations at independence were, as elsewhere in French-speaking Africa, the local versions of the union federations in France. The Confédération Générale Africaine du Travail (CGAT) was heavily influenced by the Communist-controlled Confédération Générale du Travail (CGT) in France; the French Socialist-controlled Fédération Ouvrière (FO), was the parent organization of the Confédération Africaine des Syndicats Libres (CASL); while the Confédération Africaine des Travailleurs Chrétiens (CATC), including half of the unionized Congolese workers (Desjeux, 1980), was the offshoot of the Confédération Française des Travailleurs Chrétiens (CFTC). Normally, such a diversity of backgrounds would have kept the unions divided, but the confluence of government mistakes and ineptitude, corruption, arbitrariness and economic decline (which included 40-50 per cent unemployment) did bring them together in August 1963, when they united to stage a general strike which brought about Youlou's resignation and the intervention of the military. Prior to the strike, Youlou had been moving towards the creation of a one-party state. In August 1962, the National Assembly had given him the power to rule by decree. He had immediately announced his intention to declare one-party rule. This seriously worried the increasingly marginalized Mbochis (including those dominating the military) and the frustrated Vilis, who feared political irrelevance. The unions feared that their influence would be reduced. This combined with frustration over the poor performance of the economy. A ban on public meetings followed by the arrest of two CATC leaders on 12 August was the spark which led to the general strike by the three unions. The strike led to riots and attacks on government buildings. Not surprisingly, in light of the urban nature of the unions and the general character of Congolese politics, the entire affair was limited to Brazzaville, Loubomo and Pointe Noire, largely involving union workers, the unemployed and, an ominous sign of things to come, the youth (Desjeux, 1980). It is important to point out that the three union federations did not object to the establishment of a single-party system in principle, they hoped that they could influence if not control it. What they wanted was participation in political and economic life as a separate and well-defined entity.

The riots escalated quickly and the gendarmerie, badly outnumbered, soon lost control. Despite the crowds and the insurrectionary atmosphere, there were only three fatalities—'Les Trois Glorieuses' had found their three 'martyrs', and an avenue was later named after them (*Jeune Afrique*, 17-24

August 1983, pp. 74–5). The army, French-led but far from controlled, refused to intervene; more importantly, however, despite Youlou's pathetic requests, De Gaulle also declined to become involved. Despite Congolese political mythology, France probably could have saved Youlou, as it saved Leon M'Ba of Gabon the following year, even without the support of the indigenous troops, merely by using the Pointe Noire-based Bataillon des Tirailleurs Congo–Gabon. The reasons for Paris's indifference were many, but Fulbert Youlou's pre-1960 anti-French demagoguery, his incompetence and corruption, as well as the mistaken assessment of the nature of the opposition to his rule, all played a part.

Although the military did not play a particularly active role in the 1963 'revolution' of 13–15 August, their interest in political change was a significant influence on developments. Mostly Mbochis, the soldiers had a stake in a radical change of regime, inasmuch as it promised to become an opportunity for its own officers to replace the French. It is probable that young officers, like Lieutenant Marien Ngouabi, then posted in Pointe Noire, had a clearer understanding of what could follow Youlou's political demise than did the French.[7]

The failure of the army or the French to support him and the lack of success in negotiating with the unions, led Youlou to resign and effectively hand power to the army rather than the unionists. It was the Chief of Staff Félix Mouzabakani who accepted his resignation. Youlou fled the country, first to Zaïre and then to Spain, where he died in Madrid in 1972. Contemporary myths aside, Youlou, while only enjoying minority, and largely Lari support, had built himself a solid, stable and relatively committed constituency; this created persistent problems for successor regimes.

The Second Republic, 1963–8

Massemba-Debat and the Radicalization of the Military

The riots and general strike the of 13–15 August 1963 'revolution' marked a decisive turnaround in the modern Congolese history (Obenga, 1977, p. 38) initiating a period of radicalization. The three-day period is still celebrated as 'Les Trois Glorieuses'. The overthrow of Youlou marks a move away from the generally pro-Western stance adopted by Congo. The events of August indicated that diverse groups such as students, trade unions and sections of the army would play an increasing role in political life and serve as sources of leftist influence.

At the age of thirty-nine, a socialist-inclined former teacher and a

Protestant in a largely Catholic, Matsouanist and animist country, an ex-UDDIA deputy and pre-independence leader of the National Assembly and a Youlou cabinet member until his resignation in January 1963, Alphonse Massemba-Debat, had the asset of a reputation for honesty and was more radical than his predecessor. Massemba-Debat was initially appointed prime minister. However, his authority was subject to the approval of the military.

The collapse of the Youlou regime was followed by the establishment of a provisional Conseil National de la Révolution (CNR) which included union leaders, some army elements and the Marxist Union de la Jeunesse Congolaise (UJC), some of whose leaders were also prominent in the CGAT. In December 1963, following the approval of the new constitution, a new National Assembly was installed, and Massemba-Debat was made president, with Pascal Lissouba as prime minister. The new system was supposed to imitate that of Gaullist France, but it was immediately evident that Massemba-Debat was no De Gaulle and that the CNR and army exerted huge influence. The president's powers included the selection or dismissal of the prime minister and cabinet members, the right to dissolve the Assembly and theoretical control over the CNR, to which the Assembly was also subordinated (Racine, 1982, p. 232). In stronger hands and different circumstances such a system could have provided long-term stability; as it was it became a recipe for factional struggle and institutional competition. But there is little documentation of the political struggles of the 1963-8 period because of the government's tight control of the Congolese media and policy of restricting foreign journalists.

In July 1964 the Mouvement National de la Révolution (MNR) was established as the sole legal party in the country; it was a pro-socialist movement organized on the lines of democratic centralism. It established its own 'mass organization' including a youth group, Jeunesse MNR (JMNR), a women's group, Union Révolutionnaire des Femmes Congolaises (URFC) and a trade federation, the Confédération Syndicale Congolaise (CSC) (Desjeux, 1980, p. 22; Racine, 1982, p. 232; Decalo, 1976, p. 254). These organizations were intended to be tools for passing on MNR ideology and for mobilizing support for the policies of the MNR. In fact, the JMNR, the CSC, and the newly relabelled Armée Populaire (AP) all became power bases for groups competing for power and influence. Having a broad membership, the MNR provided a convenient entry point into national politics for diverse groups. But the MNR gradually became narrower in its membership as the Massemba-Debat regime grew older.

A number of different rivalries emerged: between the JMNR and the army, between northerners and southerners and between traditional, conservative Catholic groups and the essentially radical government. Massemba-Debat's main task was to try to balance the competing forces and to use the divisions to entrench his own power. The main conflict which developed once he had opted for a clearly socialist approach was with the Catholic trade unions. Representatives of these conservative forces (many of them Youlou sympathizers) were removed from the government and the MNR. This purge of rightists strengthened radical pro-Marxist groups, which were able to increase their influence over the direction of MNR and government policy. It was at this time that Youlou was able to flee the country.

The gradual isolation of pro-Catholic forces was a major cleavage in national unity—the Catholics having a substantial following. The Catholic church increasingly became a target for criticism from the radicals in the youth movement. The radicals got their way in 1964 when Massemba-Debat ordered the abolition of all Catholic youth groups and the establishment of the JMNR as the sole legal youth organization. The next blow to the pro-Catholic and conservative forces came at the end of 1964 when the National Assembly banned all the trade unions and formed a single, government-dominated movement, the Congolese Trade Union Confederation (CSC).

The JMNR, which began to receive financial aid from the newly established Soviet and Chinese embassies, soon became the most influential political force in the country. The JMNR was allowed to start organizing its own militia force. The militia, picked from among the JMNR's most radical groups, was trained by Cuban military advisers. Many of the advisers were part of a group of volunteers who went to Congo-Leopoldville with Che Guevara to assist leftist groups against Tshombe and Mobutu. This mission failed and the Cubans were welcomed in Congo by Massemba-Debat. They also played an important role in training the pro-communist MPLA (Popular Movement for the Liberation of Angola) liberation movement. Close links developed between the MPLA, the JMNR, radical Congolese army officers and the Cubans.

The JMNR gained further political power when its Marxist-Leninist leader, André Hombessa, was appointed interior minister. The JMNR-dominated militia took on itself the role of hunting out and harassing perceived opponents and 'counter revolutionaries'. The militia was not under Hombessa's total control: other leaders, including Claude-Ernest Ndala, Ambroise Noumazalay and the as yet little noticed Ange Diawara all competed with him within the organization. The JMNR became known as the Jeunesse and gained a reputation for having eyes and ears everywhere. But it increasingly competed with the army to be the vanguard and chief defender of the revolution. Tension increased in April 1966 when the JMNR-backed militant wing of the MNR succeeded in getting one of its leading figures, Ambroise Noumazalay, appointed prime minister when the MNR Political Bureau forced the resignation of Lissouba. Noumazalay and Ndala were representatives of a leftist group associated with the journal *Dipanda* (Independence). Right-wing elements accused the group of using political violence against its opponents and of murdering the President of the Supreme Court, Joseph Pouabou, and Attorney General Lazare Matsocota in 1965.[8] Although never attaining the highest office, Noumazalay proved to be a durable political operator and in 1988 still had a cabinet rank as minister of industry, fishing and crafts.

In the military, whose resentment of the JMNR activities grew by leaps and bounds, the Saint-Cyr-Coëtquiddan officer group became more and more important. By 1965 Yhombi Opango was Massemba-Debat's main military adviser; Captain Marien Ngouabi was the AP's representative on the MNR Central Committee; and Lieutenant Louis Sylvain-Goma was in command of a company. These three officers together represented the combination of increasingly serious and open grievances of the military. Ethnic origin had no influence over the coalition (Ngouabi was a Kouyou, Goma a Lari and Opango a Lari born and brought up in the Owando area of the north, and a cousin of Ngouabi). Most soldiers, as Mbochis and Kouyou, resented the growing domination of Brazzaville politics by the JMNR, which the army saw as usurping the military's role in the revolution.

At the time of Noumazalay's appointment as premier, Ngouabi, as the military representative in the MNR, openly attacked Massemba-Debat in the Central Committee. For such behaviour, the government reduced Ngouabi's rank and posted him to Pointe Noire, to which he refused to go. The move was jointly organized by Massemba-Debat and Noumazalay, and it backfired against both. The Kouyou troops, Ngouabi's non-Mbochi colleagues and northern politicians used the opportunity to support Ngouabi for their own reasons—chiefly hostility towards Massemba-Debat and Noumazalay and only partly related to ethnic allegiances (Goma, Raoul and other officers all supported Ngouabi). Much of this confusing but essential period is still misunderstood today; it seems that Ngouabi's criticism of Massemba-Debat was centred on the latter's 'associates' within the JMNR who were trying to force the army into a submissive position and reduce its political influence. It was this institutional approach, as much as Ngouabi's command of the paratroop/commando regiment, that unified most of the army behind him. The immediate result was the mutiny of the paracommandos, the arrest of senior AP officers and the seizure of MNR leaders. Although some reports say that the Cubans and the MPLA were prepared to oppose Ngouabi and to support the MNR, there is no evidence to support this; rather, Ngouabi seemed to have good relations with Cubans and he supported the MPLA's struggle in Angola. Ngouabi's move did not lead to the immediate removal of Massemba-Debat, rather he became increasingly impotent politically and the ideological, financial and political balance decisively shifted to the military. Ngouabi was reinstated, and the government was humiliated and weakened. Indeed, one of the putschist's demands was met: the loyal chief of staff, Moutsaka, was replaced by a low-ranking and insignificant officer, Lieutenant Kimbouala. By then, the end of the government was clearly being plotted. As Ngouabi later admitted, 'Faced with the total insecurity of the masses, the uncertainty for the revolutionaries, the progressive forces of the youth, workers, and intellectual revolutionaries, the militants, students, etc., have seriously prepared the end of the Massemba-Debat regime, in order to reiterate the irreversibility of the socialist option' (*L'Homme du 31 juillet*, 1976, p. 11). Simply put, the previous quotation indicates that by 1967 Ngouabi and his civilian and military associates were already operating on the assumption that Massemba-Debat was politically dead.

According to Obenga, the group of plotters, or the 'revolutionary nucleus' around Ngouabi included, after 1966, such leftist intellectuals and politicians as Pierre Nze, Noumazalay, Lissouba, Martin Mberi, Justin Lekoundzou Ithi Ossetoumba, as well as military officers like Nicolas Okongo, Sassou-Nguesso, Yhombi Opango and Gaston Eyabo (Obenga, 1977, pp. 46-7). All of these personalities certainly played a role. That Lissouba and Noumazalay, both former prime ministers under Massemba-Debat took part, was a clear indication of the regime's loss of most of its political base of support. Noumazalay's role is surprising given his JMNR links and his dismissal as premier in January 1968. Even more important, however, and a factor not admitted by Obenga, whose view of Congolese political history is consistent with that of the current ruling group, was the dissatisfaction of elements of the JMNR with Massemba-Debat. Some of the most radical of those elements were the basis of the People's Militia, soon to reach 2,000 members, on a par with the army (Decalo, 1976, p. 149), and led by Ange Diawara. Half-Malian, half-Kongo, Diawara was a radical, widely considered as 'Maoist'. It was his joining the Ngouabi group of plotters, as a result of disenchantment with the vacillating Massemba-Debat and hatred for his erstwhile colleagues in the JMNR, that helped to seal the fate of the regime. His political outlook was not dissimilar to that of Noumazalay, who was increasingly pro-Chinese. The growing opposition meant that Massemba-Debat's days as president were numbered. Competition to succeed him grew apace.

The 1968 Coup and the Third Republic

The Politicization of the Military and the Militarization of Politics

The main competitors for the post of president were Hombessa, dismissed as interior minister in early 1968 and with significant support in the MNR; Noumazalay, dismissed as prime minister at the same time; Diawara's civil defence (People's Militia) forces, and the military united around Ngouabi, Opango and Goma. Certainly, the rhetoric of all the competitors sounded similar, or at least equally to the left of the government. They were all stridently anti-French, advocating nationalization, particularly of foreign enterprises, 'anti-imperialism' and support for world revolution, without taking clear sides in the Sino-Soviet conflict.

In the hope that his enemies could not unite and choose a successor, Massemba-Debat announced on 22 July 1968 that he was prepared to resign if a successor could be found. None came forward, since no consensus existed within the opposition; a *putsch* intended for the following week failed because the elite armoured unit supposed to spearhead it failed to move (Desjeux, 1980, p. 26). Some street demonstrations in support of Massemba-Debat took place, while his opponents remained divided over the division of the political spoils.

On 29 July 1968 Marien Ngouabi was again arrested, together with Eyabo, accused of plotting a *coup d'état*. Two days later, on 31 July, according to Ngouabi himself, it only took eight unarmed soldiers to free him (Obenga, 1977, p. 49). They took him to the Maya Maya paracommando base, close to the airport, from where the army staged the coup which ended the Massemba-Debat regime. The time was ripe for his removal with massive army opposition and demonstrations against him in Brazzaville by the JMNR. The growing crisis led Massemba-Debat to suspend the Assembly and dissolve the Politburo.

The events started on 31 July were the beginning of a slow-moving coup. Officially, Massemba-Debat remained president; Ngouabi was appointed army commander; and Ange Diawara, from his barracks at 'Camp Biafra', negotiated with the military. At the same time, however, a disgusted Massemba-Debat retreated to his home village of Boko, waiting for further developments. Only at the end of August a solution, temporary as it turned out, was found, and Alfred Raoul, a Cabindan and former colleague of Ngouabi at Saint-Cyr was chosen as prime minister. As a Cabindan, Raoul had no personal political or ethnic power base; as an old friend of Ngouabi he was a reliable military figurehead. Meanwhile, Ngouabi became the leader of the Conseil National de la Révolution (CNR) the real power centre in the country (on 31 December of the same year he was formally nominated as president with Raoul as prime minister).

Diawara's civil defence forces were to be assimilated into the military following the August events with Diawara becoming a sub-lieutenant but also political commissar of the army; Louis-Sylvain Goma became chief of staff of the army. However, the JMNR militia refused to submit to army authority and a conflict ensued. The army attacked the 'Camp Biafra' of the JMNR when Hombessa refused to surrender the weapons in JMNR possession. Some 100–300 JMNR militants were killed by Ngouabi's commandos (Decalo, 1976, p. 155). The camp was captured on 1 September. On 4 September, Massemba-Debat resigned; Raoul became acting president.

While by the end of 1968 the military, and Ngouabi in particular, clearly had the upper hand, it was clear that his control was not absolute in circumstances of factional competition. Nobody seemed to have any real long-lasting power. In fact the following year, the practice that continues to this day was established of periodic purges taking place to ensure control by the president resulting in the elimination of the political enemies of the strongest group. The purges and struggles are indicative of the varying ideological positions of factions within the ruling group, the army and the active political organizations such as student and labour groups. Ideological differences between orthodox Marxists, Maoists and out-and-out opportunists have muddied the waters and made labelling of groups nearly impossible.

On 31 December 1968, the CNR named a new government. Ngouabi was chief of state, and his former Saint-Cyr colleague, Alfred Raoul, was chief of the State Council—the equivalent of prime minister. Much of 1969 was spent by Ngouabi in consolidating his political control and in preparing the groundwork for the oft declared transition to socialism. The regime laid great stress on national unity and eschewed tribalism, though it was accused of this by opponents. Despite the presence of Raoul as a figurehead, the 1968 coup was widely seen as a northerners' coup, and thus a threat to the Kongo. The result was that some Lari elements within the military and the gendarmerie were hostile to the Ngouabi group. In February 1969 the government claimed that a plot to bring back Youlou had been discovered, led by the 1963 chief of staff, Félix Mouzabakani and a Lari paratroop instructor, Captain Pierre Kikanga (Mouzabakani had recently been sacked as interior minister by the CNR). By November of the same year, another Lari plot was alleged. The commander of the gendarmerie, Major Norbert Tsika, was demoted to private as a result. Finally, on 23 March 1970, a small group of rebels, led by the same Pierre Kikanga, crossed the river from Zaïre and attempted to rally the Lari against the northern-based regime. The rebels unsuccessfully offered the presidency to a fellow Lari, but one born and educated in the north, Yhombi Opango, then a paratrooper commander (*Jeune Afrique*, 15 April 1977).

The various plots from the 'right', whether alleged Youlouists or 'tribalists', served to strengthen the far left in the armed forces, particularly those formerly associated with the JMNR but who had rallied to the side of the army during the 1968 events. Some of those former youth leaders, like Claude Ndala, Ange Edouard Poungui, Diawara, Justin Lekoundzou, were among the Politburo members elected at the founding Congress of the PCT (Parti Congolais du Travail) (29–31 December 1969). The nucleus of the PCT was the left wing of the MNR. One of the most active and influential members of the leadership was Ange Diawara. Incorporated in the ranks of the army as a lieutenant in 1968, the next year Diawara became the first commissar of the newly established Political Directorate of the army. His role was to purge ideologically unsound elements. He and his deputy, Captain Kiboula-Kaya, had extensive powers and used them to attempt to create their own power base within the military. Through them and in order to further his ideological aims, in 1969 Ngouabi launched a politicization campaign within the APN (Armée Populaire Nationale).

Following the Kikanga affair, the gendarmerie was dismantled and replaced with a People's Militia. The old spectre of a paramilitary force challenging the military emerged and his more 'professional' colleagues pushed Ngouabi into crushing it (*Afrique Nouvelle*, 25 March 1971).

By the spring of 1970, following the defeat of Kikanga, the socialists were clearly in the ascendent, as demonstrated in March–April that year, during the PCT's First Extraordinary Congress. Denis Sassou-Nguesso and the omnipresent Noumazalay were added to the Politburo, strengthening what looked like a pro-Chinese faction, with which Diawara and Claude Ndala were also associated. But it may be too simplistic to describe them purely by reference to their wish for close ties with China. As far as domestic policy was concerned, they called consistently for the implementation of radical socialist policies.

The only serious challenge to the new regime so far had come from civil servants, who went on strike in August and September 1969. Ngouabi dealt ruthlessly with the strikers, detaining several and dismissing others. He also sacked the minister of finance, in whose department the strike took place. To curb possible opposition from the unions, he dissolved the executive committee of the CSC. Ngouabi personally attacked the civil servants in a national address in which he accused them of being members of the exploiting classes. In this he had some justification and popular support; public sector employees ate up around three-quarters of the national budget and enjoyed a far higher standard of living than most Congolese.

On 3 January 1970, Ngouabi symbolically proclaimed Congo to be a People's Republic and put into effect a new, Soviet-style constitution drawn up by the leading organs of the PCT. Ngouabi was president of the party and of the state. Below him was a vice-president of the Council of State (a post to which Raoul was appointed) who was theoretically responsible to the PCT Central Committee but in fact to Ngouabi. Under the new constitution, the president was committed to governing the country according to the principles of Marxism-Leninism. The PCT was structured along orthodox Marxist-Leninist lines with a Politburo at the top of a pyramidal structure; below it was a forty-member Central Committee (ten of the members being candidate members). Following the civil service strike, the next threat to the regime was the student riots in Pointe Noire in November 1971. These were put down ruthlessly by the army, several students being killed in the process. At the time of the riots, Ngouabi purged possible opponents from party and state bodies. Raoul and Ndala were dismissed from the Politburo; many of those purged from the Central Committee were on the radical wing of the party.

The most serious test of Ngouabi's strength came in February 1972, when Ange Diawara, with support from the People's Militia, attempted a coup to forestall his dismissal from the PCT leadership. Some reports said that he was advised in his bid for power by members of the French Communist Party. Units led by chief of staff Opango crushed the coup. Diawara initially tried to disguise his coup by claiming to have been protecting Ngouabi against an Yhombi Opango coup; Ngouabi in turn ordered the arrest of the latter. Fortunately for Ngouabi, Yhombi Opango escaped arrest and was able to smash the Diawara *putsch* (Desjeux, 1980, p. 28; Decalo, 1976, p. 165). The fact that Diawara escaped, and that his Mouvement du 22 février (M-22), also known as the Parti Communiste Congolais (PCC), survived, was a worrying experience for the Ngouabi regime, and so was the fact that thirty to forty guerrillas survived in the Pool and Brazzaville regions for almost one year. Finally, in April 1973 Diawara and three of his colleagues were cornered and killed by the military. Ngouabi denounced Diawara, calling him both a CIA agent (*West Africa*, 17 March 1972) and likening him to Trotsky and Lin Biao (*Africa Contemporary Record*, 1972-3: B534).

Once again, purges and trials followed, with the predictable results.

Noumazalay was purged, Ndala was sentenced to life imprisonment, and Raoul was sentenced to ten years. According to a number of observers, after the Diawara affair the regime centred around four persons of unequal rank: Ngouabi, Yhombi Opango as colonel, the highest rank in the military, Pierre Nze, a former educator and the ideologue of the regime and Kondo, the CSC boss (Desjeux, 1980, p. 29). In fact, Ngouabi controlled most of the army himself.

The weakening of the radical left after the Diawara affair, politically demonstrated by the M-22 members engaging in 'self-criticism' for 'entryism', seemed to indicate by the end of 1972 that the military had finally won the struggle for power. The twin problems confronting the new regime, however, remained the same: the desire to legitimize itself through Marxist ideology, and to be perceived as a national rather than an ethnically-based entity. The first required the appointment of civilians to leading party and state positions and the transformation of the PCT into a credible Marxist party; the second involved non-Mbochi-Kouyou personalities participating equally in politics as well as in military units. By the end of 1988 the regime had not managed to find a permanent solution to either of these dilemmas.

During his rise to power, Ngouabi had been transformed from a left-inclined officer sick of the shortcomings of politicians into a political animal speaking Marxism–Leninism *à l'africaine* as its language. Quite obviously, he had read Lenin's works, which is plain not just because his own writings constantly quote him, but because of his ability to use Leninist language, organizational methods and slogans. His adherence to Marxism was more than just an *ad hoc* justification or legitimization of his seizure of power. What is in question is his ability to apply Marxist–Leninist theories which he assimilated to the realities of the Congolese situation and his claims to have created a genuine Marxist–Leninist party. He stated very clearly his adherence to orthodox Marxism–Leninism rather than some form of African socialism. In an interview with *World Marxist Review* in 1975 he stated that 'there is only one socialism—scientific socialism, the foundations of which were laid by Marx and Engels ... One can speak of ways to socialism, but certainly not of an African socialism' (*World Marxist Review*, Vol. 8, No. 5 May 1978). In the same interview he spoke of the primacy of the working class, which he said was the most exploited group in Congo. He referred to the peasantry (the poorest and most numerous portion of the Congolese population) as allies of the working class. As in many African states, there was only an embryonic working class and it was more prosperous than the peasantry. The few workers were essentially part of an urbanized elite. Inordinate stress on this class led to the marginalization of the peasants in political terms. Many workers and, in particular, civil servants, joined the Marxist party led by Ngouabi but did so for material or political gain rather than for ideological reasons. The party was not a strong ideological force. Its influence was generally limited to urban areas and it was led from above with little real commitment on the part of many members.

The death of Diawara brought about a certain relaxation in Congolese politics and renewed attempts to institutionalize the Ngouabi regime. A new constitution in July 1973 was approved in a referendum, with 73.5 per cent of the votes cast in favour; it provided for a National Assembly, a State Council (government) and resulted in the appointment of a new prime minister the following month. The new chief of government, Henri Lopes, a writer and technocrat from the south without any political base of his own, acted within the narrow limits imposed by Ngouabi and his associates, particularly the military. Among the policies introduced was a 50 per cent increase in the salaries of the civil servants, and increasing investments in industry, all on the basis of oil revenues. Little investment or interest was directed towards agriculture.

Despite attempts to institutionalize itself, the elimination of Diawara and control over the elite army units, the Ngouabi regime remained vulnerable to internal challenges and to threats to its leader. Student demonstrations in 1971 and again in January 1974 brought military crackdowns, while the PCT had its political role and influence strictly limited by the army.

Between 1974 and 1975 Ngouabi was challenged by the unions and as a result dismantled the UGEEC. He also had practically to destroy the PCT through purges in 1971 and 1975 in order to maintain control. Insecure in his role as president, Ngouabi kept even the military under close surveillance. To maintain his primacy he periodically demoted Yhombi Opango, and Sassou-Nguesso, both fellow northerners and popular among the military rank and file. This weakened his own support among the northerners. The 1975 appointment as prime minister of his former Saint-Cyr colleague, Louis Sylvain-Goma (a Lari) was intended as a concession to the south; it was instead seen by many in the PCT and army as a further demonstration of his oligarchic tendencies, since Goma was a member of Ngouabi's 'clique of four', along with Raoul and Yhombi Opango. Feeling under ever greater pressure, in September 1975 Ngouabi decided to engage in a 'radicalization campaign', which involved a massive purge of many of the remaining PCT cadres, particularly civilians, and virtually destroyed the PCT as the 'revolutionary vanguard'.

The entire episode also had important external connotations, related to developments in neighbouring Angola, and particularly to the Cabinda enclave. Pointe Noire and the adjacent areas have a large number of Cabindan immigrants, particularly of mixed blood. They have traditionally had some political influence, as demonstrated by the career of Alfred Raoul. The Cabindans are ethnically closer to Congolese groups on the Atlantic coast than to those across the Zaïrean border. Furthermore, the Cabindan oil industry has attracted many Congolese. When Prime Minister Henri Lopes made a statement in Paris in 1975, in support of Cabindan 'self-determination', it represented more than his personal opinion. The fact that Auguste Tchioufou, leader of a faction of the Front for the Liberation of the Cabinda Enclave (FLEC), a movement advocating secession from Angola, received some discreet support from Brazzaville (*Africa Confidential*, 9 January 1976, pp. 5–6), also demonstrated Congolese interest in Cabinda. None of this, however, was compatible with either the MPLA policies, or with those of Moscow and Havana, both of which had large numbers of military personnel in Congo at the time. Nor was it consistent with Brazzaville's longstanding support for the MPLA. Ultimately, the links with the MPLA proved stronger and Congo became a vital staging post for the Cuban expeditionary force which intervened in the Angolan civil war on the MPLA's side.

In August 1975 members of the union federation supposedly controlled by the PCT, began openly to criticize the party leadership, and implicitly Ngouabi, for 'bourgeois behaviour'. The leadership responded by starting a series of 'self-criticism' sessions and preparations for a massive purge (ibid.). In September, Ngouabi set up a Purge Commission, led by Henri Lopes, and started a series of anti-French and anti-'imperialist' rhetorical attacks, in contradiction to Lopes's relatively pro-French stance. Furthermore, Brazzaville's public statements of support for the MPLA became more frequent than ever. Internally, Ngouabi attacked the *extravagance vestimentaire* and *le comportement hippy* of Congolese youths and students—his most vocal opponents at the time. Finally, in December 1975, he struck. After a week-long meeting of the PCT Central Committee, the Politburo was dissolved and replaced by a five-member Special Revolutionary General Staff (EMSR), including Ngouabi, Sassou-Nguesso, Louis Sylvain-Goma, Jean-Pierre Thistère-Tchikaya and Jean-Pierre Ngombe. Lopes, the head of the Purge Commission, was the major victim of the purges; he was sacked as prime minister, being replaced by Louis Sylvain-Goma. One of the new government's first decrees was to ban political meetings during working hours—a blow to the radical firebrands among the union leadership.

Ngouabi promised to continue the revolution and to restructure the party, saying: 'The Central Committee continues to exist. The functions of its secretariat and Politburo are temporarily being exercised by the EMSR, until the next extraordinary congress of the party, which will give the Congolese Revolution a new, efficient and truly revolutionary political leadership: new Central Committee, Politburo, Central Committee secretariat members' (*Afrique-Asie*, 1976, p. vi). For all practical purposes, the 'radicalization campaign' was a reassertion of total control by the small group of radical officers which was Ngouabi's chief source of support. In November 1976 a party conference 'legitimized' the military takeover represented by the formation of the EMSR. Once again, party institutions had been used to rubber stamp military decisions.

But Ngouabi's concentration of power in the EMSR and his purges of suspected opponents did not neutralize his opponents, who began to build a coalition against the government, which had only one recourse—violence. The result was Ngouabi's assassination on 18 March 1977. According to the official communiqué of the Military Committee of the party, signed by Sassou-Nguesso, Marien Ngouabi 'found his death in combat, with weapons in his hand on Friday, 18 March 1977' (in Obenga, 1977, pp. 99–100). The death of the Congolese president remains today both a mystery and a political minefield, since it was never fully explained.

The official version was that a 'suicide commando' led by ex-Captain Barthélemy Kikadidi, former chief of military intelligence under Massemba-Debat, with support from members of the presidential guard, assasinated Ngouabi. A Kongo, like Massemba-Debat, Kikadidi was allegedly motivated by 'tribalism' and acted under orders from imperialist enemies of the revolution.[9] One of the questionable aspects of the assassination was the odd inability of the authorities to capture Kikadidi (he was shot dead on 13 February 1978 in Brazzaville), while at the same time, in the absence of the accused, a thorough settling of accounts took place immediately after the assassination. The circumstances of Kikadidi's death strongly resembled those of Diawara's convenient killing in 1973; in both instances the victims clearly had some support, as was proved by their ability to survive in Brazzaville for almost a year, and knew far too much to be captured. The rumours in Brazzaville, a city dominated by rumours, were that the assassination of Ngouabi may have had more to do with the followers of Diawara still retaining an underground infrastructure known as the M-22 (Mouvement 22 du février—22nd of February Movement, after the date on Diawara's failed *putsch* in 1972). Interestingly, in September 1987, Sassou-Nguesso was clearly jolted by an otherwise minor rebellion in Owando, led by retired Captain Pierre Anga, a member of the eleven-man Military Committee of the Party established immediately following Ngouabi's death. Among Anga's actions was the circulation of a tape cassette, accusing Denis Sassou-Nguesso of having planned both Ngouabi's assassination and the judicial murder of Massemba-Debat in 1977. The regime's overreaction, which included the arrest of Yhombi Opango, clearly recalled the memories of the spring of 1977. It is very likely that the truth surrounding Ngouabi's death will never be found, since too many parties have a stake in hiding it or blaming others, and the murdered leader had alienated so many powerful groups in the Congolese society that the list of possible culprits is very long indeed. It includes ethnic elements among the Kongos, the supporters of Massemba-Debat, the 'historic Left' of the Congo, represented by Diawara's followers as well as those of Lissouba, Noumazalay and Nze, Youlouists, disgruntled Cabindans, and PCT *apparatchikh* shunted aside during the 'radicalization campaign' of 1975.

Following the assassination, a series of rapid and puzzling events took place. Cardinal Emile Biayenda was killed the following day, allegedly by Ngouabi's relatives, who suspected him of using magic to overcome the president's own 'invulnerability' to bullets. In light of the PCT's traditionally good relations with the Catholic Church, as well as of Ngouabi's personal close ties to the cardinal, it was an unexpected and rather puzzling event. More importantly still, and well within the pattern established by Ngouabi himself, the assassination 'inquest' was used as a pretext for a wide-ranging purge of politically influential personalities seen as threatening a smooth succession by other members of the military. 'Rightists' and 'leftists', former union leaders and politicians all became victims of the purge. Some leading members of the military hierarchy were suspected of having used the assassination as a pretext to settle old scores. Among those arrested as a result of the 'inquiry' into Ngouabi's death were Lissouba and Noumazalay, both former prime ministers under Massemba-Debat, and the latter also an influential member of Ngouabi's initial PCT leadership group; union leader Kondo, seen as one of the four most powerful members of the regime in 1972-3; Félix Mouzabakani, who as chief of staff received Youlou's resignation in August 1963; the ubiquitous Claude Ndala; Moutsaka, dismissed following the 1966 Kouyou soldiers' mutiny on behalf of Ngouabi; and most spectacularly, Massemba-Debat himself. Lissouba was sentenced to life in prison; Massemba-Debat to death. A week after his 'conviction' Massemba-Debat was executed, together with four members of Ngouabi's bodyguard squad; and two days later two members of Ngouabi's extended family were also shot for the murder of Cardinal Biayenda. Massemba-Debat allegedly gave a confession shortly before he was shot.

Ngouabi's successor was Brigadier-General Joachim Yhombi Opango—

the former army chief of staff and minister of defence. At the time of Ngouabi's death his political career was in decline. He had been dismissed from the PCT Central Committee in December 1975 and was in the shadows. He emerged from them to become president. He claimed to be following Ngouabi's Marxist policies, though under Opango the military accumulated even more power at the expense of the PCT. He ruled through what was called the Military Committee of the PCT. He appointed Henri Lopes, the former premier, as finance minister—Lopes had been one of the victims of Ngouabi's radical period. Louis-Sylvain Goma was prime minister and Denis Sassou-Nguesso defence minister. Soon after the assassination Sassou-Nguesso became first vice-president and Goma second vice-president. With the exception of Goma—a southerner—most members of the new leadership were from the north. The purge of the party and of state institutions—which undoubtedly had a personal side—was also intended by Opango to reduce corruption and nepotism and to reshuffle or replace local PCT officers. Opango issued repeated calls for greater political and work discipline and for higher productivity.

Many people were surprised when the successor to Ngouabi was selected, since Sassou-Nguesso had been clearly the most influential person with both army and party. He also seemed to be in charge in the hours following the assassination: he signed the official communiqué on the events of 18 March in the name of the Military Committee. The reasons for Opango's succession were mostly related to the Byzantine arrangements, cliques and intrigues within the Congolese military, the peculiar circumstances surrounding Ngouabi's assassination and the personal roles of the main actors. While Ngouabi and Sassou-Nguesso were both northerners, and Yhombi Opango was an Owando-born Lari, the intricacies of Congolese ethnicity and politics played a hidden but none the less important role. Thus, with the Kongos clearly in the political saddle since the 1950s, tribal clashes between them (Lari versus Vili) dominated the scene. With the northerners' victory in 1968, and their unshakeable grip on the military, it was their turn to clash along tribal lines, once ethnic solidarity was no longer a prerequisite for taking power. The result was that tribal (Mbochi versus Kouyou) and sub-tribal, or clan considerations (Yhombi was related, by clan ties, to Ngouabi) became natural vehicles for personal jockeying for power within the 'northern'- dominated army. Yhombi Opango sought power by allying himself with groups such as the paramilitary and police people, some of them Kongo. In the case of Sassou-Nguesso, his political alliances were ideological, with the mostly Lari-Vili intellectuals of the PCT.

Of the eleven Military Committee members, Sassou-Nguesso, Thistère-

Tchikaya, Okongo, Katali, Tsiba and Ngollo were clearly the most ideologi-
cal, closest to the PCT and most committed to Marxism–Leninism. Opango,
however, was the most senior officer, had been widely associated with
Ngouabi, a former colleague of Goma and was enthusiastically supported by
Anga, also from Owando. Thus, while the numerical balance within the
Committee was clearly in Sassou-Nguesso's favour, the combination of ranks
(Opango being the most senior officer), ethnicity (Sylvain-Goma, a Lari,
being needed by both sides, and initially supporting his erstwhile colleague,
Opango) and experience all served to establish a balance, albeit a temporary
one within the political elite.

However, it was clear from the start that Opango was in a peculiar
position: his office was supposed to be part of a new, 'collegial' form of
government—an inherently unstable arrangement. Indeed, Opango's
strength, initially at least, was largely among the military rank and file and the
bureaucrats, the latter tired of ideological convulsions and the former loyal to
the man whom they saw as the closest friend of their dead Kouyou leader. In
fact, what seemed at the time to be a collegial leadership was nothing but a
dual one, in which power among the eleven-member Military Committee
was divided between Yhombi Opango and Sassou-Nguesso, both northerners but unequally gifted for political manoeuvring in a radical political
environment. Of the Committee members, it was clear that some were far
more equal than others; Sassou-Nguesso, first vice-president in charge of
party matters, propaganda, control and organization as well as defence
minister, was clearly in control of the military and the centre of party plots
against the relatively apolitical president; the second vice-president, Louis
Sylvain-Goma, was not only of the wrong ethnic origin, as a Lari, to challenge
Sassou-Nguesso but was by statute expected to implement CNR policies
(Owona, 1978, p. 61), although he was relatively powerless in that body. His
lack of political clout made him little else but a Lari figurehead in a largely
northern officers' clique. Of the remaining members, most of them
northerners, Ebaka, Ngollo, Okongo,[10] Florent Tsiba, Jean-Xavier Katali
provided a majority for Sassou-Nguesso—a majority whose ambitions for
power had to be temporarily checked by Opango's popularity in the army.
'Collegiality' in that sense and time, meant that each side was looking for
ways to eliminate the other, whether through popular or elite manoeuvres. It
was obvious for Congolese political observers that the political skills and
ideological commitment of the Opango camp were clearly inferior to those
of the Sassou-Nguesso group, and that it was just a matter of time before the
latter would gain power.

The distribution of tasks among the Military Committee members indicated from the beginning that the most radical elements of that body were in control of the sensitive positions: Sassou-Nguesso as defence minister retained a strong influence over the military, supported by his two deputies, Ngollo as chief of staff and Okongo as chief of the political directorate of the APN, in fact the main political commissar. The propaganda sector of the PCT came under the control of Jean-Pierre Ngombe, and that of organization was led by Justin Lekoundzou, while Tsiba became Sassou-Nguesso's deputy in charge of the coordination of party activities. Only Pierre Anga among Yhombi's loyalists had a significant position, as political commissar for the Brazzaville area.

Like Ngouabi and Massemba-Debat before him, Opango also had to face the threat of coups, some real and some imaginary. The most significant, according to the regime, and widely doubted by the population, was the '15 August Plot' of 1978. According to the government, a plot involving foreign mercenaries and local politicians was hatched to overthrow the government on the eve of the anniversary of 'Les Trois Glorieuses'. The timing and the description provided by the officials, including the alleged role of 'foreign intelligence agencies' and agents, including a Frenchman, a Ghanaian and a Zaïrean-Togolese-Ghanaian citizen, sounded suspiciously similar to the 'international imperialist plot' in Benin the year before (*African Contemporary Record*, 1978-9, p. B554). At any rate, whether real or staged, the plot resulted in the arrest of a number of formerly prominent politicians, including Dieudonné Miakassisa, former assembly speaker under Massemba-Debat, and Félix Mouzabakani, the former commander of the army. They were kept in detention, never tried and released by Sassou-Nguesso the following year. There were even reports that an unnamed foreign state had put combat aircraft at the plotters' disposal.

Yhombi Opango inherited an unstable economic situation, the result of the dislike of foreign investors for the radical policies pursued by Ngouabi and poor relations with the main aid donor, France. His attempts to reduce the size of the civil service, limit the salaries of unionized workers (by eliminating the annual bonus, equivalent to one month's salary) and achieve a *rapprochement* with France and the United States immediately made Yhombi Opango unpopular with the entrenched employees of the government and with the relatively privileged wage earners in Brazzaville and Pointe Noire, from students to unions and bureaucrats. At the same time it provided his enemies on the left with ammunition, which they were to use against him soon. Compared with Ngouabi—not to mention Sassou-Nguesso—Opango was not a radical and was more concerned with regime stability than ideological goals. In addition, Yhombi Opango's own ostentatious life style further alienated members in the military and the population at large.

Despite Opango's weakness, it was apparently impossible for his opponents to mobilize enough support within the military alone to oust him. The radicals reversed the post-1968 pattern of change in Congolese politics: instead of using the army as the ultimate instrument of pressure, barely concealed by party slogans, they began to use the party apparatus to legitimize what amounted to a palace coup against the president. The leading organs of the PCT began pressing Opango to account for his far from impressive record in charge. Apparently convinced that the PCT apparatus was too weak and submissive to oppose him, Yhombi Opango acceded to 'popular demands' for the convening of a Central Committee session on 5 February 1979, over two years since the body's previous meeting. The 'popular demands' were in fact the result of the activities of and public criticism of Opango by two Central Committee members, Florent Tsiba and Thistère-Tchikaya. Both had just returned from an ideological training course in Guinea, where they clearly learned the techniques of intra-party manœuvring. A better Leninist and politician than Opango could have easily removed the two for breaking the rules of 'democratic centralism' and party discipline by searching for support outside the PCT; he did not, and allowed the Central Committee meeting to take place.

The Sassou-Nguesso Regime and the Institutionalization of Radicalism

The 5 February 1979 CC meeting produced a clear majority for Opango's critics and the president was forced to resign. Supported by a coalition of radicals, military as well as civilians, Denis Sassou-Nguesso was elected to the leadership of the party and the presidency. An extraordinary party congress was convened on 26-9 March the same year, with the aim of legitimizing the new regime, and to purge the losers of the February meeting. Purge it did, as twenty old members, including Anga and Ngombe, were replaced, and thirty-five new ones elected. Opango was placed under home arrest, his property confiscated. A party inquiry was launched to investigate the property owned by Opango and his lieutenants. The new ruling troika appeared to be composed of Sassou-Nguesso, Thistère-Tchikaya and the union boss, Bokomba Yangouma; prominent Central Committee and Politburo members included Tsiba, Katali, and Pierre Nze. The door was also open to former members of the M-22, Diawara's followers, among them

Camille Bongou. On his accession to power, Sassou-Nguesso had a strong following in the unions and some popular support. He was seen as a committed socialist.

On 8 July 1979, elections were staged, combined with a referendum on a new constitution to replace Ngouabi's 1973 document, declared void by the CMPT in 1977. The only list of candidates was, naturally, that of the single party, the PCT. On 16 August 1979 Sassou-Nguesso was sworn in as president, and one of his first decisions was to provide amnesty to those accused of involvement in the murder of Ngouabi and Biayenda, of harbouring Kikadidi and of trying to overthrow Opango in August 1978. The only exceptions were André Hombessa, who remained in prison, and Opango and his followers. While one may in part agree with Sassou-Nguesso's assessment of the '5 February Movement' as 'a resolute retaliatory measure by all our country's leftist forces against the rightist movement' (*Bulletin Quotidien de L'ACI*, 17 August 1979, p. 3) that assessment should be taken with caution. To begin with, some of the 'rightists', including Finance Minister Henri Lopes, sacked by Ngouabi in 1975 and brought back by Opango, retained their jobs; and even though the 'leftist' credentials of Goma could be doubted, he also retained his position as prime minister. Sassou-Nguesso's stated aim on coming to power was to fight corruption, tribalism, regionalism and conservatism.

The Extraordinary Congress of the PCT in March 1979 resulted in a Politburo which represented the division of political influence between various elements of the radical wing of the party. Thus, while Sassou-Nguesso became the clear winner, Thistère-Tchikaya became the *de facto* second most powerful leader, in his capacity as Politburo member in charge of education and ideology; Lekoundzou, secretary in charge of planning and economy; Yangouma, secretary in charge of organization; Ngollo, chief of the political commission of the army; Nze, secretary for foreign affairs (and minister of foreign affairs since 1979, replacing the Ngouabi loyalist Obenga); François-Xavier Katali, in charge of security; and Florent Tsiba became propaganda chief. Camille Bongou was promoted from relative obscurity to be secretary-general of the presidency of the Central Committee. All of these personalities had claims to power, whether by virtue of long service in the party, their role in 1968, 1977 and 1979, ideological purity, base of support among politically relevant groups like youth, unions, party apparatus or the military. All of them were potential competitors for influence and power. As Sassou-Nguesso entrenched his power, he purged, detained or demoted most of the possible threats to his position. Once again, the Sassou-Nguesso regime demonstrated that 'collegial' leadership in Congo cannot last beyond a short honeymoon period following a victory; ultimately, power has to be centralized and personalized.

In his swearing-in speech in August 1979, Sassou-Nguesso, as a good Congolese Marxist–Leninist, described the pressures on his regime. In explaining the amnesty he offered, he stated that: 'It would be false to believe that the purpose of these measures is to please certain regions, districts . . . Although words like "kouilou," "les grands niari', "Cuvette", "Pool", "nord-sud", and so on recall geographical and administrative realities, they are without doubt counterrevolutionary and essentially reactionary concepts as far as politics and ideology are concerned' (*Bulletin Quotidien de L'ACI*, 17 August 1979, p. 3). But Sassou-Nguesso has not ignored the need to maintain some sort of balance between region and ethnic groups. This was not the be all or end all of policy and Sassou-Nguesso sought to avoid decisions or appointments that were overtly aimed at such a balance, but neither did he ignore these realities. The result of such awareness is that many of Sassou-Nguesso's erstwhile radical allies in 1979 were purged, demoted or otherwise eliminated from positions of real power and influence. Unlike his military predecessors (Ngouabi and Yhombi Opango), or Massemba-Debat, Sassou-Nguesso combines political astuteness and a precise sense of survival with a realistic assessment of the importance of foreign connections, cultivation of the military rank and file and his ability to run a leftist political party.

Sassou-Nguesso's means of dealing with actual, former and perceived opponents within the party and the army were the time-honoured purges. They started quite soon after 1979, but only by 1984 had the pattern become clear. In that year, Florent Tsiba and Jean-Pierre Thistère-Tchikaya were purged from all party functions. These two were the most active PCT leaders in preparing for the removal of Yhombi Opango in 1979. At the same time, Pierre Nze lost his position as foreign minister, and on 30 November 1986 was also removed from the Politburo (*Afrique-Asie*, 12–25 January 1987). Louis-Sylvain Goma was removed both from the Politburo and as prime minister (*YICA*, 1984, p. 10). During 1986 and 1987 purges and demotions involving formerly prominent leaders continued unabated. In August 1986, the death sentence was passed against Claude Ndala, accused of plotting a bombing campaign in the capital in 1982. Ndala had been one of the most prominent radicals in the country since the mid-1960s and had been a consistent critic of the regime from a leftist position. At the same trial a suspended five-year sentence was imposed on Jean-Pierre Thistère-Tchikaya, until 1985 the second most powerful man in the country (*FBIS, Africa*, 18 August 1986, p. 54). The fact that Thistère-Tchikaya only received a suspended sentence may indicate that he retained enough support domestically not only to have his life spared but perhaps to come back in the future.

In July 1987 a new 'restructuring' of the Politburo resulted in the *de facto* demotion of the regime's number two, Camille Bongou. A former Diawara follower and apparently the leading light of the M-22, Bongou was at the time Politburo secretary in charge of organization and coordination, the first providing control over the party apparatus and the second over the 'mass organizations'. He retained, for the time being the least important of the two positions, that of coordination, but lost control over the party apparatus to a Sassou–Nguesso loyalist, André Obami Itou (*Jeune Afrique*, 2 September 1987, p. 30). In a characteristically Stalinist form of humiliation, at the end of August 1987 Bongou was sent to talk ex-Captain Pierre Anga out of his rebellion in Owando, while the regime was said to be spreading rumours connecting the two (*Jeune Afrique*, 7 October 1987, p. 3).

Sassou–Nguesso came to power as a result of the victory of the left-wing, most orthodox Marxist–Leninist sectors of the PCT, APN and trade unions. Many of them were hoping for a rapid and far-reaching socialist transformation. But for all his ideological commitment and political abilities the president had to operate in a very unfavourable economic environment. Falling oil prices and rising import prices, combined with high international interest rates, meant that Congo's financial position was very precarious. He needed foreign aid and a sympathetic attitude from international financial institutions and so had to mould his economic policies to take note of these factors, which were beyond his control. His relatively conservative economic policies were similar to those which the Marxist regimes in Angola and Mozambique were forced to adopt. Such policies were unavoidable but were not to the liking of many of Congo's leftists. But for Congo there was no alternative. The history and structure of the Congolese economy tied it to the world capitalist system. The socialist bloc and China had neither the resources nor the inclination to offer a real economic alternative to Congo or similar Third World regimes.

The Sassou–Nguesso government has had to introduce austerity measures and shelve whatever plans it has had to introduce radical, socialist policies. He has attempted to restrict spending on civil service salaries and to crack down on loss-making parastatals. These policies have not always been totally consistent as Sassou–Nguesso has frequently appointed his supporters to head state companies for political rather than managerial or economic reasons. Nevertheless, the major and most explosive problems were not caused directly by him. The main one is the over-manning of the state or parastatal companies. Any cutbacks in the employment levels would upset the unions and provide ammunition for ideological hardliners on Sassou-Nguesso's left. Privatization would also result in personnel reductions and, in the almost total absence of Congolese investors, would bring back foreign companies and thus 'neo-colonialism'; this would be in contradiction to his stated policies and would further provoke his critics. Foreign aid, the chief source of which is the West in general and France in particular, can only provide temporary relief, as is the case with the International Monetary Fund (IMF), and the World Bank (IBRD).

In such circumstances, and considering the unstable, radical and frequently personalized character of post-independence Congolese politics, Sassou-Nguesso's hold on political power is remarkable, and the numerous purges and plots do not appear to have weakened him. The fact that, as OAU Chairman between July 1986 and July 1987 Sassou-Nguesso had to travel extensively, always a dangerous activity for African chiefs of state, and survived in power, is another proof of his political astuteness and the reward of his successful cultivation of the military and his retention of some radical credentials. On the other hand, it is also important to note that it was precisely during Sassou-Nguesso's stint as OAU Chairman that the two most dangerous threats against his regime were revealed. In June 1987 a large number of senior military officers were arrested; it was plausibly claimed by the regime that they were linked to the PCT's number two leader, Camille Bongou, and the M-22 organization. At the end of August the Pierre Anga affair broke out and soon became a major headache. This affair, strange even by Congolese standards, started when, it appears, the investigators of the June 1987 plot, led by state security (Sûreté d'État) general-director, Colonel Gouelo-Ndele, tried to organize another '*tous azymuts*' purge, by alleging links between those arrested and Pierre Anga, a former CMPT member in 1977, arrested after 1979, and since 1984 under house arrest in his native Owando—a fate he shared with Yhombi Opango. In August, the two were summoned to Brazzaville for interrogation; Yhombi Opango went, Anga refused and started recruiting young Kouyou for his cause against the Mbochis—a north versus north conflict was clearly in his mind. Brazzaville reacted by sending a number of envoys to reason with him; Colonel Jean-Michel Ebaka, a former CMPT colleague of Anga in 1977, under arrest since July 1987 (*Jeune Afrique*, 16 September 1987, p. 20); former prime minister and ex-Politburo member, Colonel Louis Sylvain-Goma, to whom Anga responded that his actions were not the business of a Lari (Goma's ethnic group among the southern Kongos) (*Jeune Afrique*, 7 October 1987, p. 33); and the outgoing Camille Bongou.

The Anga affair reflects a number of intriguing and relevant aspects of present Congolese politics. The obscure ex-CMPT member taped a statement about the Ngouabi assassination, and had it made available to Brazzaville's rumour-loving population, in which he accused Sassou-Nguesso of involvement, and explained his own dismissal from the CMPT at the end of 1977 as a result of his report on the murder (ibid.). That indicates a clear regime sensitivity to that matter, particularly since most of the alleged authors of the assassination were conveniently executed after summary trial (Massemba-Debat), or without any trial (Kikadidi), and the clear beneficiaries were the leftists led by Sassou-Nguesso himself. Furthermore, Anga's answer to Goma, if true, is another indication that Congolese politics today, far from being chiefly influenced by social-class conflict, as the official ideology would have it, or by a north–south ethnic division, as most academic analysts would claim, has become a truly tribal matter between ethnically related northerners, who dominate and control the country, but among whom the differences between Kouyous and Mbochis are becoming increasingly relevant. In fact, Anga's rebellion, although it superficially resembles those of Diawara and Kikadidi, both of whom survived in the bush but close to the capital for almost a year after their bid for power failed, is neither ideological nor ethnic. It is an interesting and fascinating result of rapidly diminishing spoils in an ethnically diverse, economically declining African state. Some protagonists may act out of ethnic considerations but others, and Anga could be an example of this, manipulate ethnic differences for their own political reasons. But Anga's career came to an abrupt end when he and two companions were killed in a clash with the Congolese army in the Ikongo Forest (Owando district) on 4 July 1988. Following this clash, the army commander warned that any further threats to peace would be dealt with ruthlessly.

3 Ideology and the Institutional Landscape

Congolese radical politicians, and often just frustrated citizens searching for a way of putting their country on the map, tend to point out that Congo was the first African state formally to adopt 'scientific socialism' as its official ideology, in 1969, and to proclaim itself a 'people's republic'. It is also true that Congo, like Benin, another of the five African 'people's republics', is a rather peculiar case of a small country, heavily urbanized and with a disproportionately large intelligentsia, a relatively well-educated urban populace and an active and influential trade-union movement. In addition, as in Ethiopia in 1974 or Benin in 1975, Marxism–Leninism, or 'scientific socialism', was adopted in Brazzaville as a result of what was essentially, although not exclusively, a decision taken by the ruling military junta. By contrast, in Angola and Mozambique the adoption of Marxism–Leninism was the result of genuinely socialist liberation movements, the MPLA and FRELIMO, respectively, coming into power as a result of the Portuguese collapse in 1974. Thus, while Marien Ngouabi, Mathieu Kérékou and Mengistu Haile Mariam were all essentially military coup makers and junta leaders, as well as professional military officers, Agostinho Neto in Angola or Samora Moises Machel in Mozambique were basically civilians, committed to Marxism–Leninism for at least a decade before taking power. In Congo, Joachim Yhombi Opango, president of the people's republic between 1977 and 1979, was plausibly said to make no secret of his aversion to Marxism–Leninism and to boast of his ignorance of Marx and Lenin (*Jeune Afrique*, 15 April 1977, p. 24). In addition to such examples or instances of doubt about Congo fitting into the traditional image of an 'orthodox' Marxist–Leninist system, there are a number of instances in which local African traditions resulted in some quite 'unscientific' behaviour on the part of the people's republic vanguard party of the proletariat. Thus, Ange Diawara's corpse was publicly exposed in Brazzaville in 1973, to prevent the rise of another Matsoua-type cult (Decalo, 1976, p. 166; Desjeux, 1980, p. 29). During the confusion of the few hours following Ngouabi's assassination in 1977, a number of his 'relatives' (which may simply mean close friends and supporters) murdered Emile Cardinal Biayenda, Archbishop of Brazzaville, accusing him of using magic powers to neutralize Ngouabi's alleged 'invulnerability' to bullets. Finally, in 1987, ex-Captain Pierre Anga, a former member of the 1977 Comité Militaire du Parti and of the PCT Central Committee, was alleged to have used magic potions to become invulnerable to government bullets (*FBIS, Africa*, 7 October 1987, p. 1) a repetition of the superstition in the other Congo republic (now Zaïre) during the mid-1960s utilized by followers of another self-styled Marxist–Leninist, the 'Maoist' ex-education minister under Lumumba, Pierre Mulele.

All these facts may raise serious doubts as to the extent to which the PCT, the official and only bearer of ideological purity in Brazzaville, is a 'true' Marxist–Leninist party, and of Congolese dedication to Marxism–Leninism in general. Some observers have in fact claimed that it was 'the personal conviction of the military leader [Marien Ngouabi] and of a small clique of military and civilian associates, [that] accounted for the conversion to Marxism–Leninism' (Ottaway & Ottaway, 1981, p. 95). There is a good case to be made against that argument in the instances of Benin and Ethiopia, and an even better one in that of Congo. To begin with, and despite Obenga's fantastic claims to the contrary, Ngouabi was not known to be a Marxist ideologue before his accession to power and although his speeches and addresses published *post mortem* demonstrate familiarity with Lenin's work, though less with regard to Marx, he showed no originality in interpreting them or in trying to put them into practice. Yhombi Opango was no Marxist or Leninist and clearly mouthed the right sentiments for political reasons. Sassou-Nguesso, on the other hand, has maintained a commitment to socialism during his period in power despite his economic pragmatism. But he and his supporters have not successfully applied the tenets of Marxism–Leninism to Congolese society or built a durable party. This is partly due to the fact that political activity is limited to the urban elite (civil servants, teachers, students and trade unionists) and the military and little real attempt has been made to mobilize or educate the mass of the peasantry. Furthermore, many party and state officials are clearly guilty of entryism. They have joined the PCT to achieve personal advancement and not to advance the 'revolution'. Their approach to ideology is limited to parroting socialist slogans.

While it is very easy, and indeed tempting, to dismiss the 1968 events as another example of 'revolution by word',[1] it is difficult to explain why an economically vulnerable country like Congo has chosen to risk its main source of foreign aid (France), its economic future (through central planning and nationalization), its security (by following a foreign policy at odds with those of all but one of its neighbours) and its general international standing by adopting a radical ideology. Unless one believes that it is all a matter of rhetoric, of the magic of the word, one has to find other explanations for Congo's particular ideological direction.

Perhaps a very good explanation can be found by looking less into the motivations of Marien Ngouabi and his supporters in 1968, and further into the development of Congolese politics since independence. Indeed, the radicalization of the country's body politic had already begun by the late 1950s, during the last years of the colonial period, both among the intelligentsia and, more importantly and politically potent, among the increasingly active trade-union movement. It is thus significant that two of the three major union federations in the country in 1960 were ideologically, financially and organizationally linked to left of centre French parties—the communists and socialists. Even more significant, albeit natural, was the primary role played by the union leadership in overthrowing the Fulbert Youlou regime during the 'Trois Glorieuses' of August 1963. Since that time the development of Congolese politics was guided—and it was development dominated by continuous radicalization—by a form of political legitimacy derived from claims of adherence to increasingly radical socialist ideologies, or at the very least promising to continue a 'true revolutionary' path (Yhombi Opango in 1977). At the same time, at least after the 1970 failed 'Youlouist' *putsch* against Ngouabi, all major attempts at political opposition, mostly via coups or guerrilla warfare, were also from the left or were factional struggles justified by claims of leftist authenticity, from Diawara's in 1972 through the June–July 1987 'M-22' plot and the Pierre Anga affair.[2] The implications of this phenomenon are clear: no matter how deep their convictions may be— and we know that Yhombi Opango was indifferent to Marxism–Leninism, his stint in Moscow notwithstanding, and that there is no reliable data on the depth of Ngouabi's interest, let alone acceptance of that ideology prior to 1968—their language, political style and rhetoric have to be radical, if the entrenched elements among the intelligentsia, military, unions and students are to be placated. It is also clear that for those elements 'scientific socialism' is a cherished set of beliefs and has a concrete content, related to statism, a controlled economy with little room for the private sector, and alignment with the communist states, including military and political, as well as party-to-party cooperation.

It is the presence and influence of such entrenched elements within the military, bureaucracy and the party apparatus that have made all Congolese leaders since Massemba-Debat captive to Marxist–Leninist rhetoric and policies. While the rhetoric is clearly more striking than the policies, hence the claim by many observers that Congolese Marxism–Leninism is basically a farce, 'communism by word', an African adaptation to current ideological fashions, there is a clear substance in such rhetoric, and it has gone largely unnoticed. The substance of Congolese Marxism–Leninism demonstrated by the regime's social, economic, ideological and, to a far lesser extent, regional and external policies.

There is no rhetorical body *per se* defining the Congolese version of Marxism–Leninism, despite repeated declarations by Ngouabi, Sassou-Nguesso, Ngombe, Bongou, or Nzé that the Brazzaville regime applies the general theories of scientific socialism to Congolese reality. The factional nature of the PCT and affiliated groups such as M-22/PCC has meant that no single, dominant Congolese application of Marxism–Leninism has emerged. One reason is the fragmented ideological scene of Brazzaville ever since 1963, in which each faction attempts to interpret Marxism–Leninism in a 'truly orthodox' manner, as opposed to the alleged 'right-wing deviationism' or 'infantile leftism' of its opponents. The other is that, no matter how much lip service Brazzaville tries to pay to the 'applicability of Marxism–Leninism to Congolese realities', the PCT's legitimacy is based upon its claim to be the sole arbiter of 'scientific socialism'. Hence, Ngouabi flatly stated that: 'One can speak of African paths to socialism but certainly not of an African socialism' (Ngouabi, 1975). That type of statement, reiterated ever since Ngouabi, clearly places Congo, at least rhetorically, in ideological opposition to the hybrid attempts to define and implement an African form of socialism, derived partly from African communal traditions, as was tried by Sékou Touré in Guinea, Julius Nyerere in Tanzania or Kenneth Kaunda in Zambia. In fact, and this may be precisely the reason behind such ultra-orthodox statements, PCT ideologues have specifically accused Massemba-Debat of 'going astray . . . into Bantu socialism and other similar theories. But, since the fall of Massemba-Debat, we have put in place a Marxist-Leninist party, a vanguard party which fights alongside the working class' (Jean-Pierre Ngombi, interview in *Jeune Afrique*, 7 December 1976, p. 39). Similarly, in his apologia for Ngouabi, Obenga claims that one of the factors bringing the conspirators of 1968 together was the danger of Massemba-Debat's regime moving too far towards 'Bantu socialism' (Obenga, 1977, p. 45). The basic claim of the PCT since the Ngouabi period is that Congo is at the stage of 'national, democratic and people's revolution', and that claim was first formalized during the extraordinary congress of the party in 1972 (Sassou-Nguesso, 1978, p. 63). According to Sassou-Nguesso, the Congolese revolution is national because it is a continuation of the anti-French, anti-capitalist, anti-colonial 'struggle'; it is democratic because it 'mobilizes the vast majority of the people', and is the 'people's' because 'we have decided to advance socialism. To this end we must lay adequate economic, cultural and psychological groundwork' (ibid.).

The most influential theory of stages to socialism, the first stage being the 'people's democracy', was formulated in Moscow during the Comintern period but refined towards the end of World War II and put into practice by communist leaders like the Bulgarian Georgi Dimitrov and used ideologically to justify the communist parties' takeovers in Eastern Europe largely achieved as the states were liberated from German occupation by the Red Army. The 'people's democracy' stage, according to Soviet-style ideologues from Dimitrov to Mikhail Suslov and Karen Brutents, was characterized by political and economic control by the 'vanguard' Marxist-Leninist party and the elimination of 'class enemies' of the proletariat by the coalition of workers and peasants, nationalization of all main means of production and a foreign policy based upon proletarian internationalism. At one point or another the PCT, and even the Massemba-Debat regime before 1968, tried to implement one or another of these goals, but seldom all at the same time or with the same intensity.

The Congolese Party of Labour (PCT)

The PCT is structured along traditional Marxist-Leninist lines, a structure perfected at the 1983 Third Extraordinary Congress. The president of the Central Committee is in charge of the management and coordination of party activities, and ensures the permanent functioning of the party between each congress. He is ex-officio chairman of the party and the PCT's presidential nominee. The top leadership consists of the party chairman, the Army's Permanent Commission (renamed the General Political Directorate in 1985) and five departments of the Politburo: ideology and education, planning and the economy, organization, external relations, and press, propaganda and informations (*Elikia*, August 1983, pp. 26–7). Department heads are appointed and removed by the chairman, on the advice of the Politburo.

The PCT finances are supposed to be secured through members' dues, payments by party enterprises such as the Hotel Panorama, the restaurant-bar La Congolaise, a car service station, etc.; in fact, as Camille Bongou himself has admitted, those enterprises are no more profitable than other state-run enterprises. The result is that although the party budget has increased by 600 per cent between 1979 and 1983, and from CFA fr. 424 millions to CFA fr. 3,050 millions, it is the government itself which actually provides the funds (*Elikia*, August 1983, pp. 28–30).

By 1986 the PCT had indeed made some big strides in its quest for international recognition as a bona fide Marxist-Leninist party; the year started with effective Soviet recognition of the Leninist 'vanguard' nature of the PCT, together with the ruling parties in Benin and Ethiopia (*World Marxist Review*, January 1986, pp. 43–5). In a *World Marxist Review* article PCT Central Committee member Kouka-Kampo was quoted as saying that the party had the same number of members as it did a few years ago, about 9,000, because it was engaged in continuous purges directed at 'alien elements' (ibid.). The Soviet commentator on the issue also observed that of the three parties the PCT was the most deeply implanted at the grass-roots level—a factor which, if true, may be explained by the relatively large number of members in relation to the total population; this being related to the relatively high level of urbanization and of education. Kouka-Kampo also implied that the purges were related to the process of ideological purification accelerated since the beginning of a series of early 'theoretical colloquia' between the PCT and the CPSU, the last of which (the sixth) took place in 1985 in Brazzaville. In fact, and beyond his rosy rhetoric, Kouka-Kampo was accurate in his description of the PCT as a party dominated by frequent purges in his admission that it has to expand its membership if it is to remain more than a fig leaf for ambitious officers, mostly of northern origin. On the other hand, the spectacular membership increase claimed by Kouka-Kampo, from the 250 members at the height of Ngouabi's 'radicalization' purges in 1975 to the 9,000 members claimed in 1986, can only be explained by a certain relaxation of admission standards, which is characteristic of the PCT even at leadership levels. With a small pool of ideologically acceptable cadres, it is easy to understand Ngouabi's admission that after his 'radicalization' he expected the new CC and Politburo members to be, 'new members, which is to say old cadres who accept the new [party] orientation and cadres newly recruited by the party, all expected to work for the revolution with a maximum of efficiency and impact' (*Afrique-Asie*, 3 May 1976, p. vi).

Ever since the PCT was founded, its leaders have attempted to justify its self-proclaimed 'vanguard' and 'people's' status. The PCT Third Congress of 1984 made it clear that social structure and pragmatism had nothing to do with Congolese realities. The Congress described party membership as shown in Table 3.1. This social structure by itself demonstrates the 'vanguard' nature of the party and its tenuous representatives. The two most over-represented groups, the 'intellectuals' (mostly teachers) and the military, together representing 37 per cent of the total membership, are the real power in the party and the state. However, their absolute numbers are so small as to guarantee that the party itself remains small. This is clearly demonstrated by the available data on its size (see Table 3.2).

However, the small size of the PCT only underscores the concentration of

Table 3.1 The social composition of the
PCT, 1984

Workers	13.90%
Peasants	17.25%
White-collar employees	31.68%
Intellectuals	25.00%
Soldiers	1.42%
NCO's	5.45%
Officers	5.30%

Source: 3ème Congrès, p. 31.

Table 3.2 PCT membership, 1971–86

1971	1975	1982	1984	1986
227	1,427	7,000	8,685	9,000+

Sources: Thompson & Adloff 1986, p. 188; YICA, 1984, 1987.

power in very few hands. In theory, the party members exercise influence only once every five years, when they select the delegates to the party congress. In fact, even that selection process is controlled by the leadership. The real power is in the hands of the seventy-five member Central Committee, which the soldiers and the northerners have dominated since the party's inception. The ten-member Politburo (reduced from thirteen in November 1986) and the eight members of the Central Committee Secretariat (most also Politburo members) actually control both the government and the ordinary party decision-making, in addition to the party chairman, who is ex-officio president of the Republic, chief of government and commander-in-chief.

Considering Sassou-Nguesso's claim in his *Report* to the Third PCT Congress in 1979 that the 1974 Congress introduced 'the famous thesis on the creative role of the masses and the determinant role of cadres' (p. 46), and the small pool of superior cadres available, it is natural that the convulsed history of the PCT and its periodic purges involved rejection and acceptance of the very same persons, often within a very brief time span. With no choice between party cadres, 'heretical' or otherwise, rehabilitation was a frequent occurrence. The unending series of purges, rehabilitations and reinstatements since the 1975 'radicalization', all signify less the benign nature of PCT purge tactics than the realization that radical purges, including the killing of ideological enemies would create new Matsouanist or M-22 movements, deprive the regime of politically-educated cadres, including technocrats, and exacerbate ethnic conflicts. On the other hand, the admission that cadres are all that count is not only a recognition of the true nature of Leninism, but also of Congolese political realities, which include the existence of a very small number of ideologically and technically competent Marxist-Leninists. The leaders of the PCT, within the principles of 'democratic centralism', which they cherish and use to their advantage, justify their government of the country through their ideology.

Intended by its ideologues, if not by its founder, Marien Ngouabi, as a 'vanguard', class-based party of the Leninist type, the PCT has not really succeeded in going beyond personal, factional and regional competition. As the single party in the country, it became the focus and centre of all those divisions, and it has reflected them from the very beginning. Instead of transcending social, ethnic and geographical divisions and becoming a unifying institution, the party simply reflects all those divisions within its own ranks, so that ideological conflicts are often inseparable from the other causes of division. Furthermore, social and ethnic divisions are magnified by personal ambitions and sectarian, narrow interests, all disguised by lofty ideological, 'revolutionary principles' and slogans. On the other hand, the Congolese political elites remain a small group, so small indeed, that their internecine fights are often prevented from becoming deadly from the sheer fear that physical elimination of rivals would threaten the very existence of the PCT. Indeed, at the peak of the 1975 'radicalization campaign' the party total membership was only about 250, and that after a relative increase in membership following the even more drastic purges of the 1971-2 Diawara crisis when, as described by a close observer, 'the Central Committee and Politburo were reduced to only five and three members respectively, and most party branches closed due to lack of leaders or members; total membership of the PCT declined to barely 160' (Decalo, 1979, p. 258; *Le Monde*, 18 December 1971). All of these factors explain why Congolese politics under Ngouabi and since have been characterized by rapid leadership turnovers, purges, rehabilitation and renewed purges.

Not even the major figures, other than Ngouabi himself, were spared periodic disgrace, even arrests and heavy sentences. Thus, of the main leaders of the 1968-77 period, Noumazalay became a Politburo member in 1970 and head of the planning secretariat of the Central Committee; after the Diawara *putsch* he was arrested, tried and sentenced to death; released, he was once again arrested, sentenced to death, released after the assassination of Ngouabi in 1977 and by the end of 1987 he was still a member of the cabinet. Claude Ndala, a leading Maoist of the 1960s, charged with embezzlement in 1966 and fired as youth minister, was rehabilitated by Ngouabi and in 1970 became the Politburo member in charge of propaganda and was widely considered the regime's second most powerful member; in 1971 he was purged with Diawara, sentenced to death after the 1972 *putsch*, and again released and brought into government by Sassou-Nguesso (Thompson & Adloff, 1986, p. 88), only to be purged and sentenced to death again in 1986 (Radu, 1987, p. 8). Pierre Nze, a former professor at the Lycée Savorgnan de Brazza in Brazzaville, became minister of education in 1969 and Politburo member in 1973; purged in 1975, he was arrested in 1977, released by Sassou-Nguesso in 1979 and appointed foreign minister the same year. As Politburo member and foreign minister Nze was one of the most powerful Congolese leaders until he was again purged in November 1986. Yhombi Opango, a prominent officer by 1963, was sent into comfortable exile as military attaché to Moscow in 1965-8, recalled by his cousin, Marien Ngouabi, played a major role in putting down the Kikanga and Diawara coup attempts; by 1972 was a Politburo member and chief of staff of the army and had been promoted to colonel, the highest rank in the APN. At the time he was also considered to be the regime's number two. The following year, in September 1973, however, Yhombi Opango was demoted to the strictly honorific post of Inspector General of the Armed Forces; in October 1974 he was once again put in an important position as State Council member in charge of military and internal security, only to be once again demoted to Director of Public Works following the 'radicalization' campaign of 1975. Nevertheless, following Ngouabi's death Yhombi Opango became a member of the Provisional Military Committee and president of the republic (*Jeune Afrique*, 15 April 1977, p. 24). Overthrown in 1979, he was placed under house arrest until 1984, when he was released and sent to his native town of Owando. Following the Anga affair of 1987 Opango was arrested and brought to Brazzaville. Finally, Sassou-Nguesso himself, a member of the original PCT Politburo in 1969, as 'coordinator with the masses', attracted Ngouabi's anger as he was suspected of being a behind the scenes manipulator of the 1971 student disorders, was briefly purged from the Politburo following the Diawara affair in 1972, but came back as one of the five members of the Special Revolutionary General Staff (État Majeur Spécial Révolutionnaire—EMSR) established in September 1975 (*Africa Contemporary Record*, 1978-9,

p. B542). Since then, his career has advanced steadily, as second in command under Yhombi Opango and as president and PCT leader since 1979. He has maintained his power by building coalitions with prominent political and military figures or with particular factions. At times this has meant alliance with the M-22/PCC, at other times mending his fences with Opango.

The Military and Society

The Armée Populaire Nationale (APN), the People's Republic of Congo's army (so named since 1969) started, like most post-independence African military institutions, at least in francophone Africa, as an *ad hoc* creation largely intended as a simple accoutrement of the newly acquired sovereignty. In fact, strictly speaking the newly independent Congo did not even have a national army until 1962, and at the time of the so-called 'revolution' of Les Trois Glorieuses in 1963 it numbered a mere 1,500 men, still commanded mainly by French officers.

The reasons for this situation were complex, but they were closely related to the peculiarities of the process of independence of most francophone countries. One of those peculiarities was the signing of a defence accord with France at the time of independence which generally meant that external threats would be answered by direct French involvement. The second was the assumption that African armies, like the French one, were to be only the defenders of state sovereignty, not involved in domestic disturbances. The latter were to be dealt with by the gendarmerie, with the military at best a last resort.

Some African troops were trained by the French during the pre-independence era, and most of those later played a prominent political role. As a rule, they were ambitious youths from among the most backward ethnic groups of the country; in the case of Congo, particularly, although not exclusively, Mbochis. The career of Marien Ngouabi himself is enlightening in this respect, as it followed a rather common pattern of those Congolese who could not follow a business or public sector career for lack of means, local traditions or access to education or influence.

Born in 1938 in Owando (then Fort-Rousset), Ngouabi finished his primary and secondary schooling in that locality, and in 1953 was admitted to the 'General Leclerc' cadet school in Brazzaville (now 'Cadet School of the Revolution') which served both as the equivalent of high school and the entry ticket for a military career. Significantly, among his classmates was his fellow Owando native, Joachim Yhombi Opango, later to become his successor as president of the country. After four years at 'General Leclerc', with the rank of corporal, Ngouabi received his diploma, and with it the obligation of serving five years in the French army. Between 1958 and 1960 Ngouabi served in Cameroon, and was involved in counter-insurgency operations against the Marxist-led Union des Populations du Cameroun (UPC). Promoted to sergeant, on the eve of Congo's independence Ngouabi and Yhombi Opango, at the same time, were selected for further training at the Strasbourg Military School, as a preparatory step towards entrance to the French Military Academy at Saint-Cyr-Coëtquiddan. At Saint-Cyr Ngouabi and Yhombi Opango met fellow Congolese Alfred Raoul and Louis Sylvain-Goma, both southerners (and Kongos). In 1962, with the formal establishment of the Congolese armed forces, Ngouabi and Yhombi Opango were sent back to Congo following graduation as lieutenants; Raoul and Louis Sylvain-Goma followed them the next year (Obenga, 1977, pp. 20–37).

Two members of the above mentioned quartet were to become presidents of the Congo; the other two became prime ministers and served in other cabinet positions. It is hardly coincidental that the two future presidents were relatives from the same small northern town; the two future prime ministers were both southerners. The fate of the Saint-Cyr-Coëtquiddan group is highly symbolic and representative of the Congolese military and their political role. On a personal level, camaraderie made them a tightly knit group, which later political expediency may have temporarily divided but never destroyed. At a different level, however, the hierarchy within the group had nothing to do with academic or military performance and everything to do with their ethnic bases of support within the military. Finally, that group was the first group of highly-trained Congolese officers in a newly established army; therefore they received rapid promotions and built up their influence; it also established a pattern of behaviour by Congolese officers that remains important today. In fact, the 'quartet' itself played an important, often dominant role in Congolese politics at least after 1966: Yhombi Opango was president until 1979, Louis-Sylvain Goma was prime minister until 1984. In other words, out of Congo's twenty-eight years of independent statehood, the same four men trained by the French in Brittany in the early 1960s dominated or strongly influenced the national political scene for sixteen years.

In fact, for a young country like Congo, the continuity of the military (and political) elites is surprising in light of the number of coups, attempted coups, changes of rulers and, less often, assassinations and murders which have occurred since 1960. It seems that the thoroughly politicized army still retained a certain sense of institutional integrity and *esprit de corps* to ensure a degree of continuity. That fact was naturally encouraged by the increasingly clear Mbochi ethnic domination of both the rank and file and the officer corps. In fact the often mentioned claim to the effect that the initial Congolese army was Kongo-dominated in terms of the officer corps, and Mbochi among the rank and file (Decalo, 1976, p. 146) is far from correct: a majority of the officers trained by the French after the late 1950s were Mbochi—Ngouabi and Yhombi Opango were far from being exceptions.

While the first generation of officers and political leaders in Congo came from the same narrow, Mbochi-dominated but basically multi-ethnic group of French trainees, the second one, represented by Sassou-Nguesso, was trained after 1963 and therefore a mixture of French, Chinese and Soviet bloc training. Clearly most important is the present generation of APN officers, most of whom were trained in communist countries, and the overwhelming majority in the Soviet bloc, including Cuba. It was a process already completed by 1975, by which time some 825 Congolese military personnel had already been trained in the Soviet bloc; (CIA, 1977, p. 6). Today, the majority of the reserve officers and NCOs of the APN have been trained in the Soviet bloc. More importantly still, the weapons available to the APN are predominantly Soviet bloc or Chinese-made, and thus provide a further incentive for the military to continue close relations with the Soviet bloc or, to a lesser extent China, at the expense of the West, including France.

The APN strength at the end of 1986 was 8,750, of whom 8,000 were in the army, 250 in the navy and 500 in the air force. In addition, there are 1,400 gendarmes and 4,700 in the People's Militia. Most equipment is Soviet or Chinese made, including all tanks (thirty-five Soviet T-54s and fifteen Chinese-made T-59s) and combat aircraft (twenty MIG-17s and 1 Mig-15) (International Institute for Strategic Studies, 1987, p. 125). The transport aircraft, extremely important for a relatively large country with a small army, are divided between aircraft made in the Soviet Union (five Antonov 24s, one An-26 and two Ilyushin-14s), France (one Noratlas, one Frigate, two Brous-sards) and the United States (two converted DC-3s); while the small, Pointe-Noire-based navy includes small Chinese, Soviet and Brazilian-made vessels. The five helicopters available to the military were all made in France (ibid.). Military service is voluntary, for a two-year period. The cost of the army is, despite its small size, very high indeed: the defence budgets for 1984 and 1985 were, respectively CFA fr. 21.6 and 25 billion, or $49.43 and $55.6 millions (ibid.). Considering the obsolete equipment available and the static strength of the APN, one may naturally assume that most of the budgetary increases go towards higher pay; and the fact that in a period of clear economic hardship the defence budget increased by almost 20 per cent between 1984 and 1985, in the conspicuous absence of any external threat, is another major indication of the APN's political clout and of the regime's recognition of it. Pay and privileges maintain military support or at least acquiescence.

The APN today is a far cry from the immediate post-independence military, which was little more than a glorified constabulary. Not only has it grown from 1,500 to its present strength of 8,750, a rate of growth far beyond that of general population increase, but its nature has also changed, politically as well as ideologically. In December 1984, 660 Congolese military personnel were undergoing training in the Soviet bloc; in 1975 there were 850 Congolese doing military training in communist countries (350 in the Soviet Union, seventy-five in Eastern Europe and 425 in China); and in 1976 the figure was 855, with China training ten less and Eastern European states training ten more; by 1979 the Soviet Union was training 505 and the East Europeans and Chinese remained at the previous figures.[3]

Relative as they are, such figures should be compared with the decline to zero of the number of Congolese officers trained in France; it is also important that the number of Chinese-trained personnel has consistently decreased over the past decade, while that of Soviet bloc trainees has increased dramatically.

The importance of the previously described pattern cannot be over-estimated; never in Africa has a Soviet-trained officer led a non-leftist coup. The fact that the APN hardware is largely Soviet-made, and thus requires the presence of Soviet-bloc technicians to maintain it—350 of them were in Congo at the end of 1984—is another long-term incentive for the officer corps to use their enormous political influence to ensure the continuation of present ideological and military alignment patterns. Finally, the absence of external threats, the APN's long experience of political involvement and relative ethnic homogeneity virtually guarantee that it will remain a radicalizing, ideologically orthodox force in Congolese politics.

In view of Congo's peculiar political situation, and the army's role, such considerations are both important and relevant for future governments in Brazzaville. The military's political position and role ever since 1966 are a clear indication in this respect. On the other hand, while the APN's present structure, doctrine and indoctrination clearly demonstrate that it will remain committed to 'scientific socialism' in Congo for the foreseeable future, the particular form, content and rhetoric of the regime it will support are all dependent upon the balance of forces within the military. Indeed, and paradoxically at a first glance, the present doctrinal and ideological homogeneity of the Soviet-bloc or Chinese-trained officer corps means that, while

Marxism–Leninism is unanimously supported, its specific version or application to 'Congolese realities' could serve as a pretext for factional clashes just as pro- and anti-'imperialist' attitudes did during the 1960s. Marxist-Leninist trained and pro-Soviet or not, the APN remains a highly regionalistic and ethnically conscious institution, whose allegiances are divided between personalities, ethnic origins, unit or service loyalties, ties with civilian groups and politicians. These influences compete with or exacerbate ideological differences.

The relationship between the military and the party in Congo is clearly demonstrated and defined by the history of the PCT since 1968. In fact, every single time the regime was threatened from the left or, far more seldom, from the 'right', it retreated into its military base of support, a perfect demonstration of the ultimately military nature of Brazzaville regimes since 1968. What was clear from the beginning of the People's Republic of Congo, at least for non-ideological observers, was that the new regime, its ideological claims and rhetoric notwithstanding, was basically a military regime which had adopted a Marxist stance. That it was a junta was demonstrated both by the manner of taking power—Ngouabi's paratroopers and commandos moving in from their barracks in Brazzaville in 1966 and again in 1968—and by the background of the main leaders: Ngouabi, Yhombi Opango, Sassou-Nguesso, Alfred Raoul, Louis Sylvain-Goma, etc.

In September 1975, besieged by students and unions, the Ngouabi regime undertook a 'radicalization campaign', the immediate result of strikes by the 'official' unions of the USC and the tension arising from the escalating conflict in neighbouring Angola. A Central Committee meeting on 12 December 1975 complained about the 'blocking of the revolution', accused the unions of being 'too demanding', and generally found the PCT's performance unsatisfactory. The result was that the Politburo, Central Committee and other party organizations were suspended and a five-member Special Revolutionary General Staff including Ngouabi, Sassou-Nguesso, Louis Sylvain-Goma, Jean-Pierre Thistère-Tchikaya and Jean-Pierre Ngombe was established as the supreme ruling institution. Once again, the formalities of a vanguard party were preserved since Thistère-Tchikaya and Ngombe were civilians, while the reality of the military regime was demonstrated by the background of the other three members. Cornered and threatened, the PCT retreated into its real political shell: the military. It was the first such instance, and it was repeated following Ngouabi's assassination in 1977. Indeed, the 5 April 1977 Fundamental Act abrogated the 1973 constitution and established an eleven-member Military Committee of the PCT (Comité Militaire du PCT–CMPCT) which included the following:

president, Yhombi Opango; first vice-president in charge of party activities and national defence and security, Commander Sassou-Nguesso; second vice-president, and prime minister, Commander Louis Sylvain-Goma; members (in addition to the above), Commanders Jean Michel Ebaka (control commission), Raymond Damasse Ngollo (chief of staff), Pascal Bima (economic department) and Martin Amin; three captains (Nicolas Okongo (political department), François-Xavier Katali, and Florent Tsiba; and Lieutenant Pierre Anga, CC member. In other words, every challenge to the ruling group of the Congo resulted in a resort to the military, the ultimate source of power, while some thin ideological pretext was maintained—hence the PCT's Military Commission.

After 1979 it appeared for a while that the institutionalization of the party had advanced far enough to limit power struggles to that institution alone. Nevertheless, it seems increasingly clear that what actually happened was that party factions returned to the pre-1968 pattern instead, and tended to search for support within the military in the name of lofty ideological slogans. It is significant that in 1986 Thistère-Tchikaya's five-year suspended sentence was also given to army Colonel Blaise Nzalakanda since it indicated that the intra-party rivalries had spilled into the military and that the present leadership cannot be completely sure of the loyalty of even prominent military officers (*FBIS*, 19 August 1986). That the problem was serious was underscored by President and Secretary-General Sassou-Nguesso himself during his address to servicemen on the occasion of the twentieth anniversary of the ANP (Armée Nationale Populaire, National People's Army). He stressed the importance of political indoctrination of the military and the need for increased party control over it. The speech was considered important enough to be picked up by the Soviet army's own journal.

In July 1987 the same pattern was repeated once again during the first stage of the political fall of the regime's number two, Camille Bongou; not only did Bongou lose his main position in the Politburo, but his military associates, apparently all former JMNR-Diawara cadres and M-22 members, were arrested. Among them were prominent officers like Colonel Jean-Michel Ebaka, a former CMPT member in 1977 and police chief; deputy chief of staff Lieutenant-Colonel Henri Eboundit, Colonel Nzalakanda, ex-commander of the Congolese 'buffer-force' in Chad in 1979; Lieutenant-Colonel Apollinaire Yoka; Commander Félix Ongouya, the navy chief of staff; air force commander Luxon Obambo; police Captain Lambert Elenga and a few assorted civilians, including a trade-union leader, Jean-Pierre Iboko. This spectacular list, even allowing for the traditional Congolese pattern of purges *à tous azimuts*, established by Ngouabi, also tends to indicate that factions, based on common origins (in this case the JMNR rather than the regular army) and loyalties (Diawara and Bongou respectively), could persist in the APN for quite a long time, and they may surface only at a critical point, sometimes too late to achieve their objectives.

In theory, the system of party control over the military, as defined by the PCT Politburo during its 26 January 1985 meeting is based on nuclei at section or company level, cells at company or battalion level and committees at battalion, regiment or corps level (*Mweti*, 29 January 1985, p. 2). At the leadership level, the entire army is under the political control of a General Political Directorate, which is represented by political directorates for the army, security forces, state security, public security and military zones; a political section supervises ideological activities at corps, service and autonomous formation level, and a political deputy does so at unit level (ibid.).

Auxiliary Organizations and Pressure Groups

Congolese youths have been thoroughly radicalized ever since the Youlou regime, and have seen it as their self-assumed 'right' to attack successive governments from the far left, in the name of 'idealism', revolutionary purity, and nationalism. During the first years of the Ngouabi regime, the Union Générale des Étudiants et Elèves Congolais (UGEEC) and particularly its Pointe Noire branch, was in the forefront of leftist opposition to the government. Student strikes occurred in Pointe Noire in 1970, and at the end of that year a UGEEC 'colloquium' proposed the establishment of a 'people's school', allegedly adapted to 'the realities of the country', and rejected the French-type curriculum which ensured automatic recognition of Congolese diplomas by the French government (Desjeux, 1980, p. 28). In January 1974 the UGEEC again opposed the government and organized riots and demonstrations; the result was the intervention of the army, and the forced drafting of its leaders into the military for six months. At the same time, the UGEEC was officially dismantled and its infrastructure included in the UJSC. The same pattern continued under the Yhombi Opango and Sassou-Nguesso regimes. Any attempt to transform the largely parasitical and overpaid educational system of the country into what was it supposed to be from the beginning—a source of technically trained domestic cadres, rather than a career path towards political power, regardless of academic accomplishments—was resisted, often in a violent manner. When the Sassou-Nguesso regime decided, on 6 November 1985, to impose competitive

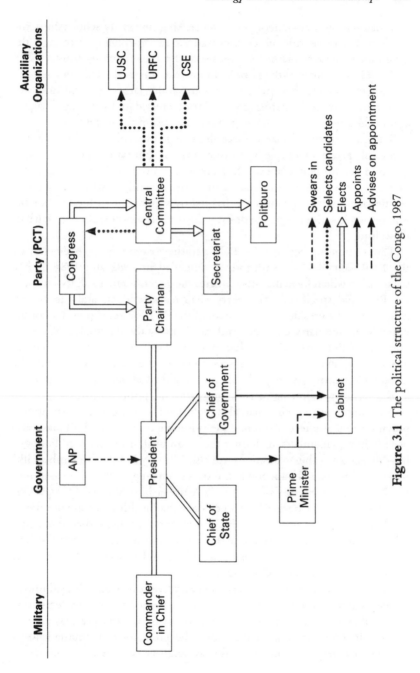

Figure 3.1 The political structure of the Congo, 1987

examinations on high-school graduates seeking university scholarships, the result was massive student demonstrations in Brazzaville. Although the government chose to blame 'religious sects' for those demonstrations (*FBIS, Africa*, 18 November 1985, p. B6), the impact was both clear and serious. Congolese students, beneficiaries of one of the largest expenditures for education as part of the state budget in Africa, pressed for their alleged 'rights' against the government, at the expense of the rest of the society.

Students remain a major force in Congolese politics. They do not necessarily play a direct role in decision-making, but rather act as a pressure group in certain policy areas. They are more radical and idealist than the military or the trade unions and openly criticize policies which they see as reactionary. Students protests are frequently suppressed ruthlessly, but the suppression has never served to destroy the student movement nor to curb its radicalism.

The relationship between the PCT and the government is made clear by the 1979 Congolese constitution, as amended in 1982 and 1984. It is a relationship which formally subordinates the government, in all its forms, to the PCT and specifically the party chairman-president, and the central committee. The president or chairman of the PCT is elected president of the Republic by the party congress, and sworn in by the Assemblée Nationale Populaire (ANP–art. 63). In that position he is also *ex-officio* chief of government, and appoints the prime minister after consultation with the Central Committee (art. 65). The members of the Cabinet are also appointed by the president following consultations with the prime minister.

It is important to notice that, although there is no specific constitutional provision to that effect, all Congolese prime ministers since 1969 have also been Politburo members, including the incumbent, Ange Edouard Poungui. In addition, key cabinet positions are also filled by Politburo members like Itihi-Ossetoumba Lekoundzou (rural development and economy) and until the November 1986 loss of Politburo membership, Antoine Odinga-Oba (foreign affairs) and Bernard Combo Matsiona (health and foreign affairs). Furthermore, all ministers are PCT members, meaning that the entire cabinet is subject to party discipline first and to ministerial discipline last. The prime minister himself is responsible not to the rubber-stamp ANP but to the president–i.e., to the PCT Chairman.

The ANP is selected by popular vote every five years from a list submitted by the Central Committee of the PCT. It is supposed to consider legislation proposed by the prime minister during two sessions every year, lasting two months at most (art. 49). Furthermore, the president can impose (mostly economic) emergency measures for as long as two years, without the

Assembly's approval. The same arbitrary requirements regarding the PCT's social composition apply to the ANP as well. Thus, of the 153 members of the ANP ten must be military, eighteen workers or state employees, peasants or trade unionists, and in fact all deputies are members of the PCT (and therefore subject to party discipline) or of its auxiliary organizations. Cabinet members cannot be ANP members.

At the time of independence in 1960 Congo was a country with poor economic prospects. The population was small but relatively well educated, but over time these two advantages were largely lost because of the maldistribution of population and resources. Indeed, while the main export commodity, tropical wood, was largely concentrated in the sparsely inhabited northern half of the country, a very large percentage of the population lived in just three major cities located in the southern half of the territory. Even today, the urban concentration of Congo's population is quite peculiar for Africa south of the Sahara as demonstrated by Table 4.1.

Furthermore, the relatively impressive educational level of the Congolese hid a most serious problem, and one that has grown worse ever since: while better educated in academic terms and extremely articulate, the highly urbanized population lacked the technical and practical skills necessary for handling a modern economy. In 1960 that situation could largely be blamed on the nature of the French colonial educational system, centred on producing black-skinned Frenchmen rather than well-adapted and useful Congolese cadres. Since then, however, a whole new generation has been educated not only in the independent Congo, but also under the guidance of increasingly 'progressive' and 'revolutionary' regimes, but the gap between the products of the Congolese schools and university and the skills required by the economy has, if anything, deepened. The flooding of the labour market with radical, articulate and increasingly numerous high-school and university graduates in social sciences is paralleled by the scarcity of economic and scientific skills. Thus, the *1983-1984 Yearbook* of the Marien Ngouabi University in Brazzaville indicates that there were 2,046 students in the Department of Human and Social Sciences (FLSH), and 881 in that of Sciences and that there were 241 students in the Rural Development

Table 4.1 The population of major cities, 1983

Brazzaville	521,000
Pointe Noire	214,500
M'Kayes	40,500
Loubomo	33,600

Department, compared to 207 in Physical Education.[1] Obviously, a developing country whose only university produces more philologists and sociologists than scientists, and almost as many graduates in physical education as agronomists has a serious problem in maximizing the use of its human and physical resources.

In 1983 a national census revealed that Brazzaville had over 500,000 inhabitants, out of a total national population of 1.62 million, and that the capital had grown by 200,000 since 1974 (*QER*, April 1984, p. 21). At the same time, the rural exodus towards the cities, particularly Brazzaville and Pointe Noire, encouraged by the oil boom of the early 1980s and often forced by the government's neglect of the rural areas and economy, continued unabated, even after the collapse of oil prices in the mid to late 1980s. The 'scientific socialism' of successive regimes since 1963, and particularly the wave of nationalizations of the early 1970s, as well as deeply rooted Congolese traditions, have made the government the only significant employer in the country. It was the government which had to try to satisfy the high expectations of the rapidly growing mass of urban youth. Not to do so would have meant courting the danger of further radicalization of that critical sector of the population; satisfying its growing demands and expectations, however, was always beyond the means of the government, and the declining oil prices only made that fact more painfully obvious. What was done to help urban groups was to the detriment of rural ones.

The 1984 Congolese budget is perhaps the best symbol of the inescapable bind any ruler in Brazzaville finds himself in. Of the total CFA fr. 412 billion in expenditures (*QER*, 1984, p. 18) CFA fr. 123.5 were to be borrowed from abroad, CFA fr. 3.3 were expected as grants, and CFA fr. 279.5 were to be raised internally (*QER*, 1984, p. 19). Of the amount to be internally generated, CFA fr. 90 billion were to come from oil companies' taxes, and another CFA fr. 74 billion from oil royalties, thus making oil the source of some 59 per cent of internal government revenues (ibid.). The difference was to be made up from domestic sales and income taxes (CFA fr. 56.5 billion), and another CFA fr. 36 billion were to come from customs and excise duties (ibid.). A sales tax is always an inherently regressive form of taxation, but it is even more so in a country like Congo, since it hits the rural population far harder than the urban one. Indeed, the agriculturalists' dependence on the government-controlled distribution system is decisive, as they have to buy from it fertilizers, tools, seeds, clothes and food, all taxed.[2] Furthermore, at least until very recently, government-imposed prices for agricultural commodities remained geared toward subsidizing supplies for the urban population, thus creating a disincentive for greater agricultural production.

Equally important is the budget makers' open recognition of the fact that a third of the revenues were expected to come from abroad, mostly through borrowing, virtually all of it from the West, and a major part from France. The implication is as clear as it is unpleasant to the ideologues of the PCT— the regime's survival is essentially dependent upon 'imperialist' support, whether that support comes from the French or the IMF and the World Bank. Furthermore, it means that the Congolese socialist state, and the benefits it provides and of which it boasts, are a function of Western, and largely French assistance, self-interested as that might be. Equally significant for the Brazzaville regime's approach to economics is the fact that, despite the obvious government inability to pay its bills and of the decline in oil revenues, the share of pubic sector salaries in the national budget increased from CFA fr. 35.7 billion, or less than 19 per cent, to 27 per cent or CFA fr. 64.3 billion in the 1984 budget (*QER*, Annual Supplement, 1983, p. 23).

The conclusion from all these data is that the Congolese revolutionary, Marxist-Leninist regime is characterized by a persistent policy of redistribution of resources from the countryside to the cities, and of maintaining a highly artificial standard of living for the politically influential urban dwellers at the expense of depending upon those viewed as ideological enemies (France, World Bank, IMF). Under successive regimes in Brazzaville the economy has become less rather than more diversified in its structure and revenue base,[3] and increasingly dependent on regressive taxation for the small part of the national budget still internally raised. Rhetoric aside, Congo is more dependent today on the Western economic system than it was in 1968, but still paralysed by the incompatibility between economic realism and ideological goals. The whole economy has been thrown into imbalance by the oil sector.

The State Sector

In 1978 the Sassou-Nguesso government decided that the Société Industrielle et Agricole du Congo (SIAN), probably the largest agricultural employer in the country, with over 80,000 employees in the sugar, oil seeds, flour and animal fodder sectors, had to be dismantled. Since the outright closing down of SIAN was political dynamite, the corporation was broken into three smaller parts, the most important of which, the sugar monopoly of SUCO (Sucre du Congo), was to be managed by a joint French–Dutch managerial team (*QER*, Annual Supplement, 1983, p. 21). Sugar production, tradition-ally Congo's main source of hard currency and its major export crop until the discovery of oil, had collapsed by 1978, with the result that the 1978 EEC quota of 10,000 tons was unfulfilled, production barely reached 4,957 tons. The result was a loss of the EEC quota, awarded to Zimbabwe in 1980 (*QER*, Annual Supplement, 1980, p. 17). The collapse, partly a result of Ngouabi's policies, was as abrupt as it was dramatic: in 1975-6 Congo produced 29,000 tons of sugar, but it only took nationalization and Cuban management to reduce that amount by over 80 per cent in less than three years. By 1981-2 sugar production was 28,450 tons (*QER*, Annual Supplement, 1983, p. 19), although it had no chance of again becoming as important as it was before the discovery of oil. Similarly, in 1978 the Congolese palm oil production plunged to its lowest level ever, and groundnut production only allowed the oil mills to operate at 30 per cent capacity (*QER*, Annual Supplement, 1983, p. 14).

The SIAN story is significant in so far as it demonstrates the level of inefficiency of state corporations. The country's shortage of technical and managerial skills rendered the running of large parastatals almost impossible. Most of the state corporations are the inheritance of Marien Ngouabi's campaign of large-scale, precipitate nationalization of foreign, mostly French, assets in Congo. Slowly and carefully, successive regimes, and particularly Sassou-Nguesso's, have had to retreat from Ngouabi's inheritance, for the sake of economic survival. That such a reality was obvious was demonstrated by Ngouabi's behaviour as well: his anti-French brinkmanship stopped when it came to the newly discovered bonanza for Congo's economy—oil. Indeed, from the beginning, ELF and AGIP controlled Congo's oil resources, and enjoyed better terms than in 'neo-colonial' but less oil-dependent Gabon.

Oil is not, however, the only sector where a retreat from the orthodox nationalization campaign has been obvious. The Office Congolais du Bois, intended as the exclusive exploiter of timber resources, has been plagued by managerial and over-manning problems, and in 1983 a French consortium was given a one-million-hectare timber concession in the north (*QER*, Annual Supplement, 1983, p. 19)—now the most productive part of the Congolese timber industry. By 1987 it was clear to everyone in Congo, excepting the most dogmatic radicals on the left, that the parastatal sector is one of the main reasons the country cannot pay its bills, remains dependent upon foreign aid, and has to import most of its food.[4]

5 Policies

Education

For any country with Congo's enormous percentage of school-age citizens education would be a major policy challenge. In the case of Congo, moreover, the problem was further exacerbated by the disproportionately large number of civil servants the country had at the time of independence, all attracted by the advantages of education and determined to ensure that their children will also enjoy it.

Some ethnic groups were long attracted by the advantages of education, foremost among them the Lari. As the inter-ethnic balance of power shifted towards the northerners and Congolese politics became increasingly radicalized, other groups began to compete for better education. The important political role played by the radicalized youth during the 1960s and 1970s made the issues related to education even more politically poignant and sensitive. The result was that all revolutionary governments since 1963 had to deal with a radical youth whose numbers have swelled continuously and whose expectations and demands have relentlessly increased, while the resources available tended either to grow far more slowly or decline in relative terms.

The politics of Congolese education have since 1963 tended to be indistinguishable from the national politics as a whole. In ideological, political and economic terms they are a direct extension of the internal debates over the nature and direction of the Congolese revolution in general. Since that of Massemba-Debat, all Congolese regimes have tried to find a way of both satisfying and controlling the demands of youth. None have really succeeded so far.

In 1965, Massemba-Debat nationalized the mission (mostly Catholic) schools. Lay teachers, mainly expatriates, were brought in. By 1972 the French (mostly Communist Party members) teachers numbered 323, with Soviets as the second largest contingent with 83 (Thompson & Adloff, 1984, p. 63). School attendance between ages 6–16 became compulsory, and all high-school graduates became entitled to government grants and fellowships for higher education. Under Ngouabi all university graduates and most university students were entitled to a government job.

It soon became clear that the cost of such policies was enormous. Between the mid-1960s and the early 1980s primary school attendance grew by 5.1 per cent a year, that of secondary schools by 20.3 per cent, and that of university students by 17.9 per cent (ibid. pp. 68–9). As a result, the cost of fellowships and grants alone grew from CFA fr. 1.2 billion or 5.5 per cent of the national budget in 1972 to CFA fr. 2 billion or 7.5 per cent in 1974 (Gakosso, 1983, p. 303). With Congo's high population growth and the politically immutable decision to make education free at all levels, the costs were escalating while the political influence of the youth made government attempts to control the contents of the curriculum increasingly difficult and politically dangerous. Furthermore, it became apparent by the early 1970s that the country simply did not have the human resources to sustain such an effort. Nor were the results of the high investments encouraging, whether in practical or political terms.

By 1972 it became clear that something drastic had to be done; there simply were not enough teachers and the dropout rate was 30–40 per cent in secondary schools and an astounding 70 per cent at university level. Ngouabi's response was to impose an oral examination at the end of high school and the suppression of the automatic admission to university of all high school graduates (Thompson & Adloff, 1984, pp. 70–1). At the same time, the curriculum was 'radicalized' in 1974–5, including the introduction of compulsory Marxism-Leninism classes at the university level (Kissisou-Boma, n.d. p. 97).

At the political level there were both ideological and nationalist pressures for change in the educational policy. Hard line Marxist-Leninist ideologues bemoaned the youth's selfishness by attacking the policy which made '[university] diplomas a piece of paper opening the way to the public sector … It suffices to show one to be automatically offered a job in the state apparatus' (Kississou-Boma, n.d., p. 59). Worse still, from that viewpoint, these spoiled youths were exhibiting a clearly non-socialist attraction for Western clothes, dances and music, and considered French or other Western degrees far superior to those from communist countries and even more so to those awarded by their own country's higher education institutions (ibid., p. 97). In fact, there was and still is a strong student (high school as well as university) opposition to any attempt to 'Congolize' education, since that would threaten the students' chances of being accepted by French or other Western (primarily Italian) institutions. It was in this respect that the question of the education medium has to be seen, and where regime rhetoric and pragmatism clashed.

French was the language of Congolese education during the colonial era and continues to be so today. Half-hearted attempts to change that were made under Ngouabi, mostly at the rhetorical level. It was only in 1981 that the Sassou-Nguesso regime took the first timid step to introduce native languages, by making Lingala and Munukutuba compulsory in secondary schools (Thompson & Adloff, 1984, p. 69). The PCT Third Congress in 1984 proclaimed those two languages compulsory at all levels of education—alongside French and, in fact, for secondary languages. In fact, even the most ferocious ideologues requesting a larger role for native languages do so in French and are published in France. On the other hand, Sassou-Nguesso's decision to send 600 Congolese teenagers for study in Cuba in 1969 provoked such a strong domestic and external reaction that it forced Brazzaville to deny it and made it both reluctant and discreet in repeating it since.

Under the Sassou-Nguesso regime both the accomplishments and the political implications of the haphazard educational policies of previous Brazzaville governments became clearer. Education improved in quantitative terms with 93 per cent attendance in 1979 in 1,992 educational establishments (by 1987), of which 1,773 were primary schools in 1987 (*QER*, March 1987) placing Congo at or close to the top among African or even Third World countries in general.

At the same time the attempts to control the students politically were paralleled by a relative decline in educational expenditures. Thus the summer labour camps for students, the Chantiers Vacances Organisés (CVO) were proposed as a condition for receiving fellowships during vacation time (Kississou-Boma, n.d., p. 107). Students abroad in the West were threatened with a cut in their fellowships and some were called back home for political reprisals—mostly for being leftist enemies of the regime, and without success, as France and Italy refused to extradite them.

At the economic and financial levels, the revised five year plan for 1982–6 provided for an educational expenditure of CFA fr. 22,565 millions, compared with CFA fr. 37,000 for defence, CFA fr. 36,560 for the interior (police, security and secret police) and CFA fr. 27,183 for health and social services (*L'Économie congolaise*, 1983, p. 138). This drastic relative drop in educational expenditures was matched by decrees limiting automatic admission to the civil service or state enterprises to graduates of university, rather than students, stricter standards for graduation, and denial of automatic grants to university students (*QER*, January 1987).

Finally, the Third Congress of 1984 made, and so far has enforced a number of drastic educational reforms. It stressed the importance of 'Peoples' Schools' for dropouts, illiterate or semi-literate adults and evening classes. More politically sensitive, it established clear (and largely political) standards for recipients of state fellowships. Those standards are political, academic and social, in this order. The political standards include Congolese citizenship, 'respect for national institutions', talents for sports or cultural activities, and most importantly effective participation in party-sponsored or mass organizations' activities. In academic terms, proper age, a 'brilliant record' and the 'right choice' of a discipline 'related to development' are required. Socially, priority for fellowships is given to children of 'martyrs', the handicapped, orphans and children of very large families (PCT 1984, *3ème Congrès Ordinaire*, pp. 299–345).

The Economy

The World Bank officially classifies Congo as one of the four sub-Saharan 'middle-income oil exporters', together with Angola, Gabon and Nigeria (World Bank, 1986, p. 184). Despite being clearly the smallest oil producer of the four, it has a GNP per capita of $1,140, far higher than Angola, higher than Nigeria and a large majority of the sub-Saharan states (Gabon is one prominent exception). Among black Africa's radical, socialist or scientific socialist regimes, Congo is far and away the most economically prosperous.

The general characteristic of the Congolese economy since independence, and certainly since the early 1970s, is its increasing dependence upon one major commodity—oil. The structure of the economic production of the country between 1965 and 1984 is indicative in this respect. In 1965 agriculture provided 19 per cent of the GDP, industry 19 per cent, manufacturing close to zero, and services 62 per cent; for 1984 the same figures were 7, 60, 6 and 33 per cent, respectively (World Bank, 1986, p. 184). Such figures demonstrate that in less than two decades the country has undergone a revolutionary economic change; from being an equatorial backwater heavily dependent on transportation fees from its northern neighbours, with no industry (a term including the oil sector), it has become a significant oil producer. Largely unsuccessful efforts were made in the 1960s to develop a major potash mining sector.

Oil, unlike other basic raw materials, is a stable and essential one, and in this respect Congo has a decisive advantage over Cuba and her sugar-dominated economy, or other countries' reliance on copper, tin, bananas or similar commodities. Furthermore, although not an OPEC member, Congo has consistently taken advantage of that organization's temporary ability to control international prices and supplies, while at the same time avoiding the obligation of maintaining cartel prices. Indeed, Brazzaville has often sold its crude for less than the OPEC prices, even before the current slump in world demand and prices.

Dependence on oil, however, has had the same, or worse, negative impact on the economic and social structure of the country as it did in practically all other major oil suppliers of the Third World, from Kuwait to Nigeria, Mexico to Libya and Venezuela to Gabon. It has created excessive expectations of future income based upon inherently unreliable estimates of the behaviour of the oil market; it has brought about a rapid and massive influx of wealth into the hands of the politically influential classes and civil servants who, through the state, control oil revenues, and it has further exaggerated the role of the small number of Congolese directly employed in the oil industry, whether as workers or, more often, as bureaucrats. In other words, oil in Congo exacerbated the already dangerous economic and political imbalances between the politically relevant, urban organized and militant minority and the politically irrelevant peasant majority. It has led to greater neglect of the vital agriculture sector.

The economic distortions produced by oil also included the skyrocketing prices for urban housing and consumer products; an irresistible, additional pull to the towns for the rural population (a phenomenon common throughout Africa, but exacerbated in Congo); growing inflation; political miscalculations on the part of the regimes in power and their opponents on the left, both of whom counted and still plan on higher revenues and therefore greater resources for the state sector and for grandiose plans for 'building socialism'.

The other major problems with Congo's dependence on oil are that the national reserves, all so far off-shore, and thus more expensive than on-shore

Table 5.1 Changes in Congo's volume of trade with main
partners, 1985–6

Country	1985	1986	% change
France			
Imports	1,017	968	−4.8
Exports	2,355	1,829	−22.3
United States			
Imports	645.6	397.9	−38.4
Exports	19.4	10.1	−47.9
United Kingdom			
Imports	2.8	2.4	−14.3
Exports	21.5	9.2	−57.2

Source: QER, April, 1987.

deposits, are not very large by international standards. True enough, scares of oil running out did occur before, in the mid-1970s and again at the beginning of the 1980s, and were proved incorrect by new discoveries. Nevertheless, Congo's narrow coast and the likelihood that no significant on-shore deposits exist, clearly eliminate serious hopes for further major discoveries. For Congo, oil is running out, and the *l'après petrole* era is a worrying but inevitable reality. This is a fact the Sassou-Nguesso regime admits publicly, and most Brazzaville inhabitants claim to have nightmares about.

The nature of oil's impact upon Congo's economy, and implicitly on politics is both clear and representative of certain realities, all unpalatable for the ideologues of the PCT. The most obvious is that central planning on the Soviet pattern, ideologically desirable as it may be, is simply not realistic in a largely one-commodity, export-orientated economy, where world prices are decided by world, primarily Western, demand and where there is a severe shortage of managerial personnel.

By 1987, quite clearly the main preoccupation of the regime was the economy, which had worsened steadily, the result of years of poor management and collapsing oil prices. The seriousness of the situation was demonstrated by the decision to cut the state budget in half (*FBIS, Africa*, 24 March 1987, p. 52). Although the salaries of the inflated number of state employees were not touched, the regime had to ask its Western creditors to reschedule its debts. Following negotiations with its major creditors (France, the United States, Brazil, Great Britain and Switzerland) a ten-year repayment schedule was agreed upon in July 1987. The agreement was the result of previous Congolese acceptance of the IMF demands for restructuring the state sector and for giving a larger share of the economy to the private sector, as well as a more responsible approach to the size and structure of the government budget. In large part as a result of this forced reassessment of the economic realities, the regime also proclaimed its intention of shifting emphasis from the urban industrial/service sector to agriculture, with the declared goal of improving rural life, eliminating 'backwardness' and, most importantly, of stopping urban growth (*FBIS, Africa*, 29 April 1987, p. 82).

As part of the Structural Adjustment Programme adopted by the government and directly linked to the twenty-year agreement signed with the IMF, a politically risky measure was adopted: the imposition of a highly unpopular tax on urban dwellers intended to fund efforts to enhance food production. Finally, what in different circumstances would have been very promising news, the discovery of the rich Tchiboula oil field, had little impact in an era of cheap oil and a scarcity of investment capital for the industry.

Foreign Policy

General Patterns

The foreign policy of Congo since independence has been characterized by the sudden shift in 1963 and relative continuity ever since. The Youlou regime was conspicuously pro-French and anti-communist and an active member in the conservative 'Monrovia' group. Youlou was closely involved in the events in neighbouring Congo on the side of Kasavubu and against Patrice Lumumba and his followers. The Youlou foreign policy, however, turned out to suffer from a number of fatal drawbacks, which explain in part the radical shift of Brazzaville's external policies after the 1963 'revolution'. The first problem was that it did not take into account the large and radical-ized urban strata, precisely those which played a decisive role in the overthrow of Fulbert Youlou. Their sentiments were, rhetorically at least, clearly 'pro-gressive' and anti-French, a rather common phenomenon throughout Africa at the time. Second, De Gaulle's blunt refusal to save Youlou—an attitude in sharp contrast with France's prompt military intervention in support of Leon M'Ba's regime in neighbouring Gabon—tended to discredit pro-French policies in general.

With such a background, it was no big surprise that the Massemba-Debat regime decided to move closer to the Soviets and Chinese, while relations with France cooled abruptly and those with the United States were soon broken off at Congo's initiative.[1] The very same fragmentation and radical-ization of the Congolese body politic that brought Fulbert Youlou down prevented Massemba-Debat, a weak politician to begin with, from ever establishing full control over the government or its alleged 'mass organiza-tions', and hence over foreign policy. Indeed, Massemba-Debat's first prime minister, Pascal Lissouba (1963–6), was largely seen as 'pro-Chinese', while his second, Ambroise Noumazalay (1966–8), enjoyed a reputation as 'pro-Soviet'. In fact, the extent to which Lissouba was 'pro-Chinese' was the result of the revolutionary fervour of August 1963, and the need to radicalize drastically and rapidly all important institutions if the new 'revolutionary regime' was to retain power. As for Noumazalay's 'pro-Soviet' reputation, it was largely a Western perception resulting from his faction's success in gaining the upper hand over Massemba-Debat in 1966, allegedly with Cuban support—directed via the training and arming of the JMNR. The pro-Chinese or pro-Soviet labels had little if any significance domestically.

Both cases were simple reflections of the momentary and inherently unstable balance of forces between various radical factions within the politically relevant institutions of the time: the MNR, JMNR and the army. The MNR as well as army factions were trained, and, in the case of the latter, equipped by both China and the Soviet bloc. The JMNR militia received ideological and military training from Cuba. Each and every momentary shift in the relative balance between those factions led to Western speculation on the 'trends' of Congolese international politics and misled everyone, including the leaders of the various factions. What was, and has remained ever since, an important characteristic of Congo's foreign policy was Brazzaville's ability to maintain a roughly equal distance between Moscow, Beijing and Havana, receiving support from each without being subject to undue influence. The explanation was that since 1963 and to date (1988) none of those foreign allies provided substantial *economic* aid; at the same time France, supposedly the main enemy, still played a major economic role and was effectively a source of the inflated salaries of the civil servants, public employees and bureaucrats.[2] Despite the pro-socialist alignment in foreign policy, successive regimes were careful not to alienate the French totally.

Time, however, and the cumulative experience of the impact of foreign ideological and politico/military interference in Congolese politics, resulted in a steady but discernible shift in Congo's foreign policy, and so did the dawning realization of the Brazzaville leaders that theirs is a small country in a complex regional environment. The 1966 coup attempt, the role of the JMNR in general throughout the Massemba-Debat period and of Ange Diawara afterwards, indicated to Ngouabi and some of his closest military advisers that wild-eyed radicalism is both unproductive for the country and a deadly threat to themselves.[3]

The three pillars of Brazzaville's foreign policy, each corresponding to a specific set of interests, are relations with its neighbours, secondarily with other African states, relations with the Soviet bloc and other communist states and ties with France and the West in general. The first corresponds to immediate security and strategic concerns, the second is related to ideology, while the third is decisively influenced by the need for economic aid and by tradition.

Africa

Brazzaville's relations with its five neighbours have always been as much linked to Congo's relative size and strength compared to each of them as with domestic, economic and ideological considerations. On the other hand, inherited colonial patterns of regional relationships have also played a role, as have ethnicity and personality.

Cameroon has been the neighbour with which Congo has had the least interaction, largely since the common border is remote and isolated and there are no bilateral communications or transport links of any significance. After a brief flirtation with supporting Marxist opponents of the Ahmadou Ahidjo regime in the early days of the Massemba-Debat government, Brazzaville's relations with Cameroon stabilized and currently remain correct if not that close.

Relations with Central Africa reached a clear low during the Bokassa regime, when Bangui was unable to pay its transport bills within the Central African Community (Chad, Congo, Cameroon, Central Africa) and at the end seemed to be cast out even by Paris. That latter fact allowed Brazzaville to strengthen its radical credentials, by supporting Abel Goumba's Front Patriotique d'Oubangui-Parti du Travail (FPO-PT) against Bokassa, and by threatening to refuse transit facilities to Central African Freight via the Zaïre River to Pointe Noire, given Bangui's bankruptcy. Once France and domestic opponents had cooperated to oust Bokassa in 1979, Brazzaville again became a 'good neighbour' and its support for the FPO-PT became strictly rhetorical. Indeed, when Claude-Richard Gouandjia of the FPO-PT was arrested in Brazzaville in September 1987, he was neither expelled to Central Africa, nor allowed to continue his activities against the Kolingba regime (*FBIS*, 9 September 1987, p. A1).

Congo's relations with Gabon have been the most consistently stable and friendly, despite Libreville's close political and security ties with France, Morocco and the United States. Indeed, Gabon guaranteed to send a share of Moanga's manganese exports via Pointe Noire even after the completion of the Transgabonaise railway (*QER*, Annual Supplement, 1983, p. 23). Economic interests have overcome ideological differences.

Among Congo's neighbours it was Angola that raised the most dangerous, important and significant problems for Brazzaville. A supporter of the MPLA since 1963, Congo was the headquarters of that organization until it gained power in Luanda in November 1975 with the assistance of Cuban troops. Ngouabi and Agostinho Neto were fond of proclaiming their friendship, although the former is suspected of not having abandoned totally the idea of Cabindan secession and of retaining links with secessionists. Cuban troops landed at and used Loubomo's airfield for operations in Angola, and MPLA guerrilla units, were active in Cabinda from the late 1960s, using Congolese bases. On the other hand, FLEC also used Congolese territory for its operations, and even attacked Congolese installations in retaliation for Brazzaville's support for the MPLA in 1977; hence doubling the projected cost of the realignment of the Congo–Ocean railway, from CFA fr. 33 billion to 75 billion (*QER*, Annual Supplement, 1983, p. 22).

Despite such a long history of MPLA support, the PCT leadership seems to have been extremely careful to avoid becoming involved in hostilities with its huge neighbour, Zaïre. Zaïre was militarily involved in fighting the MPLA in 1975 and currently supports UNITA.

Traditionally, or at least until 1963, Congo was the main beneficiary of massive diamond smuggling from Zaïre, to the extent that diamonds were a major 'export'. That has largely ceased since Kinshasa cracked down on 'freelance' smuggling—most of the smuggling is now carried out by government officials, who do not need to use Congo as an outlet. The old ideological disputes between the two neighbours, whereby Zaïre supported the 'Youlouists' and Brazzaville the anti-Mobutu 'progressives', seem to have ceased; coexistence and cooperation have increased to the extent that in 1987 direct communication links between the two capitals were established, replacing the old patterns of using Paris and Brussels as routes for telephone calls.

In a more general vein, and as a counter to accusations of leftist bias, Congo has greatly improved relations with Egypt, which has offered economic aid, and with such moderate francophone states as Senegal and Togo.

By 1987 the most important and difficult development was President Sassou-Nguesso's election as chairman of the Organization of African Unity (OAU). Despite his relatively skilful handling of this position, the president had no choice but to alienate certain African countries, as well as some Western states, while making little headway in solving such perennial African conflicts as those in Chad and Western Sahara. Thus, by receiving the 'president' of the Saharan Arab Democratic Republic in June, Sassou-Nguesso indicated his preference in the dispute. Nguesso was respected as OAU chairman but not seen as even-handed over Chad by Chadian President Hissein Habrè. This resulted from Congo's good relations with Colonel Gadaffi and with the then Libyan-backed Goukouni Oueddei.

Congo and the Communist States

On 20 March 1984 Congo celebrated the twentieth anniversary of official relations with the Soviet Union. On that occasion the Soviet embassy in Brazzaville estimated total Soviet loans to Congo since 1964 at $85 million, and grants at some $20 million; that would make an average of slightly over $5 million per year, compared with French average annual aid disbursed during the 1980-3 period of some $60 million (*QER*, April 1984, p. 18).

In theory, and according to the official PCT ideological line, foreign affairs in general, and relations with communist states in particular, are part and parcel of the party's Marxist-Leninist nature, inasmuch as proletarian internationalism is a defining characteristic of a vanguard party at the stage of the 'national, democratic and people's revolution'. Thus, for Yhombi Opango, who tried to shore up his shaky revolutionary credentials with a flurry of foreign trips to communist states, ranging from Cuba to the Soviet Union and Eastern Europe, 'any influence exerted over the first socialist country in the world [the Soviet Union] would . . . only be beneficial to these struggling countries' of Africa (*Africa Contemporary Record*, 1977, p. B554). As for Sassou-Nguesso, proletarian internationalism is a *sine qua non* condition for victory over international capitalism and imperialism, as well as 'one of the irremovable characteristics of the Congolese Party of Labour' (*Afrique-Asie*, 6 August 1979, p. 54). On the other hand, Ngombe publicly expressed the frustration of the PCT and of other revolutionary regimes in Africa and the Third World in general with the amount and quality of Soviet bloc assistance to its underdeveloped ideological siblings, when he stated: 'We wish that the socialist countries continue to adhere to the principle of internationalist solidarity, which is expressed, among other ways, in practical aid to Third World countries that have chosen the socialist road. The world revolution cannot succeed if any of its contingents is ignored; the strength of a chain is the strength of its weakest link' (Ngombe, 1977, p. 38). For Sassou-Nguesso, his application to join the CMEA as an observer was a result of Congo's policy of seeking 'privileged relations with the socialist countries', which would 'accelerate our political and economic liberation' (Sassou-Nguesso, interview in *Afrique-Asie*, 30 April 1979). In other words, close economic ties with the Soviet bloc and massive aid from Moscow and Eastern Europe were seen as related to the ideological claims of the PCT, at least as much as an alternative to dependence upon France or the 'Western imperialism', as represented by the IMF, the World Bank and aid from Paris, Bonn or Washington.

Ever since 1963, Congo's relations with the communist states have consistently been characterized by attempts to maintain an intricate balance between their ideological, military and political influence and the continuation of economic ties with the West; between China and the Soviet bloc, including Cuba; and between political, military and security considerations. As already mentioned, the amount of economic assistance received from communist states has never been very important economically and that obtained from the Soviet Union was proportionally the lowest. It is highly doubtful whether any Congolese regime since Ngouabi really had very high expectations regarding Soviet bloc economic assistance. As for China, the general retrenchment of Beijing's Third World commitments following the Cultural Revolution and Mao's death have prevented Beijing from maintaining its aid levels to the Congo. Nevertheless, Congo may well be one of the few developing countries where China has retained a certain parity with the Soviets, both in terms of general relations and in terms of economic assistance. Chinese aid is small but is seen as effective and valuable. China's economic limitations are well understood by African states. At the height of China's influence in Congolese politics, during the last years of the Massemba-Debat regime and the first period of Ngouabi's, China surpassed the Soviet bloc in economic assistance to Brazzaville. Thus, between 1963 and 1974, of a total of $42 million in communist economic assistance (credits and grants) was extended to Congo, China provided $25 million; of the total of $163 million received by 1978, $75 million was provided by Beijing, compared with $28 million from Moscow and $60 million from Eastern Europe (CIA, 1974).

After 1975, when Mao's death and party in-fighting in China further lessened Chinese interest in foreign relations and Congo's role in the Angolan civil war magnified Soviet interest in the country, the trend was reversed. The East Europeans provided $10 million in assistance in 1975 alone, and by 1984 their collective assistance amounted to $65 million; by 1984 total Soviet credits and loans reached $75 million, with $30 million being offered in 1981 (US Department of State, 1986, pp. 10-14). These patterns seem to suggest that while Chinese economic assistance fluctuated depending upon Beijing's own priorities and declining resources, Soviet bloc aid had clear political connotations. While Congo remained a rather unstable and insignificant backwater, Soviet bloc support was minimal. With the prominence Brazzaville reached during the 1974-6 events in Angola and the relative radicalism, particularly in foreign policy, of Ngouabi, Warsaw Pact and CMEA (Council of Mutual Economic Assistance) interest was promptly followed by increased aid. Just prior to and immediately after Congo signed a Treaty of Friendship and Cooperation with the Soviet Union in 1981, Moscow almost doubled its aid commitments. This coincided with a period of greatly increased Soviet interest in central and southern Africa and enhanced involvement in supporting liberation movements.

In terms of the specific projects supported, financed or supervised by communist states, the differences between China and the Soviet bloc are again clear. The Chinese have concentrated their efforts, usually involving a far higher proportion of grants than loans and extensive use of skilled labour, on infrastructure and prestigious projects such as stadiums and 'people's palaces'. In 1977 China installed the first of four generators at the Bouenza Dam, and paid one-third of the project's total $54 million cost. The Bouenza hydroelectric station is by far the largest in the Congo, with its 74 MW capacity. Indeed, the second largest such station, at Djoué, only has a capacity of 15 MW (*QER, Annual Supplement*, 1983, p. 21). By contrast, CMEA projects are centred around prospecting for and exploitation of natural resources, particularly minerals. Romania and Bulgaria provide assistance in phosphate prospecting (the former was also briefly interested in the timber industry), while the Soviets are involved in the declining copper, lead-zinc and gold extracting industries (*QER, Annual Supplement*, 1983, p. 20). The presence of 440 communist, mostly CMEA, economic technicians in Congo by 1984 was limited to such projects and had a marginal impact on the country's economy. The marginal nature of Soviet bloc economic assistance and their small overall roles in Congo are reflected in the insignificant amount of trade between Congo and the Soviet Union which, at less than 3 per cent in 1984 was far smaller than that with Brazil or the United States, and less than one-tenth of that with France (*QER, Annual Supplement*, 1983, p. 24).

The impact of Congo's relations with the communist states in the educational field is extremely important. By 1976, 880 Congolese students were already being trained in the Soviet bloc. The number grew rapidly to 1,385 in 1977 and 1,665 in 1984 (CIA, 1977; US Department of State, 1986). Almost all of those future civil servants, state-company managers and party workers trained on Cuba's Island of Youth, at the 'Marien Ngouabi School' or at various institutions in the German Democratic Republic, Romania and the Soviet Union. It is hoped that they will return home imbued with Marxist-Leninist, economic, political and ideological theories and thereby reinforce the already strong statist, radical and 'internationalist' nature of the Congolese political elite. In practice, this does not always prove to be the case. In light of the nature of the Congolese political system, a mixture of military and Marxist-Leninist vanguard party rules the role of the Soviet bloc trainees is very important. That of their military colleagues trained by the Soviet Union, GDR, Cuba or China is more important still.

With its low population and correspondingly small military establishment, Congo is host to a large number of Soviet bloc advisers and has a proportionately high percentage of Soviet bloc-trained personnel. As of December 1984, 660 Congolese had undergone Soviet bloc (including Cuban) military training, compared with 2,120 Ethiopians, 380 Angolans and 530 Mozambicans (US Department of State, 1986, p. 14). Considering the fact that Ethiopia has a population almost thirty times larger than Congo's,

Angola six times, Mozambique ten times, and they have standing armies respectively fifteen, six and twice as large (International Institute for Strategic Studies, 1987, pp. 89-110), the APN is indeed the most thoroughly Soviet-educated military establishment in Africa, with all that that entails in terms of ideological influences and the likely political outlooks of trained military cadres.

Equally important is the fact that, unlike economic ties, military and military-training relations between Congo and communist states are not balanced between China and the Soviet bloc, but show an increasingly clear domination by the latter. Thus, of the 825 Congolese military personnel trained in communist states by 1976, 400 were trained in Warsaw Pact states, and the rest in China; by 1979, 590 were trained in the Warsaw Pact and 425 in China, and by 1984 the total trained in the Soviet bloc reached 660 with Chinese trainees dropping to zero (CIA, 1977; US Department of State, 1986). To this one may add the fact that virtually all of the 350 communist military technicians and advisers present in Congo in 1985 were Soviets, East Europeans, Cubans or North Koreans. In recent years, the North Koreans have had a much increased presence in Africa as military and economic advisers.

The radical rhetoric is likely to be maintained even though actual policy, particularly in the economic sphere, is likely to be more pragmatic. None of these facts imply that Congo meekly follows Soviet dictates in its foreign policy: regional and African considerations, and most importantly financial ones related to the vital French economic assistance, have a permanent and important role in influencing foreign policy, as does Congo's commitment to non-alignment. Congo did not support the Soviet invasion of Afghanistan at the United Nations; it consistently abstained, to Moscow's annoyance.

More recently, and particularly in 1987, Brazzaville's relations with the communist world continued as before, with the gradual development of closer party and government ties to the Soviet bloc and warm relations with China. Both Moscow and Brazzaville celebrated the fifth anniversary of the signing of the Congo–Soviet Union treaty of friendship and cooperation, with the Soviets pointing out their economic and technical aid, from the PCT party school to the Cosmos Hotel and the training of hundreds of cadres (*Izvestiya*, 13 May 1986). During the year such ties were further strengthened when a new accord was signed between the two ruling parties, providing for joint colloquia and Soviet training of Congolese cadres (*Pravda*, 8 April 1986). Even more specific was the August meeting in Brazzaville between the deputy chairman of the CPSU control commission, Voropayev, and high-level PCT leaders (*Pravda*, 19 August 1986). Interestingly enough, that very same month a PCT control commission delegation met its Mozambican counterpart in Inhambane for an exchange of views and experience (*World Marxist Review*, August 1986). A PCT Politburo delegation headed by ideological chief Goma Foutou visited China in March and met their Chinese counterparts (*FBIS, China*, 18 March 1986, p. 14). In July, a Chinese delegation led by the deputy minister for information visited Congo and signed an agreement of cooperation between the two countries' information agencies.

Congo and the West

By and large, since the radicalization of Brazzaville politics in 1963, Congo's relations with Western states have continued to remain stable, as has the flow of aid. The latter was the main topic of discussion as late as the May 1987 meeting in Brazzaville between French cooperation minister Michel Aurillac and Prime Minister Poungui. Certain realities, strongly resented but at the same time widely accepted in Brazzaville, have consistently forced successive radical Congolese regimes to tread carefully in their relations with the West and particularly with France. The trade balance is one of the most important

Table 5.2 The structure of Congo's foreign trade, 1985

	$ million
Principal exports	
Crude oil	979
Petroleum products	35
Timber	28
Total exports	1,087
Principal imports	
Machinery	139
Food	112
Metal products	101
Transport equipment	63
Chemicals	46
Total imports	581

Source: *QER*, March, 1987.

of those realities: in 1984 France provided 55 per cent of Congolese imports and bought 13.3 per cent of exports; followed by Italy with 39.1 per cent of exports and 3 per cent of imports; the United States bought 12.9 per cent and Brazil 17.3 per cent of Congo's exports, and provided 3 per cent and 8 per cent respectively of Brazzaville's imports (*QER Annual Supplement*, 1983, p. 24). Some 70 per cent of Congo's foreign aid comes from the European Economic Community (EEC), either directly, with France the largest donor, or indirectly, with Paris the decisive supporter for such community aid. French companies, including ELF, exploit Congo's major resource, oil.

Equally important is the fact that, official ideology notwithstanding, educated Congolese still see themselves as French-speaking elites, and regard local languages, such as Lingala, as inferior. To speak French is a sign of education and, ultimately, of high social status. French-educated lawyers, doctors, educators and even military officers still despise the *sauvages* – the ubiquitous northern soldiers patrolling the capital. In 1980, during Brazzaville's centenary, not only was Jacques Chirac, the mayor of Paris, the guest of honour, but he was also the most popular guest by far, clearly putting in the shade any Soviet bloc representative; common language was clearly a factor there, though. The fact that Sassou-Nguesso asked for and received French military support during the Ouesso disturbances of 1987 is the ultimate example of the persistence of France's influence.

Since the United States has never had any strong interest in Congo, whether economic or political, bilateral relations have consistently been dominated by the prevailing ideological winds in Brazzaville, rather than mutual interests. The Youlou regime, considering itself a bastion of African anti-communism, established good ties with Washington, culminating with

Table 5.3 The Structure of Franco-Congolese trade, 1986
(F fr. million)

Exports to France		Imports from France	
Oil	758	Machinery	294
Timber	115	Electrical Equipment	267
Coffee	30	Pharmaceuticals	163
		Iron and steel	127
		Vehicles	110

Source: QER , March 1987.

Youlou's visit to the United States in 1962. American aid to Congo, however, was insignificant and political interests did not always coincide. Indeed, Brazzaville was a consistent supporter of the Katangan secessionists, while the United States played a major role in supporting the Leopoldville government against Tschombe. The 1963 events produced a drastic change in bilateral relations; the militants declared the United States the 'head of world imperialism'. This portrayal of the United States served to strengthen their ideological credentials at little or no risk. The result was a paradoxical attitude on the part of the Massemba-Debat regime. While the former colonial power, France, was largely spared the ideological fury of the radicals—not least because it was still paying most of their salaries through large subsidies to the Congolese national budget—Washington unwillingly assumed the role of a lightning rod for anti-imperialist rhetoric. That was made easy by the fact that American aid was minuscule, as was the threat of retaliation. Indeed, when revolutionary thugs manhandled American diplomats on the second anniversary of the 1963 'revolution', all Washington could do was to recall all its diplomats and, in effect, suspend diplomatic

Table 5.4 Direction of Congolese trade, 1984

Country	Amount	Percentage of trade
Imports by origin in CFA fr. billion		
France	136.8	52.2
West Germany	15.4	5.9
United States	14.8	5.7
Japan	9.5	3.6
Spain	8.7	3.3
Total	262.1	100
Exports by destination in CFA fr. billion		
United States	400.8	77.6
France	45.9	8.9
Belgium	12.3	2.4
Holland	11.0	2.1
Spain	9.6	1.8
Total	516.8	100

Source: QER, January 1987.

relations with Congo. Some observers suggested, plausibly, that the entire episode was an example of Massemba-Debat's diplomatic brinkmanship backfiring. Indeed, in the last months of 1964 American diplomats were expelled, as were journalists, while Brazzaville tried to put pressure on the United States to increase its aid, then less than $1 million per year (*Jeune Afrique*, 24 June 1977).

By 1973, Brazzaville, in its permanent search for more foreign aid, and with relations with Paris in one of their cool periods, began making discreet overtures to Washington, using the good offices of President Mobutu of Zaïre. It seems that negotiations were on the verge of success when the Angolan events once again put Congo in the forefront of radicalism in the region. Ngouabi's open support for the MPLA and the use of Congolese territory by the Cuban combat forces ended any interest Washington may have had in reopening diplomatic ties with Congo. In apparent frustration, Ngouabi confiscated the assets of Texaco and Mobil in 1974. Nevertheless, by the end of his life he had once again begun to seek a *rapprochement*, which explains the speed with which the Yhombi Opango regime reached an agreement re-establishing official ties with the United States in June 1977; only a month after Marien Ngouabi's assassination. The fact that the Congolese negotiator was Foreign Minister Theophile Obenga, a close associate of Ngouabi, strengthens that argument (ibid.). The agreement on resuming relations, reached in Bonn, provided for, among other things, Congolese compensation for the Texaco and Mobil assets, which was indeed paid (Mboukou, 1981, p. 17).

United States aid to Congo was a clear disappointment to the Brazzaville authorities; in 1984 total American economic assistance was $1 million in AID grants, and $33.8 million in Ex-Import Bank loans; in 1985 the figures were $1.4 and $12.1 million respectively, and in 1987 only $700,000 in grants (US Department of State, 1987, p. 82). On the other hand, a number of American companies have expressed interest in investing in Congo, including a consortium trying to reopen the Holle potash mine, some Louisiana agro-businesses studying the possibility of introducing new crops or improving the present yields of Congolese farms and a few other projects, all relatively small. The most important benefit for Congo in normalizing relations with the United States, however, was the removal of actual or potential American objections to Congolese credit and financial assistance demands from the World Bank and the IMF. Since the reopening of relations, such advantages clearly offset existing problems, such as the Carter Administration's rejection of the first Congolese ambassador-designate to Washington, Jacques Okoko, on human rights' grounds.[4]

Under the Reagan Administration, despite minor snags such as the official PCT condemnation of the American raid on Libya, and the even stronger language used in the joint communiqué with the PLO during Arafat's visit in May 1986, relations with the United States have improved. The most significant development in this respect was Sassou-Nguesso's visit to Washington in September 1986, when he met President Reagan. The meeting dispelled some of the clouds in bilateral relations.

6 Conclusion

Congo's politics, economic policies and ideological atmosphere are one of the best examples of what could be called Afrocommunism (Ottaway & Ottaway, 1981). This implies a process of adapting, adopting and modifying a basically European ideology to unusual and peculiar circumstances imposed by vastly different conditions and both internal and external political and cultural factors. In the case of the Congo, successive regimes have espoused Marxist–Leninist doctrines but have largely failed to build an effective party through which to disseminate the ideology and mobilize support.

The nature of post-independence Congolese elites has remained fundamentally unchanged almost thirty years later, with an entire new generation repeating the patterns of political behaviour evident ever since 1963, without appearing to learn from errors. The result has been a continuing push towards greater radicalism without the basic understanding that ideology has to be applied to concrete 'objective' conditions in order for a realistic set of policies to be drawn up and implemented. Congo's leaders clearly have a strong commitment to socialism but have not come to terms with the need to match theory and practice.

Congo's radical political culture goes far beyond what some authors have defined as 'socialism by words': the rhetoric of 'scientific socialism' is not only the dominant political vocabulary in Brazzaville, it also has concrete economic and social content. For the entrenched groups such as the military, party officials, government employees, trade unionists and the burgeoning number of students, central planning, state control over the economy and huge subsidies represent a precondition for maintaining their legitimacy and their living and social standards. There are clearly many who have jumped on the socialist bandwagon for purely materialistic rather than political reasons.

The ruling PCT's history is one of consistent attempts to walk a tightrope between trying to institutionalize itself in orthodox Marxist fashion and having to face internal and external pressures it could only cope with by increasing its dependence upon the military. The apparent symbiosis between the military and the party was never more than a façade for the ultimate control of the former over the latter. The fact that all Congolese leaders since the proclamation of the People's Republic in 1969 have been military men is no coincidence. The military, as in many African states, has remained the most potent political force as well as one of the most progressive.

For all practical purposes, the PCT, military and government are under the control of a group which is doubly a minority: ethnically, the northerners are clearly a minority, and the membership of the PCT, as befits a 'vanguard party', is exceedingly low. But there are no reasons to believe that this group's domination will be threatened from outside, since its grip over the military is strong. Factionalism is a problem within the military, but the factions are shifting ones and they have continuing faith in radicalism—even though they interpret it in different ways. Factional conflict breaks out frequently but it assumes forms which may threaten individual regimes but not the socialist tradition within the military elite. The economic crisis the country is facing since the collapse of the oil prices has clearly resulted in a decline in revenues available to the ruling group. Scarcity and budget difficulties have forced difficult choices for the Sassou-Nguesso regime, and thus resulted in the alienation of some important constituencies of the party and government. Socialist and statist policies have had to give way to economic policies which have enabled the government to maintain at least limited international confidence in the economy. Inevitably, that has provided political ammunition for the president's enemies on the 'left', and led to the purge of Camille Bongou in 1987. Purges have over time resulted in the reduction of the PCT's base of support, support which periodically is renewed; as in the last years of Marien Ngouabi, or during the Yhombi Opango regime, they backfire and lead to the growth of sufficient support within the PCT and other politically active groups to defeat the president. What has proved abundantly clear is that radicalism is far too well rooted in the Congolese political tradition to expect any ideological change in the foreseeable future, regardless of the person occupying the presidential palace. Strong anti-socialist forces have failed to materialize. Within groups opposed to or critical of Sassou-Nguesso, socialism is as much the ruling political idea as it is within the currently dominant group. The major problem for the PCT and the radical sectors of the military is to effectively transform a military regime into a Marxist-Leninist government. The military rulers have a clear commitment to socialist ideology but have failed to build a durable, ideologically coherent party, let alone popularize it nationally. Ideology is important to the regime but regime stability has always proved the dominant motivating factor.

Notes

Chapter 1

1 The World Bank's *World Development Report, 1986*, Table 31, p. 240, gives Congo's urban population percentage as 56 per cent, with a growth rate of 5.4 per cent in 1984; at the same time, and somewhat puzzlingly, it gives the percentage of the Brazzaville population's share of the total as 56 per cent in 1980. One can only speculate at the increase in the population of Pointe Noire or Loubomo, particularly in light of the attraction of the former, an oil boom city until a few years ago.

2 Like all tropical and equatorial soils, the Congolese is a highly erosion-vulnerable one, highly fertile in the short term and barren in the medium and long term, unless high fertilizer use is introduced. Nevertheless, tropical and equatorial areas are far better for agricultural use than most of the rest of the continent.

Chapter 2

1 This is a point consistently made by all students of Congolese politics, from Wagret (1964) to Decalo (1976, pp. 123–72).

2 *West Africa*, 19 April 1976, quoted in Decalo (1979, p. 250).

3 *FBIS, Africa*, 5 October 1987, p. 3. PCT Central Committee member Vital Balla (1987, p. 130), mentioned some 80,000 civil servants. Prime Minister Poungui estimated the cost of salaries for the civil sector in 1987 at CFA fr. 36–76 billion, cf. *FBIS, Africa*, 5 October 1987, p. 3. This figure should be compared with the CFA fr. 73.56 billion allocated to agriculture for the entire five-year plan of 1982–6. See Kissisou-Boma 1984, p. 64.

4 In 1971 Congo had a 70 per cent school attendance rate, and the highest per thousand number of university graduates in black Africa. See Morrison *et al.*, 1972.

5 The Kongos were divided into Lari (some 21 per cent of the Congolese population), Vili (slightly fewer), Yombwe, Dondo and other marginal Kongos; the Mbochi were divided into Mbochi and Kouyou, and marginal elements, for a total of some 11 per cent of the total population (see Morrison *et al.*, 1972, p. 211. Within groups differences are dialectal and traditional, or 'tribal'. Hence Kouyou and Mbochi are as different as Swedes and Norwegians, despite linguistic similarities.

6 One of Matsouanism's tenets is that no spiritual leader is actually dead until his

corpse is seen by the faithful and receives proper burial. Since Matsoua died in exile, he is still considered to be alive; that explains why the Ngouabi regime exposed the corpse of Ange Diawara in public in 1972: to prevent the birth of another 'Matsoua'-type cult.

7 In this respect, Obenga's *La Vie de Marien Ngouabi*, sycophantic as it is, may be accurate in claiming that in 1963 Ngouabi had ties with Aime Matsika, the main organizer of the general strike that brought Youloy down (p. 39).

8 Desjeux, 1980, p. 22; according to Obenga, 1977, p. 44, they were tortured and killed at the JMNR Makala-Djoue camp. For Ngouabi's own, self-serving version of the facts, see *Etumba*, 9 April 1977, p. 13.

9 The role of 'imperialism' (read 'France') was probably, although never specifically, centred round Kikadidi's alleged role as a French intelligence asset (*Africa Confidential Record*, 1977–8, p. B552). Considering the close relationship between French and Francophone African military intelligence officers, the accusation is largely meaningless, even if true, as it could be.

10 His job as prosecutor in the trial of Massemba-Debat allowed him to know more about the circumstances of Ngouabi's death than most, and provided a significant leverage over the major personalities of the post-1977 regime.

Chapter 3

1 This is a widely perceived opinion and a significant body of publications has been dedicated to it; see Pierre Erny, 'Le socialisme de la parole', *Le Monde*, 11 November 1969.

2 For an analysis of this phenomenon, see Radu, 1984, pp. 15–40.

3 US Department of State, 1986, Table 12. This publication, the only one available in the West, is often confusing, inasmuch as it barely distinguishes between personnel already trained and those undergoing training, or between those personnel trained in the Soviet Union, Cuba and Eastern Europe. This is the reason for some of the discrepancies apparent in this chapter.

Chapter 4

1 République Populaire du Congo, Ministère de l'Éducation Nationale, *Annuaire de l'Université Marien Ngouabi, 1983–1984*, Brazzaville, 1983, p. 79.

2 The most typical of such regressive taxes was the 1978–80 National Solidarity Fund, a general tax on incomes reaching CFA fr. 3 billion in 1978 and CFA fr. 7.8 billion in 1979, until it was discontinued following serious political pressure in 1981 (*Quarterly Economic Record*, Annual Supplement, 1983, p. 23).

3 In this respect Congo is far from unique among Marxist-Leninist regimes in the

Third World. Indeed, Cuba is far more dependent upon sugar today than it ever was under Batista.
4 Indeed, the indigenous production of two of the main staples of the traditional Congolese diet, maize and rice, has declined from 17,000 tons in 1977–8 to 3,600 tons in the case of maize, and from 8,000 tons to 800 tons in the case of rice by 1981–2. At the same time, food is now the second largest import item, reaching 17.2 per cent of total imports by 1984 (*Quarterly Economic Record*, Annual Supplement, 1983, p. 24). Any visitor to Brazzaville or Pointe Noire is struck by the huge demand for French bread, wines, mineral water, and beef, exhibited even by average urban dwellers. The result is that Congo is one of the three most expensive countries in the world for foreigners—a fact which destroys any potential tourism industry.

Chapter 5

1 Decalo, 1979, p 249. The standard, and demonstrably false, official Congolese version, blaming the United States for the break in relations between 1965 and 1977, is mentioned by Alexandre Mboukou (1981, pp. 14–15), and repeated discreetly by Sassou-Nguesso (interview in *Africa Report*, May–June 1980).
2 A fact universally accepted, even by Mboukou (1981, p. 15), and by the Congolese regimes ever since 1963, at least in private but also in public.
3 One has to point out, at this juncture, that the pro-Cuban or Cuban-trained JMNR were radicals who did not take easily to, or in many instances even accept, Castro's support for the Soviet Union after the 1968 events in Czechoslovakia. Still in search of the 'true revolutionary centre', people like Diawara naturally became 'Pro-Chinese', with Beijing having little to do with them.
4 Okoko was the public prosecutor in the perfunctory trial of Massemba-Debat in 1977 which led to the latter's execution.

Bibliography

Balla, Vital 1987. Life versus dogma. *World Marxist Review*, August.

Central Intelligence Agency (CIA) 1975. *Communist Aid to Less Developed Countries of the Free World, 1974*. Washington, DC.

—— 1977. *Communist Aid to the Less Developed Countries of the Free World, 1976*. Washington, DC.

Comte, Gilbert 1969. Le socialisme de la parole. *Le Monde*, 11 November.

Decalo, Samuel 1976. *Coups and Army Rule in Africa*. New Haven, Conn., Yale University Press.

—— 1979. Rhetoric and socialism in Benin and Congo-Brazzaville. In Carl G. Rosberg & Thomas M. Callaghy, eds, *Socialism in Sub-Saharan Africa*. Institute of International Studies, Berkeley, Calif.

Desjeux, Dominique 1980. Le Congo, est-il situationiste? *Le Mois en Afrique*, October–November.

L'Économie congolaise 1983. Paris, Editions de la documentation africaine.

Erny, Pierre 1966. Parole et travail chez les jeunes de l'Afrique Centrale. *Projet*, Paris, September–October.

Gakosso, Gilbert-François 1983. *La Réalité congolaise*. Paris, La Pensée Universelle.

Hughes, Bertrand 1975. *Le Congo: formation sociale et mode de developpement économique*. Paris, Maspero.

International Institute for Strategic Studies. *The Military Balance, 1977–1988*. London.

Jowitt, Kenneth 1979. Scientific socialist regimes in Africa: political differentiation, avoidance, and unawareness. In Carl G. Rosberg & Thomas M. Callaghy, eds, *Socialism in Sub-Saharan Africa*. Institute of International Studies, Berkeley, Calif.

Kissisou-Boma, Jean Royal 1984. Restructuring the agrarian sector. *World Marxist Review*, April.

—— n.d. Classes sociales et idéologies en Afrique Centrale. Brazzaville, École Supérieure du Parti.

Legum, Colin 1971. *Africa Contemporary Record, 1970–1971*. London.

L'Homme du 31 juillet 1976. Official publication, Brazzaville.

Mboukou, Alexandre 1981. US/Congo: pragmatic relations. *Africa Report*, November December.

Morrison, Donald G. *et al*. 1972. *Black Africa: A Comparative Handbook*. New York, Free Press.

Ngombe, Jean-Pierre 1977. Toward a new upsurge of the revolutionary process. *World Marxist Review*, September.

Ngouabi, Marien 1975. Scientific socialism in Africa: Congo problems. *World Marxist Review*, May.

Obenga, Théophile 1977. *La Vie de Marien Ngouabi, 1938–1977*. Paris, Présence Africaine.

Ottaway, David & Ottaway, Marina 1981. *Afrocommunism*. New York, Africana Publishing Co.

Owona, Joseph 1978. La République Populaire du Congo après l'assassinat du Président Ngouabi. *Revue Française d'Études Politiques Africaines*, February.

PCT 1984. *3ème Congrès Ordinaire du Parti Congolais du Travail*, Brazzaville, Les Éditions du Comitè Centrale.

Racine, Andrew 1982. The People's Republic of Congo. In Peter Wiles, ed., *The New Communist Third World*. New York, St. Martin's.

Radu, Michael 1984. Ideology, parties and foreign policy in sub-Saharan Africa. In Richard Bissell & Michael Radu, eds, *Africa in the Post-Decolonization Era*, pp. 15–40. New Brunswick, NJ, Transaction Books.

— 1987. Congo. In Richard F. Staar, ed., *Yearbook of International Communist Affairs*. Stanford, Hoover Institution Press.

Sassou-Nguesso, Denis 1978. The Congo: key tasks of the current stage. *World Marxist Review*, April.

Sinda, Martial 1972. *Le Messianisme congolais*, Paris, Payot.

Thompson, Virginia & Adloff, Richard 1984 (2nd edn). *Historical Dictionary of the Congo*. Metuchen, NJ, Scarecrow Press.

US Department of State 1986. *Warsaw Pact Aid to Non-Communist LDCs, 1984*. Washington, DC, US Government Printing Office, May.

— 1987. *Country Reports on Human Rights Practices for 1986*. Washington, DC, US Government Printing Office, February.

Wagret, J. M. 1964. *Histoire et sociologie politique de la République du Congo Brazzaville*. Paris, R. Pichon and R. Durand-Auzias.

World Bank 1981. *Accelerated Development in Sub-Saharan Africa*. Washington, DC.

— 1986. *World Development Report 1986*. Oxford, Oxford University Press.

Periodicals

Africa Confidential
Africa Contemporary Record (London)
African Recorder
Afrique-Asie
L'Année Politique et Economique Africaine (Paris, Société Africaine d'édition)
Bulletin Quotidien de l'ACI (Brazzaville)
Elikia
Etumba
Foreign Broadcasting Information Service (FBIS), Africa
Izvestyia
Jeune Afrique
Krasnaya Zvezda (Moscow)
Le Monde

Le Mois en Afrique
Mweti
Pravda
Quarterly Economic Review (QER) of Gabon, Congo, Cameroon, CAR, Chad, Equatorial Guinea (London, Economist Intelligence Unit)
Revue Française d'Études Politiques Africaines
The Economist: Foreign Report
West Africa
World Marxist Review
Yearbook on International Communist Affairs (YICA) (Stanford, Hoover Institution)

Part III
Burkina Faso

Joan Baxter and Keith Somerville

Contents of Part III:
Burkina Faso

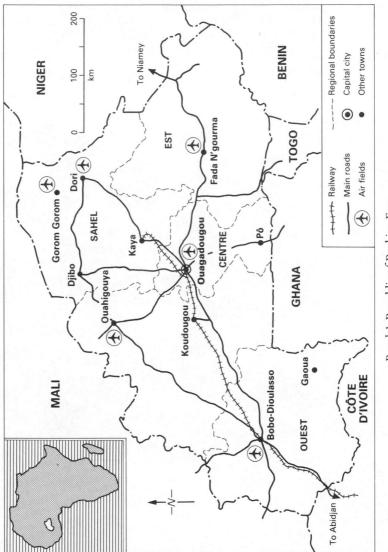

People's Republic of Burkina Faso

Basic Data

Official name	Burkina Faso
Population	7,964,705 (December 1985 census)
Population growth	3.5% p.a.
Urban population (%)	10
Total labour force	3,842,000 (FAO estimate, 1986)
Life expectancy	Male 42 years, Female 46 years (1983)
Infant mortality rate (per 1,000)	148 (1983)
Child mortality rate (per 1,000)	31 (1983)
Ethnic groups	Mossi (67%); others—Bella, Gourounsi, Peul, Bobo, Gourma, Lobi, Tuareg
Capital	Ouagadougou (population 441,514)
Other main towns	Bobo Dioulasso (228,668), Koudougou (51,926), Ouahigouya (38,902)
Land area	274,200 sq. km.
Official language	French
Membership of international organizations	UN since 1960, OAU since 1963, Economic Community of West Africa States, African Development Bank, Non-Aggression and Defence Pact
Political structure	
Constitution	Adopted in 1977 but suspended following military coup 25 November 1980
Highest legislative body	No existing legislature
Highest executive body	Council of Ministers (27 members)
Head of State	Capt Blaise Compaore (Chairman of the Popular Front)
Ruling movement	Popular Front—size and nature of membership unknown
Other main parties	Ligue Patriotique de Developpement (LIPAD—leftist); Groupe Communiste Burkinabe (GCB); Union Communiste Burkinabe (UCB); Union de Lutte Communiste (ULC); Union Democratique Voltaique (UDV—banned rightist movement); Union de Lutte Communiste Renovée (ULC-R)

Economy

GDP   CFA fr. 363,800 million (1984); CFA fr. 295,680 million (1984 estimate); $150 million (World Bank estimate 1986)

Budget   1987 Revenue, CFA fr. 83,106 million; expenditure CFA fr. 88,562 million (recurrent 75,884 million; capital 12,668 million)

Monetary unit   CFA fr. (301.03 to the $)

Trade and balance of payments

Exports   CFA fr. 31,157 million (1985)
Imports   CFA fr. 146,243 million (1985)
Exports as % of GDP   Under 10%
Main exports   Livestock, cotton, karité nuts, hides and skins
Main imports   Manufactured goods, fuel and petroleum products, cereals, fruit, industrial raw materials
Destination of exports   France, 30%; Taiwan, 17.5%; Côte d'Ivoire, 14.5%; Switzerland, 7%; China, 5%; Italy, 5%
Main trading partners   France, Côte d'Ivoire, Taiwan, China, Algeria, Libya
Foreign debt $616 million (1985)
Debt service ratio   14.8% (1985)
Foreign aid   Average $99 million p.a.

Main natural resources   Gold, manganese

Food self-sufficiency   In 1986–7, food self-sufficiency was nearly attained, but persistent drought has prevented this goal from being achieved

Armed forces   8,700 in army and air force; 1,750 in paramilitary forces
Defence budget   CFA fr. 15,338 million

Education

School system   Free education; six years primary and seven years secondary
Primary enrolment   Data unavailable but estimated in 1984 at 25% of school-age population
Secondary enrolment   Estimated in 1984 at 4% of school-age enrolment

Higher education	3,869 (1986)
Education budget	CFA fr. 16,826 million (1987); 19% of total budget
Adult literacy	13.2% (1985 estimate by UNESCO)
Main crops	Millet, sorghum, maize, pulses, cotton sugarcane, karité nuts, groundnuts
Main religions	57% of the population adhere to traditional animist beliefs; in 1986 there were an estimated 2.5 million Muslims and 974,000 Christians
Transport	
Road network	11,150 km.
Rail network	550 km. (+ 60 km. to Kaya)

Population Forecasting

The following data are projections produced by Poptran, University College Cardiff Population Centre, from United Nations Assessment Data published in 1980, and are reproduced here to provide some basis of comparison with other countries covered by the Marxist Regimes Series.

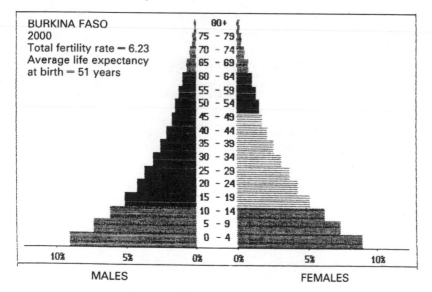

BURKINA FASO
2000
Total fertility rate — 6.23
Average life expectancy
at birth — 51 years

Projected Data for Burkina Faso 2000

Total population ('000)	10,538
Males ('000)	5,227
Females ('000)	5,311
Total fertility rate	6.23
Life expectancy (male)	49.5 years
Life expectancy (female)	52.9 years
Crude birth rate	45.5
Crude death rate	15.6
Annual growth rate	2.90%
Under 15s	44.92%
Over 65s	3.06%
Women aged 15–49	22.44%
Doubling time	24 years
Population density	38 per sq. km.
Urban population	38.4%

List of Abbreviations

CDR	Committee for the Defence of the Revolution
CE	Executive Committee (of the Popular Front)
CFP	Coordinating Committee (of the Popular Front)
CMRPN	Military Committee for Recovering National Progress
CNEC	Commando training centre at Po
CNR	National Revolutionary Council
CNTB	National Confederation of Burkinabe Workers
CR	Revolutionary Committee
CSB	Confederation of Burkinabe Trade Unions
CSP	Council to Salute the People
DOP	Political Orientation Speech
GCB	Burkinabe Communist Group
LIPAD	Patriotic League for Development
MDP	Progressive and Democratic Movement
ONSL	National Organization of Free Unions
PAI	Independent African Party
PPD	Popular Development Programme
PRP	Provincial Revolutionary Power
RDP	Popular and Democratic Revolution
TPR	Popular Revolutionary Tribunals
UCB	Burkinabe Communist Union
ULC	Union for Communist Struggle
ULC-R	Renewed Union for Communist Struggle
USTB	Union of Burkinabe Workers

1 Geographical and Political Setting

The West African state of Burkina Faso (formerly Upper Volta) lies landlocked just south of the Sahara Desert in the Sahel. It is bordered by Côte d'Ivoire, Ghana, Togo and Benin to the south, Mali to the west and north, and Niger to the east. The capital city of Ouagadougou is located in the geographical centre of the country, populated by approximately half a million people. The second major city, Bobo-Dioulasso, is the economic capital, located in highly arable territory close to the border with Côte d'Ivoire. The country is relatively densely populated, with an estimated 8 million people (official government figures) crowded into its 272,122 square kilometres. Most of this land is poor and rapidly deteriorating, plagued by deforestation, erosion and periodic drought. Government officials estimate that another 1–2 million Burkinabe citizens live abroad, mostly in Côte d'Ivoire, Ghana and Togo (interview with Blaise Compaore, December 1987).

The principle ethnic groups are the Mossi (48 per cent), Fulani (10 per cent), Lobi-Dagari (7 per cent), Mande (7 per cent), Senoufo (6 per cent), Gourounsi (5 per cent), Bissa (5 per cent) and Gourma (5 per cent). Muslims comprise 30 per cent of the populace, Christians 10 per cent, with animists the majority.

The official language in Burkina Faso is French, and the country gained its independence from France on 5 August 1960, with the French-approved Maurice Yameogo as President. Yameogo headed a civilian government heavily influenced by French advisers and rife with corruption. From the earliest days of independence it was clear that Burkina Faso was going to be a political hornet's nest. In spite of a very low literacy rate, which had only reached 10 per cent by 1988, there has always been a small number of highly educated and motivated people organized in heady and highly active political groups, mostly adhering to leftist doctrines. Historically, Burkina Faso had always been used by the French, and later the neighbouring Ivorians, as a source of manpower. As a result, even before independence, workers' rights and the goal of dismantling the colonial-imperialist apparatus were major rallying points for these activists. When Yameogo was deposed by Lieutenant-Colonel (later General) Sangoule Lamizana in a military *coup d'état* in 1966, it was largely as a result of widespread grass-roots dissatisfaction with his corrupt and neo-colonial government, which had allowed those in positions of power to enrich themselves at the expense of the vast majority of rural peasants and a few thousand factory workers.

Lamizana immediately dissolved the National Assembly, suspended the constitution and restricted political activity. In 1970 a new constitution was approved, legislating a return to civilian rule after four years. However, in spite of intense efforts to return to democracy, with an elected civilian and military national assembly, strong dissension among various leftist and labour groups lead Lamizana to clamp down once again and allow the military to take over, dissolving the assembly and suspending the constitution once again. In 1978, pressed once again by the increasingly powerful labour groups, elections were held and a new National Assembly formed. But unrest and disenchantment continued, and industrial action in 1979 and 1980 eventually led to a bloodless coup in November 1980, which saw Colonel Saye Zerbo take over.

Zerbo formed the Military Committee for Recovering National Progress (CMRPN), with thirty-one military members. Zerbo's hard-nosed and repressive military rule naturally met with vigorous opposition among labour groups, especially LIPAD (Patriotic League for Development), a broad-based Marxist-Leninist organization headed by Soumane Toure, and among a growing faction of young, revolutionary military officers, of which future presidents Captain Thomas Sankara and Captain Blaise Compaore were active. Indeed, it was at this time that Sankara first gained public attention, after accepting a post of Minister of Information and encouraging journalists to write freely and critically of the regime. He earned widespread recognition for breaking with the ministerial protocol, riding his bicycle to work and refusing the traditional perks of his post, and then made a dramatic show of resigning by announcing it on national television in a short speech in which he denounced Zerbo's CMRPN. Eventually Zerbo was overthrown in a bloodless coup in November 1982, but in the confusion following the coup a military doctor who had no strong political convictions, Major Jean-Baptiste Ouedraogo, became President. His military regime, the Council to Salute the People (CSP) was plagued by factionalism, and in an effort to placate radical military and labour groups, Captain Thomas Sankara, who was gaining popularity, backed by LIPAD leader Soumane Toure, was coerced into accepting the post of Prime Minister. In May 1983, during the mysterious visit of French President Mitterand's adviser for African affairs, Guy Penne, to Ouagadougou, Sankara and two of his closest political allies, Captain Henri Zongo and Major Boukari Jean-Baptiste Lingani, were arrested, while the fourth member of this increasingly powerful nucleus of revolutionary officers, Captain Blaise Compaore, was able to elude his captors. He subsequently led a revolt at the country's strategic military training camp in Po, on the Ghanaian border, which resulted in the freeing of the three officers. Ouedraogo's decreasing popularity and credibility, coupled with Sankara's brilliance as a crowd-pleasing revolutionary, set the wheels in motion for the *coup d'état* on 15 August 1983 that would herald the launch of the Burkinabe revolution. It was also the first coup in which blood was spilled; some fifteen people were killed.

The four years of Sankara's rule are generally agreed to be the most politically interesting period in Burkinabe history. Indeed, throughout the African continent Sankara attracted the attention of disillusioned youth who optimistically viewed him as the beginning of a wave of young second-generation leaders, who would finally take new and bold steps to dispense with the neo-colonialism and corruption that had plagued the continent since independence. Sankara ushered in sweeping and highly controversial reforms in both the style and substance of leadership. He fought the traditional 'big man' image of African presidents, dispensing with presidential limousine fleets, zealously promoting physical fitness for the civil service, personally leading his ministers in football games and exercise sessions, dogmatically flogging corruption with the Popular Revolutionary Tribunals (TPR), and rallying the people behind his revolutionary reforms with slogans which were often belligerent. His National Revolutionary Council (CNR) was an amorphous group, with secret membership (something his successors later criticized) and a core group containing himself, Compaore, Zongo and Lingani (known affectionately as the Gang of Four). The cabinet of governmental ministers appointed by the CNR was charged with carrying out the council's, mostly Sankara's policies. In addition, the Committees for the Defence of the Revolution (CDR), led by the generally unpopular Pierre Ouedraogo, were formed to bring the revolution out to even the most remote villages. Soumane Toure, the head of LIPAD and of the country's largest trade union, and the man who had worked closely with Sankara before the August coup, was bypassed for this crucial position, and subsequently fell out with the CNR (resulting in his arrest and imprisonment). This, and the recruitment of young, inexperienced and unemployed men to the CDR, were to cause much disaffection among both city and rural people, who felt that the CDR greatly abused the power (and guns) Sankara handed them. Although Sankara had begun his rule with a purely Marxist-Leninist doctrine, as enshrined in the Political Orientation Speech (DOP) of 2 October 1983, it soon became clear that the Burkinabe revolution as he personally led it, was going to be much more practical and idiosyncratic than this highly ideological and theoretical blueprint indicated. Sankara's flair for public speaking and his dogged determination to transform his country overnight into an independent and proud nation caused him to make spontaneous decisions (such as the 1987 decision to ban fruit imports made during the course of his speech at the CDR conference), angering many people who saw him as a self-proclaimed messiah (*Sidwaya*, 1987). Many of his policies are discussed later, in the section dealing with the Popular Front's current political platform.

Sankara envisioned a new economic order for his country, one of total self-reliance, which he promoted at the expense of traditional wealth and power bases. For example, he imposed clothing standards on civil servants, requiring they wear outfits made from locally grown, woven and sewn cotton. While he initially dumbfounded peasant populations with his attack on the traditional 'feudal' system of village chiefdoms, he also pleased them with his programme to build village health posts and schools by the thousands. However, like everything he did, even these dramatic improvements were beset with problems—there were health posts and schools but not enough health workers and teachers.

He persistently angered patriarchal French officialdom with his use of 'anti-imperialistic' slogans and did not hesitate to insult neighbouring conservative African leaders, notably Ivorian president Felix Houphoet-Boigny and Togolese president Gnassingbe Eyadema. By mid-1987 it was clear that Sankara's unrelenting fervour to work instant miracles in a country beset with disease, poverty and illiteracy, had increasingly isolated him from his closest associates at the top of the CNR. It was his refusal to compromise on any of his almost puritanical principles which in the end led to dissension in the military and in the CNR, and to his untimely death on 15 October 1987, at the age of thirty-seven.

2 The Popular Front

Since 15 October 1987 Burkina Faso has been ruled by the Popular Front, headed by Captain Blaise Compaore. Compaore is at once president of the Front, head of state and head of the government.

The Popular Front took power from the National Revolutionary Council (CNR), headed by Captain Thomas Sankara, after a *coup d'état* in which Sankara was killed. Convincing explanations of what precipitated the coup have never been provided. At first the Front maintained that Sankara had planned to have Compaore and top officials of the CNR liquidated on the evening of 15 October 1987, but this was never widely believed. Most evidence points to a premeditated plot to eliminate Sankara, which was carried out by commandos from the National Commando Training Centre (CNEC), headed at the time by Compaore. The Front immediately dissolved the CNR, in which Compaore had been second in command for four years, dissolved the government and dismissed all thirty provincial high commissioners.

Membership of the original Coordinating Committee (La Coordination) of the Popular Front which took office after the *coup d'état* is officially secret. However, in the early months of the Front's existence, this nucleus seemed to comprise about twenty-four men, of whom perhaps a half dozen were military, who say they formed the Front in the hours following the death of Thomas Sankara. Most of them, at least fifteen, were members of one of three left-wing political parties, including the UCB, Burkinabe Communist Union, the ULC, the Union for Communist Struggle and the GCB, the Burkinabe Communist Group. These small political parties had fallen out with former President Sankara, who criticized the divisive tactics of the 'left-wing intellectuals' operating in tiny political factions, in a country with a 90 per cent rural, illiterate population. None of the three political parties has widespread support at a popular level. The GCB, for example, is reported to have only nineteen members.

Just before his death on 15 October 1987, Thomas Sankara had been confronted by these left-wing factions at the fifth anniversary of the 'Political Orientation Speech', who—through a student spokesman—said they were against his stated intention to try to bypass this 'avant-garde' intelligentsia, in order to bring the revolution back to the masses, namely the 8 million peasants in the country (Government figures).

Two important left-wing parties were not represented in the original structure of the Popular Front. One, the Renewed Union for Communist Struggle (ULC-R) which split in 1987 from the ULC, remained close to the former president until the end. Several of its members, including former Minister of Information, Basile Guissou, and former Minister of Higher Education, Valere Some, spent the early months of 1988 in prison for alleged opposition to the Popular Front.

The second communist group excluded from the original 'Coordination' of the Popular Front, was the Patriotic League for Development (LIPAD), a broad-based popular movement allied with the Independent African Party (PAI) and closely linked to trade-union groups, and headed in spirit by the prominent trade-union leader, Soumane Toure. LIPAD and Toure were strongly behind Sankara's rise to power in 1983, but subsequently fell out of favour. Toure, in prison at the time of the coup in 1987, was released the following day and eventually reinstated in the public service. However, he was not permitted to take up his old role in the Confederation of Burkinabe Trade Unions (CSB) as general secretary, a position he lost in June 1987 during a union congress held while he was under arrest.

In addition to the obvious political partisans in the Popular Front's provisional Coordinating Committee, there were some members of that Committee, Captain Compaore himself and the current head of the Revolutionary Committees (which replace the Committees for the Defence of the Revolution under the former regime), Captain Bongnessan Arsene Ye, who have no obvious party affiliations. Both claim only to be 'revolutionaries' (author's interviews, January 1988).

It has never been made officially clear if Captain Henri Zongo, Minister of Economic Promotion, and Major Jean-Baptiste Boukary Lingani, Minister of Defence and National Security and head of the Armed Forces, both of whom were key members of the now-defunct CNR along with Compaore and the late Sankara, were also members of the Coordinating Committee of the Popular Front, but this certainly appears to have been the case. The stability of the current regime depends heavily on Compaore's ability to maintain the support of these two men. Lingani is head of the armed forces and Zongo remains Minister of Economic Promotion. When he took power, besides being the Minister of Justice, Compaore was still head of the strongest military division at Po, near the Ghanaian border, and in control of the powerful Commando Training Centre there (CNEC), which actually carried out the *coup d'état*. Since then he has had to give up these strategically important commands.

If he is to maintain control of the country he must perform a difficult political balancing act, in which no president to date has succeeded in this highly politicized country. He must manage to satisfy the desires of the factionalized left wing within the Popular Front, the military, and the resurgent right, represented by powerful businessmen and traditional tribal leaders. In addition he must convince students and trade unions, which were instrumental in bringing Sankara to power in 1983, that he means to continue the revolution they have been demanding since the 1970s when corruption was rampant. There lies the crux of Compaore's dilemma. He must give the appearance of continuing Sankara's revolution, which was popular at a grass-roots level, while finding reasons for justifying Sankara's death. In addition, he and other members of the Front, who were key actors in the revolution led by the National Revolutionary Council, have had to try publicly to absolve themselves of blame for the 'deviations' which they now say led to the downfall of Captain Sankara. And on top of this, Compaore and the Front had to spend much of their first year explaining the *coup d'état* to a confused and sceptical nation, and to a continent of youth who had come to regard Sankara as their great hope.

Popular Front Statutes and the Action Programme

In March 1988 the Popular Front published two documents outlining the statutes which govern its ultimate composition and its 'Action Programme'. These documents replace all former statutes governing the ruling forces in Burkina Faso. There has been no constitution, as such, since 1980 when Colonel Saye Zerbo took power from Colonel Lamizana, suspending the constitution and eliminating the national assembly. Thus the statutes and the action programme provide the basis for the Popular Front's 'rectified revolution'. The statues define the Popular Front as a

regrouping of political organizations, of democratic, anti-imperialist mass organiza-
tions of Burkina Faso, convinced of the necessity of uniting people in the fight against imperialism and all forms of internal domination in view of economic and social development for the veritable profit of the popular masses.

According to the published statutes, any political organization which adheres to a doctrine of 'anti-imperialism', and which subscribes to the 'action programme' can apply for membership to the Popular Front. The statutes also stipulate that the Popular Front, and any group wanting membership, must accept the political philosophy laid out in the Political Orientation Speech (DOP), delivered by Captain Sankara on 2 October 1983, just two months after he came to power. The DOP is clearly a

Marxist–Leninist platform. One of the reasons frequently offered by the Popular Front for the overthrow of Sankara's regime is his 'autocratic deviation' both to the right and to the left of this political orientation; hence the Popular Front's call for 'rectifiction processes' of the revolution.

The statutes lay out the ultimate structure of a greatly enlarged Popular Front. It will comprise:

1. A Congress
2. The Coordinating Committee (CFP)
3. The Executive Committee (CE)

The Executive Committee, which cannot be named until after the first Congress, is to consist of a president, two vice presidents and twenty-two secretaries in charge of various portfolios paralleled in the actual government ministries. In all probability, this Executive Committee will be made up primarily of those original members of the Popular Front, although the statutes demand it be elected by the Congress.

The Coordinating Committee (CFP) will be expanded to include the Executive Committee, the national elected representatives of the Revolutionary Committees (which replace the Committees for the Defence of the Revolution), the thirty appointed provincial high commissioners, and representatives of those political and trade-union organizations that are members of the Popular Front. Between meetings of the Congress, the CFP is the supreme organ of the Front. It approves the composition of the actual government, proposed by the Executive Committee. The CFP also controls all government action.

The Congress will consist of the Executive Committee, the Coordinating Committee of the Popular Front and delegates from all member organizations of the Front. Provincial delegates designated in special provincial conferences, and delegates of the Popular Front abroad, are also to attend the Congress. It is scheduled to meet every two years.

Revolutionary Committees (CRs)

The key to the structuring of the Popular Front, however, rests on the elections of the Revolutionary Committees throughout the country. These elections were begun in 1988. Revolutionary Committees replace the disbanded Committees for the Defence of the Revolution. According to a presidential decree, or Zatu, dated 16 March 1988, the Revolutionary Committees have a mission to organize, to mobilize and to enlarge the consciousness of the popular masses in the realization of the revolutionary objectives as contained in the DOP of 2 October 1983 as well as those defined in the Action Programme and the statutes of the Popular Front for meeting the goals of the rectification processes.

The Committees are also to maintain certain security functions, as they did during Sankara's rule, and they will carry arms when necessary. But their security role is to be subordinate to that of the Ministry of Defence and National Security, a step designed to prevent conflicts between the CRs and other law-enforcing bodies in the country—gendarmes and military.

The Revolutionary Committees are headed by Captain Bongnessan Arsene Ye, a medical doctor and former member of the National Revolutionary Council under Thomas Sankara. Ye's official title is National Coordinator of Popular Structures, Captain Ye unofficially ranks fourth most powerful man in the country, after Compaore, Zongo and Lingani.

Revolutionary Committees are elected in seven different categories: Youth (over 18 years of age), Women, Elders, Peasants, Workers, Civil Servants and Office Employees at parastatal or state enterprises, and Military. Each village elects a revolutionary committee composed of youth, women, elders and peasants. These committees in turn elect a 'bureau' which constitutes the village—or, in a town, the sector—council. Moving up the pyramid, to the departmental and provincial level, each of the four categories of revolutionary committee—the youth, women, elderly and peasant—elect a departmental, then provincial coordinating committee, each with seven members. These regional and provincial coordinating committees automatically become the regional and provincial sub-section of the National Unions of Youth, Women, Elders and Peasants.

On the national level, each of the four categories will have its own 'bureau', members of which are automatically direct members of the CFP. But the means of selecting these all important national bureaux had not been decided in mid-1988.

For the remaining three categories of revolutionary committees, workers, office employees and military, elections are held in each local office or division. These base committees will then elect regional and provincial bureaux. National bureaux will ultimately be chosen, in the same manner yet to be outlined for the youth, women, elderly and peasant bureaux. Representatives of these bureaux will become members of the CFP.

The CFP and the Congress, which will include all revolutionary bureaux from the base upwards, may take at least a year to form. The first Congress was not scheduled to take place before 1989.

In the meantime, the original Coordinating Committee of the Popular

Front, as described earlier, maintains ultimate power in the country, charged with carrying out the Action Programme. It meets once a week. The government consists of twenty-one ministers and six secretaries of state appointed by the Front in November 1987. It meets once a week in a cabinet meeting to approve policies, and is presided over by Compaore. At least six ministers are members of the original Coordinating Committee of the Popular Front.

The Basis for the Programme of Action

In January 1988 the Popular Front organized a national survey, carried out by the pre-existing 'Popular Structures'; Committees for the Defence of the Revolution, Presidents of Provincial Revolutionary Power (PRP) formerly elected by the CDRs, and national unions of women, elderly and peasants. Any interested individual or organization in the country was invited to present a critique of the first four years of revolution. These critiques were to include gains, weaknesses and general comments about the revolution in the areas of politics, the economy, public finance and socio-cultural development.

A three-day debate was held, attended by approximately 3,000 participants representing village farmers, trade unions, commercial interests and the civil service. Although the discussions were theoretically open, the Popular Front published guidelines for the debate shortly before it took place, and participants were cautious about deviating at all from this stated line.

Sankara's often belligerent foreign policy, which isolated Burkina Faso from neighbouring conservative states was severely criticized (see section on foreign policy), as was his dogmatic stance on promoting, through decrees, the use of local goods and food rather than imports, and his attacks on trade unions and teachers (namely the arrests of trade union leaders between 1984 and 1987, and the sacking in 1984 of 1,400 teachers who went on strike).

However, the first four years of revolution were also applauded for notable victories in the fight against corruption (through the Popular Revolutionary Tribunals), gains in primary health care, environmental programmes, cultural preservation and greater efficiency in the control of public finances.

In short, it was more Sankara's style, and the strident way he went about ruling the country than the actual goals of the revolution he led, which attracted most criticism.

The political objective of the Popular and Democratic Revolution (RDP), begun by Sankara in 1983, and to be continued by Compaore, is to 'exercise popular power to build a democratic and popular state, in destroying the neo-colonial state apparatus.' According to a document published at the end of the debate, this is to be accomplished by re-opening the 'class struggle', which the Popular Front maintains had been suppressed by the late Captain Sankara.

But, in reality, throughout the first year of the Front's rule, the leadership seems to have suffered an identity crisis. In spite of the revolutionary rhetoric, and some half-hearted attempts to resurrect some of the fervour that characterized the early years of the revolution under Thomas Sankara and the CNR, there was clearly little agreement at the top on how, or even whether, to continue the revolution.

Compaore appeared to be backtracking on policy towards traditional power structures, especially to the tribal leaders of Burkina's majority ethnic group, the Mossi. There was also intense manœuvring by conservative groups, which had at first interpreted the rectification as a chance to regain business advantages lost under the former regime. Herman Yameogo, son of Burkina's first president, Maurice Yameogo, rallied former members of right-wing parties together under the Progressive and Democratic Movement (MDP), which issued a manifesto claiming its willingness to work within the Popular Front. But this resurgence of the right was strongly opposed by the primarily communist members of the original Coordinating Committee, and Captain Ye, as head of the Popular Structures, refused any CR candidates who were leading members of any former 'reactionary' or right-wing parties. Nevertheless, the impression is that the Front has abandoned, at least temporarily, the revolutionary and populist goals espoused by the CNR under Sankara. Some revolutionary rhetoric has been retained but its emphasis has changed, with more weight being placed on centralization and control than on participation, devolution of decision-making and community involvement in political and economic activities.

Programme of Action

The Programme of Action repeats many of the development goals already laid out in the DOP, indeed it claims that political orientation speech as its theoretical basis. The apparent 'rectification' seems to apply more to the means, rather than the ends sought in the revolution. The RDP is redefined as a revolution 'which has as its primary task the liquidation of imperialist domination and exploitation, and a refinement of the campaigns against the social, economic and cultural fetters that maintain that backward state.'

Political Orientation

The Programme of Action calls for a passing of power from the exploiting classes, allied to imperialism (the bourgeoisie, retrograde forces) to the exploited classes (workers, peasants, petite bourgeoisie). However, this lofty political rhetoric is not backed up with specific programmes that might accomplish this shift of power.

Economic Objective

The Programme of Action calls for the development of a transitional stage in the evolution of a 'strong and independent' economy, described as 'state capitalism'. This would involve the consolidation and creation of more state and parastatal enterprises, and state control of the private sector.

The proclaimed idea is that this transitional 'state capitalism' would allow the rapid creation of a material base permitting the country's economy to move on to a higher stage of development.

This being achieved, the Programme hypothesizes that the main economic goals of the revolution—food self-sufficiency, the fight against desertification and the preservation of agricultural and water resources, and the requisite industrialization—would be attainable.

In the early period of the application of rectified economic policy, this involved a loosening of some of the rigid rules imposed by the late Sankara. The Popular Front lifted a ban on fruit imports, relaxed restrictions requiring civil servants to dress in cotton clothing produced locally by women weavers, lowered prices on beer, and wooed foreign business and investment with tax breaks. In June 1988 Compaore stated that Sankara's refusal to increase his country's debt burden was unrealistic for an impoverished and economically backward country, and said his country 'must go into debt'. In that month World Bank and IMF representatives visited the country for discussion on further financing for the first time since 1982.

All of these measures, which appeared to contradict the Programme's stated objectives for an independent economy, were justified by Front members as part of the transition phase of 'state capitalism'. Not all the new measures, however, even those relating to fruit imports and beer prices (which rectified Sankara's policies which had not been popular) gained wide approval. They were seen by many as bribes to allay anger over Sankara's death.

Socio-Cultural Objectives

The Programme of Action restates the DOP goals of fighting social ills in the country—illiteracy, misery, famine, begging, oppression of women and social inequality. The goal of 'health for all by the year 2000' remains unchanged.

Conclusions

Compaore and the Popular Front seemed intent on reiterating most of the idealism which Sankara embodied when he took power in 1983 in launching the RDP. However, the obvious contradictions between the stated goals of the 'rectified revolution' and the repealing of most of the most stringent measures taken by Sankara to attain these goals, led political observers to conclude that Compaore was trying to win popularity by assuming the role of a benevolent president. Instead of winning widespread popularity, these contradictions and the lack of firm application of measures intended to bring the much sought-after changes in the country, were seen as lacking political direction at the top. This earned the Popular Front criticism from all sides, and caused much confusion and passive dissent among the average people in the country.

3   The Economy

Burkina Faso is one of the ten poorest countries in the world. Statistics published by international financial institutions in mid-1986 showed that only two other countries in sub-Saharan Africa (Ethiopia and Mali) had a lower per capita gross national product—Burkinabe per capita GNP in 1986 was $160 (compared with $110 and $140 for Ethiopia and Mali, respectively). Despite strenuous attempts at development, notably by the Sankara government, the average annual growth rate of domestic product between 1973 and 1983 was a mere 2.4 per cent, compared with an average annual population growth in the same period of 5 per cent (World Bank, 1986; and FAO, 1984, vol. 38).

The country is not blessed with either substantial arable land or good grazing and has only meagre mineral resources, many of which are not viable for commercial exploitation because of the poor transport links within the country and between it and potential markets. Most of the country is a high plain, 300 metres above sea-level, which is divided by the valleys of the Black, White and Red Volta rivers (Udo, 1978).

The north and north-east of Burkina Faso is dry Sahel thorn country, which is suitable only for small-scale livestock raising. The area is subject to frequent droughts. Disastrous periods without rain in 1973 and 1974 and in the mid-1980s, which decimated herds, led to increased depopulation and exacerbated the already serious problems of soil erosion and deafforestation. The north has few trees, but those that remain are an important source of fuel and building materials, and also serve to bind the dry, thin soil. Unfortunately, the people that remain in this arid region are forced to cut down trees to provide fuel for cooking and wood for building. The United Nations Sudano-Sahelian Office, which has its regional headquarters in Ouagadougou, estimates that Burkina is suffering from a depletion of grazing land, of forest cover and of irrigation systems as a result of drought and its corrolaries (UNSO; and interviews with UNSO and Oxfam workers in Ouagadougou).

The rest of Burkina, south of the Sahel zone, is Sudan savannah. Although receiving more rain than the northern areas, the savannah is also vulnerable to drought and is suffering, though to a lesser extent, from deafforestation and soil erosion. Cattle, goats and other livestock are raised in the area and the main crops are sorghum, guinea corn, millet, maize, beans, sesame, karité nuts, sugar, groundnuts (on upland areas), rice, onions and tobacco (the latter three crops on low-lying river floodplains (Udo, 1978). In some areas cotton is grown—having been introduced as a compulsory crop for peasant farmers by the French colonialists. Since independence, the growing of cotton has continued to be encouraged and there has been less peasant resistance. Karité nuts, sesame, cotton and groundnut production have increased substantially since independence and, along with exports of live animals to Ghana and Côte d'Ivoire, are a source of export earnings.

Although the Sankara government and, following it, that of Compaore have drawn up plans for the exploitation of mineral deposits in the north of the country, there is little commercial mining. Gold deposits at Poura are worked on a small scale, while antimony is mined at Mafalou and marble at Tiara. Silver and zinc are present in commercially viable quantities at Perkoa, near to the Abidjan–Ouagadougou railway. The most promising mineral resources are the manganese ores to be found at Tambao in the far north of the country on the border with Mali and Niger. Thomas Sankara drew up plans for exploitation of manganese, but they were dependent on the building of a railway link between Ouagadougou (and thence to Abidjan's port) and Tambao. This line is under construction but exploitation of the manganese cannot proceed until the line is finished and substantial investment capital found. The Agacher strip, long a source of dispute and even of armed conflict between Burkina and Mali, is thought to contain mineral deposits, but these have still to be properly surveyed.

The industrial sector is small and concentrates generally on the processing of agricultural produce (oil mills, tanneries, shoe factories, cotton textiles), although there is a bicycle factory and a soap factory. Brewing and baking are the other main industries.

Over 90 per cent of the population lives in rural areas and is involved in subsistence agricultural production. In the countryside, the population density is very low, though it rises to 190 per sq. km. around Ouagadougou. The government estimates that 4 million Burkinabes have emigrated to neighbouring countries, some to Ghana but the vast majority to Côte d'Ivoire.

The Colonial Heritage

The basic characteristics and structure of the modern Burkinabe economy were moulded during the period of French colonial rule. Chief among these characteristics are the migration of labour to neighbouring states and extensive cash-cropping. Under the French, Burkina Faso was part of the massive French West Africa colonial and economic system, which also included the present-day states of Côte d'Ivoire, Niger, Mali, Mauritania,

Senegal and Guinea. Other parts of the colonized region had more attractive agricultural and mineral resources than Burkina and so the territory became a labour reserve for the rest of French West Africa, particularly for Côte d'Ivoire.

The French colonizers were far from gentle in their methods of encouraging migration. In 1896, taxes were imposed on the population. Payment of the taxes had to be in cash rather than produce. This forced peasants to seek paid labour (requiring that they move to areas in which such labour could be found) or grow cash crops. As little paid labour was available in Burkina, labourers had to move to other French-controlled territories to seek work. Most went to Côte d'Ivoire, where there are today about 3 million Burkinabe citizens working as migrant labourers, chiefly in the agricultural, unskilled manual or domestic sectors. Many of them work more or less permanently abroad but others stay for short periods and then return to Burkina. Remittances from migrant workers are a vital source of income for many Burkinabe families. Some Burkinabe workers go to Ghana; the numbers working there increased during the four years of Thomas Sankara's rule, when relations between Burkina and Ghana were extremely close and economic integration was a serious possibility.

Migration started in the late nineteenth century but increased dramatically after the First World War, when the demand for labour (notably in Côte d'Ivoire) increased rapidly and the French instituted a system of forced labour to ensure a steady flow of workers from Burkina to other parts of the colonial empire. The forced labour system lasted from 1919 to 1946. Village chiefs were required annually to provide men for work for a specific period to meet quotas set by the colonial authorities. Joel Gregory believes that by the end of the Second World War, migration had become 'a social and economic institution' for Burkino Faso (Gregory, 1979, p. 79).

The French colonial regime also integrated Burkina into a system of regional trade and transport, with Burkina Faso tied into a relationship of considerable dependency on Côte d'Ivoire for transport and some imports and dependency on France for manufactured and processed goods. Prior to the granting of independence in 1960, the French nurtured a small, educated elite in Burkina that could take over the government while maintaining close political and economic links with France; the newly independent state remained effectively under French economic control and was heavily reliant on Côte d'Ivoire, which had a far more developed economy and transport system.

The civil service bureaucracy grew massively in the first decade after independence—the rate of growth was totally unrelated to economic growth or the ability of the economy to support the burden of high salaries. Between 1962 and 1970 the number of salaried jobs, chiefly in the public sector, doubled. The vast majority of such jobs were in the three urban centres of Ouagadougou, Bobo-Dioulasso and Koudougou. Salaried public employees, the army, Lebanese merchants and tribal 'kings' were the chief political actors. Promotions and salary increases provided the government with important powers of patronage. Corruption was rife.

The other beneficiaries of independence were French companies with extensive interests in the economy. Political independence did not bring with it economic independence or an end to significant areas of French control and exploitation. Colonialism had been converted into neo-colonialism, aided and abetted by the political and bureaucratic elite, whose economic and political interests were bound up with the maintenance of the neo-colonial system.

Linked to continued French influence over the economy was the growth of the aid sector of the economy. Gregory estimates that between 1959 and 1971 France invested $6.4 million in Burkina through Fonds d'Aide et de Coopération (FAC) on an annual basis; in addition, a further $4.2 million was provided by France in annual aid between 1968 and 1971 (Gregory, 1979, p. 80). By the mid-1980s France was subsidizing 40 per cent of the annual government budget. Other aid was received from the EEC and other Western states, notably Italy and West Germany. The Arab states, including Libya, also became donors. In the first two decades of independence, Burkina gained the reputation of being an aid Mecca. However, this reputation did not imply that aid was benefiting the country. Rather it was felt that the substantial aid that was poured into the country benefited more the expatriate aid workers based in Burkina Faso and, in particular, the small domestic elite. Little real development or progress resulted from the aid. Addressing the UN General Assembly after his seizure of power Captain Thomas Sankara said:

Few other countries have been inundated with all types of aid as mine has been. This aid is supposed to favour development. You will look in vain for any signs of anything connected with development. [*Modern Africa*, July/August 1985, p. 20.]

One example of the way in which the misuse of aid and unnecessary expansion of the expatriate aid community, plus the combined corruption and rake-off by the ruling group, harmed the economy was through the use of valuable foreign exchange for the import of luxury commodities unrelated to the country's overall needs and development priorities. *West Africa* magazine reported that shops in Ouagadougou had on their shelves thirty-two varieties of French cheese and other luxuries for the expatriate community while much of the population lived in dire poverty. In 1980 $10.5 million was spent on wheat imports for French-style bread and a further $7 million on cheese, yoghurt and milk powder (*West Africa*, 12 September 1983). These imports of luxury food did not reach nor were ever intended for the poor, rural dwellers. These people remained on the periphery of the economic system; their existence was a constant fight against drought and poor agricultural conditions, farming as they did on the edge of the Sahara in the drought and famine-prone Sahel region.

This corrupt and inequitable economic system was one of the factors behind the 4 August 1983 coup led by Thomas Sankara and his radical supporters. He pledged to end the corruption and to distribute political power more widely while allocating more resources to rural development.

Sankara's Economic Policies: Trying to Break the Mould

Soon after the coup, Sankara said of the country's poverty and development problems that 'No real progress has been made in Upper Volta; on the contrary things just get worse'. At a press conference in Ouagadougou, he said that his primary aim was to establish food self-sufficiency—during the 1980s, drought had led to annual food deficits of anything up to 250,000 tons of grain, which is about 20 per cent of annual grain production—and to change the emphasis of previous regimes from cash crop to food production. An example of the way in which cash crops had superseded food crops is the growth of cotton production in comparison to millet/sorghum, one of the staple crops. In 1976, 55,253 tons of cotton was grown, chiefly for export, compared to 2,341 tons at independence; in the same fifteen-year period, millet/sorghum production had declined from 1,035,300 tons to 986,000 tons. The best land was devoted to cotton and other cash crops and producer prices were set by successive governments to favour cotton over food.

In addition to achieving self-sufficiency in food, the Sankara regime was intent on introducing land reforms and cutting unnecessary imports—both measures that would strike at foreign interests and the domestic elite. Sankara warned that traders who benefited from the old-style cash crop/luxury imports system would not prosper under his government. He said that such 'worm-ridden traders' who enriched themselves through corruption and bribes and at the expense of the economy 'will no longer be allowed to trade'.

Another problem that would have to be dealt with over the long term was that of migrant labour. The system of workers moving from Burkina's rural areas to Côte d'Ivoire and Ghana had continued after independence. In 1984 it was estimated that over one million Burkinabe workers were employed in Côte d'Ivoire alone. Many of them were away for periods of up to four years. Although the Burkinabe economy benefited marginally through remittances from the workers, the result of migration was to deprive the economy of vital manpower for the agricultural sector—and given the infertility of much of the farming land, labour is a vital factor in achieving higher production levels. Furthermore, it was all too often the more capable and industrious workers who sought employment abroad.

In some ways, Sankara himself was partly to blame for the migration problem. As Prime Minister in the regime of President Jean-Baptiste Ouedraogo he had lifted restrictions on migrant labour imposed by the government of Colonel Saye Zerbo, which had been unpopular. The lifting of the curbs had led to a massive outflow of young workseekers to the Côte d'Ivoire. *West Africa* estimated that the exodus would deprive the country of the labour of 100,000 workers, most of whom would never return from the migration (*West Africa*, 12 September 1983). To solve the migration problem, the National Council of the Revolution (CNR) would have to make agricultural labour within Burkina Faso a more attractive proposition through the provision of more financial and material resources and the improvement of the social and welfare infrastructure in the rural areas. But this would have to overcome the lure of prosperous Abidjan—one of Africa's most modern cities.

Another objective of Sankara's regime, enunciated in the wake of the takeover, is that of diversifying foreign economic relations—with the clear aim of cutting dependence on France and on neighbouring Côte d'Ivoire. This is for both economic and political reasons. Sankara spoke of increasing trade relations with the EEC, Japan, China, North Korea and the Soviet Union. The CNR Chairman also said that he would consider the revision of the code governing foreign investment (*African Business*, September 1983, p. 5). Increased economic cooperation with Libya, Ghana and Benin were also envisaged and small quantities of aid were provided by Libya at the time of Sankara's coup. In the early years of his rule, Sankara also showed great interest in barter trade deals with other African states that would avoid the need to expend scarce foreign currency or sell export commodities at unfavourable, Western-determined prices. In September 1986 such a barter deal was struck with Uganda—the deal followed a visit to Burkina Faso by President Yoweri Museveni of Uganda and a return visit by Sankara to Kampala following his attendance at the Non-Aligned Movement summit in Harare, Zimbabwe.

Among the development priorities identified by the CNR, with the aim of achieving food self-sufficiency and of improving rural living standards, was the provision of water supplies. In mid-1984, the government announced a plan for the construction of reservoirs in ten different areas of the country. The project was part of a rural development plan launched in October 1984 under the aegis of the Committees for the Defence of the Revolution (CDR). These bodies not only had the task of mobilizing people politically and maintaining vigilance against opponents of the revolutionary government, but also of mobilizing the population for the achievement of economic goals. The plan envisaged the establishment of local industries such as poultry farms, bakeries and light agro-industrial plants in each province which would utilize agricultural produce, create employment and supply locally-needed commodities. The concept was based on the principle of decentralizing economic activity and employment to redress the balance between urban and rural areas. Foreign aid from West Germany, the US Agency for International Development (USAID) and from the Islamic Development Bank ($7.6 million, interest-free loan) would be used to finance the water-supply projects.

One factor in the CNR's plans was the emphasis on the importance of manual work and the downgrading of the importance and privileges of the civil service elite. In August 1984, Sankara dismissed his Cabinet and a number of leading officials; fourteen of those dismissed were ordered to work on building sites rather than find other white-collar jobs. In subsequent reshuffles cabinet ministers were made to engage in manual labour. The CNR also cut the cost of government operations through reducing the pomp and ceremony associated with high government office and the perks—Sankara insists that his ministers limit themselves to Renault-5 cars (*African Business*, October 1984, pp. 24–5) and local food is served at all official banquets. While prime minister under Ouedraogo, Sankara frequently cycled to work.

The Sankara government ran into immediate problems when it tried to cut unnecessary imports, reduce the power of traders and end corruption. Traders started to build up stocks of essential goods by withholding them from the market and thereby creating artificial shortages. The shortages, particularly in rural areas, were quite severe and were compounded by the effects of drought. The government reacted by opening food stores and organizing convoys of lorries to take millet to northern rural areas, where the shortage was very serious. The food sent to the north was sold at half-price. The whole exercise was run by the Ouagadougou Committee for the Defence of the Revolution. Sankara then appealed to the international community for 350,000 tons of food aid to overcome the grain deficit result-ing from drought and poor agricultural production. This was carried out within two weeks of the takeover on 3 August 1983.

Other important objectives of the regime were included in the fifteen-month Popular Development Programme (PPD), launched during 1984, and followed by a Five Year Plan. As well as the water-supply projects, health care was to be improved. The whole programme was drawn up after intensive dis-cussions and consultations with people living and working in the rural areas. Each project was proposed, discussed and adopted by people in rural areas at village, departmental and then provincial level through the CDR network (*Africa Contemporary Record*, 1984-5, p. B441).

The PPD was split into the base programme (costing CFA fr. 7.4 billion—80 per cent of which was domestically financed) for improving water and food supplies, and a related support programme. The latter was concerned with areas such as animal husbandry, crop development, education (the rate of illiteracy was estimated at 95 per cent in 1983) and health. As well as the base and support programmes, three other projects were included in the plan—the Kompienga dam and hydroelectric power scheme, the irrigation dam at Bagre and the Ouagadougou–Tambao railway scheme linked to the exploitation of manganese deposits at Tambao. In early 1985 the West German Kreditanstalt für Wiederaufbau agreed to provide $12 million for the plan, whose total cost was put at $73 million—other donors later joined the project, including the African Development Bank ($23.5 million), the Saudi Fund for Development ($11.1 million), the European Development Fund ($6.5 million), the French Caisse Centrale de Cooperation ($9.5 million) and the Canadian International Development Agency ($7.1 million). Sankara said at a ground-breaking ceremony in June 1985 that the project would take around three and a half years to complete.

The Oagadougou–Tambao railway and the development of manganese resources proved more problematic than Sankara expected. The aim was not just to open up the manganese deposits but to use the railway to promote development in northern Burkina Faso by linking the area with the capital. Potential foreign donors were dubious about the scheme, believing it to be financially unviable. European and American governments and financial institutions looked at it purely in terms of the immediate profitability and financial returns from the manganese rather than in terms of overall national development. The cost of the project was estimated at CFA fr. 35 billion with a further 35 billion for the development of the manganese mines. The project had been mooted by previous regimes but the Sankara government took it up with greater vigour and determination. As Western donors, notably the

United States and Japan, had become involved in studies of the project with previous governments, and had pulled out saying that it was not profitable, Sankara looked to the socialist countries for help. Romania and Yugoslavia became involved in the drafting of plans for the railway and mines.

In early 1985, Sankara showed his intention to press ahead with the plan by laying the first rail in what he termed 'the battle for the railway'. At the time of the ceremony it was reported that Romania and Yugoslavia had agreed to finance construction of the railway. At the official launching of the project in January 1985, the secretary general of the CDRs, Captain Pierre Ouedraogo, said the line would also provide a line of communications for landlocked Mali and Niger. If completed, the railway would link up with the Abidjan-Ouagadougou railway and make possible a link from Niamey in Niger and Gao in Mali to the Atlantic. The revolutionary government hoped that the launching of the rail part of the scheme would encourage possible investors to put some money into the mining of manganese at Tambao, which has deposits estimated at 12-13 million tonnes with an annual production potential of 500,000 tonnes.

In addition to opening up the mining areas, the railway would also contribute to agricultural development in the Sahel regions of northern Burkina and help in fighting drought in the whole of the western Sahel—at present governments and international agencies face massive logistical problems in getting food and other aid to the interior of the Sahel (Modern Africa, May/June 1985, pp. 30-1). Compaore continued with the railway project and by October 1988 it had reached Kaya.

Other mining projects launched by the CNR to expand the economy include the Poura gold mine and the Perkoa zinc and silver mine. Speaking at the opening of the Poura mine in late 1984, Sankara said that the gold would 'shine for all Burkinabe'. The mine is expected to produce two tons of gold a year for at least eleven years. Investment in the project has amounted to CFA fr. 17 billion. The mine is being run by Soremib (Burkinabe Mining Research Company), in which the government has a 60 per cent holding—the remaining 40 per cent is divided between the French Research Company (20 per cent), the Islamic Development Bank (19.8 per cent) and the Penaroya Company (0.2 per cent). The government expects annual revenue from the mine to be around CFA fr. 5 billion, based on a gold price of $340 an ounce (*Africa Now*, December 1984, pp. 84-5).

In late 1984, Sankara instituted one of his major reforms to the economy—the abolition of private land ownership. He said that the measure was not ideologically motivated but was intended to encourage the production of more food by giving all agricultural workers a stake in the land. In conjunction with the land reform, Sankara announced the abolition of rural taxation regulations. The taxes were not huge but had to be paid prior to the annual harvest, a time when peasant farmers had little money. The measure was said to have impressed farmers even though it will have only a marginal effect on their overall living conditions. The government also introduced regulations giving women the same rights as men to lease and use land—an important measure because the bulk of the work in the agricultural sector is carried out by women, partly due to the migration of the men to neighbouring countries and to the towns (*Africa*, April 1985, p. 97).

One overriding problem that threatens Burkina Faso's plans for greater emphasis on food production and the achievement of self-sufficiency is that of drought and desertification. About 95 per cent of the country's people live in arid or semi-arid areas and the farming land is threatened by over-use, drought and erosion. Deforestation has cut fuel-wood supplies and increased the danger of desertification by reducing protection from the wind and by lowering the water table. Overgrazing by herdsmen also contributes to the overall threat to the land. The government has launched reafforestation programmes, but periodic droughts endanger the success of them and also render unsuccessful attempts to improve the overall productivity and yield of the food sector. Although better land use, increased inputs and also a better rural infrastructure will help peasants to fight drought and land erosion, the problem currently seems to be so massive that it is unlikely that any major breakthrough will occur in the near future, particularly since Compaore has lessened the emphasis on rural development.

This background to the Sankara regime's development efforts, which on the whole were pragmatic and precisely aimed at the obstacles to development of over-dependence on cash crops and too much emphasis on urban areas, has meant that although Sankara condemned past reliance on and uses of foreign aid, he had to fall back on help from abroad. He said in 1985 that he could not cut dependence on foreign financial aid (which provides 80 per cent of the country's investment funds) but intended to ensure that it was used more efficiently and that its 'perverse side' was controlled. Thus, for example, he continued to depend very heavily on French budgetary aid, as has Compaore. The CNR received aid from a wide variety of sources and for a large number of projects. Donors and projects include: Libyan aid of CFA fr. 227 million for road rehabilitation; a Chinese loan of CFA fr. 10.3 billion; Cuban assistance in the development of sugarcane growing and processing and the provision of Cuban health workers and scientists; North Korean donations of building materials and tractors; Romanian help for the railway project to Tambao, an agricultural project and trade agreements; Canadian funds for the agricultural sector; French financial aid of CFA fr. 384.5 million for mining projects; and Japanese financial assistance of CFA fr. 1.9 billion. But by 1987 Sankara's frank denunciation of 'imperialists' had taken its toll. The United States had cut aid drastically and the refusal by the Burkinabe authorities to accept World Bank financing meant a shortfall in the national budget, leading to severe cuts in the civil service and Sankara's proclamation to the people that 'we have to do it ourselves' (*Sidwaya*, 1987). The Popular Front has concentrated on seeking Western aid.

Although Burkina Faso has been closely identified with Libya and Ghana, its aid and commercial relations have been diversified and it has not been dogmatic in its internal policies or external links. Like Ghana, it has followed pragmatic economic policies. The principal thrust of the economic programme of the Sankara regime was stress on rural, agricultural development and decentralization; these aims have been watered down by the Popular Front. The CNR policies had given rural dwellers a stake in the system and an incentive to work to achieve the goals of self-sufficiency in food and overall improvements in living standards. The launching of the Ouagadougou–Tambao railway project had indicated the determination of the government to press ahead with schemes that would open up under-utilized areas and resources, even if the schemes were not to the liking of Western institutions and donor countries which in the past had been influential in guiding economic development.

Sankara tried to break the economic mould fashioned by the French and by successive regimes. Whether the Compaore revolutionary government will succeed will depend not only on the feasibility of its programmes but on the climate—both in terms of weather and the international economic climate.

Domestic Policy

The first year of Compaore's rule was not marked by landmark decisions. Most of the reforms of CNR policy were little more than retractions of laws passed by Sankara. Some of the cornerstone policies of Sankara's revolution were declared valid, to be continued, but often only nominally because of a lack of strict direction from the top, and apathy at lower levels. Divergent opinion among members of the Popular Front probably accounted for the lack of clear direction in domestic policy throughout the first year of power. Indeed, this divergence of opinion between communist factions within the Front, and between civilians and the military, led to intense speculation throughout 1988 that Compaore could not hold the regime together. There was much power-juggling at the top, resulting in a lack of confidence in the regime. This is something Compaore and the Popular Front have yet to overcome, but something they must do if they are to succeed with rectification and in the drawing up of a clear mandate for concrete domestic policies.

Trade Unions

Asked early in 1988 what he thought was his greatest accomplishment to date as leader of the country, Compaore replied 'the new détente between trade unions and the government'. Leaders of three major trade union confederations—CNTB (National Confederation of Burkinabe Workers), the ONSL (National Organization of Free Unions) and the USTB (Union of Burkinabe Workers)—were allowed to hold May Day meetings freely at the Labour Exchange office in Ouagadougou, something they had been prevented from doing the previous year under the CNR. In 1987 relations between trade unions and the ruling CNR had reached an all-time low, after government and employees of parastatal enterprises received drastic salary and indemnity cuts because of a reform of the statutes governing salaried workers. On 1 May 1987, peasant farmers were bussed into the city centre to demonstrate for the rights of unsalaried workers, who make up the vast majority in Burkina Faso. This naturally angered trade unionists and civil servants, who had planned their own May Day meetings and prepared their traditional 'Cahier de Doleances', or list of complaints, which government officials refused to receive. Shortly after that the general secretary of the CSB

(Confederation of Burkinabe Trade Unions), Soumane Toure was arrested for the second time by the CNR, and new government-approved leaders elected in his absence. The decision by the Popular Front to recognize this leadership (he was elected under questionable circumstances in 1987) has been sharply criticized by many unionists. It is also one of the reasons put forward by one of Burkina Faso's oldest and most influential leftist parties, the PAI (African Independence Party), for its refusal in May 1988 to join the Front (confidential document addressed to the Popular Front).

Under the Popular Front, the more moderate and less political trade union leaders expressed satisfaction at the new attitude towards the labour movement. On the eve of the May Day celebrations in 1988 the government held a special cabinet meeting and granted workers in parastatal enterprises almost all the benefits, retroactively, that they had lost under the CNR. This was a clear reversal of CNR, particularly Sankara, policy, which operated on the principle that as long as salaried urban workers earned more than peasant farmers they were overpaid. In addition Sankara and the CNR had slashed civil servants' salaries, pointing out that they consumed 60 per cent of the country's budget. Moves to increase state and parastatal workers' salaries and benefits greatly pleased trade unionists, but were not widely appreciated by rural and business people. They implied that the policy of giving priority to agriculture and rural people was at an end—something unwelcome to peasant farmers and many non-governmental aid agencies, which had supported Sankara's rural policies.

Women's Issues

The Popular Front, and Compaore himself, repeated statements in the DOP that placed great emphasis on the development of women's rights. In early 1988 plans went ahead for an intensive rural literacy campaign in which 10,000 women were taught to read and write. Programmes begun under the CNR to fight female circumcision and promote family planning were continued, and the National Union of Women tried, in vain, to reorganize itself. Seminars were held to discuss women's rights, with pledges to continue the struggles for emancipation of women, but there was little evidence that such 'progressive' goals had much to do with that which was happening in the country. Generally women tended not to see Compaore as the champion of women's rights he claimed himself to be, and resistance to the entire 'rectification' movement was strongest among women, who throughout 1988, openly showed their support for the former president by wearing clothing made from a patterned fabric known widely as 'Homage to Sankara' and refusing to get involved in officially organized demonstrations and projects.

Human Rights

After an initial flurry of arrests following the *coup d'état*, which resulted in official complaints from Amnesty International, the Popular Front seemed to make a sincere effort in the area of respect for human rights. Eight months after the overthrow of Sankara, only a dozen of his key men remained in detention. Pro-Sankara protests in May 1988 led to more arrests and apparent cases of prisoner beating, but efforts were made to release all but the most influential political prisoners as soon as possible.

However, it would be inaccurate to say that freedom of speech and association exist in Burkina Faso under the Popular Front, or that basic human rights are ensured by any statutes. The security forces operated autonomously throughout 1988 and people could be detained for questioning without any kind of warrant for arrest, on the basis of a mere statement made in private criticizing the authorities. Anyone suspected of writing or distributing anti-government literature was also subject to arrest. Criticism of the Popular Front was simply not tolerated, and to be on the safe side, most people avoided trouble with the authorities by avoiding political discussions outside the family setting.

Nor were there any gains in press freedom. A weekly satirical newspaper, *L'Intrus*, and a weekend FM radio station which Sankara had endorsed, were closed down. An apolitical private FM radio station and a private daily paper, which had closed in 1984 when its offices were burnt down in mysterious circumstances, were also refused permission to resume operations. The Ministry of Information justified this policy on the basis of new laws governing the press which were to make information the exclusive domain of the state. As a result the official government owned media in Burkina Faso—a daily paper (*Sidwaya*), the radio station and national television—were tightly controlled and censored by the authorities.

Justice

The Popular Front continued to enforce 'revolutionary justice' through the Popular Revolutionary Tribunals, for which Burkina Faso had become famous during Sankara's rule. In these popular courts, anyone suspected of embezzling state funds, or defrauding the state of income, is put before magistrates to defend him or herself. Proceedings of the tribunals are carried live on state radio, as an 'educational' device. Those found guilty of charges against them are usually sentenced fairly mildly, either to a few months in prison, or simply required to repay the embezzled money or to have their belongings seized.

In spite of the relaunching of the TPR in June 1988, after a hiatus of almost eight months, corruption was evidently re-entrenching itself in the country, something which angered the ordinary people and which the Popular Front will have to watch if it intends, as it claims, to continue the revolution.

The Five Year Plan

The five year development plan, which was created and implemented in 1986 is to be continued. This ambitious plan sets development goals for all ministries, with special emphasis on agricultural reform and productivity, designed to help the country attain food self-sufficiency by the year 2000. But with the loss of momentum in almost all national development projects felt after the 1987 *coup d'état*, exactly how the government is going to accomplish the goals of the five year plan was still under discussion by the Ministry of Planning and Cooperation in the middle of 1988.

Housing

Under the CNR, each year of the revolution saw a major new housing project undertaken in the capital and regional towns with local financing and local construction. The attractive suburbs built in Ouagadougou to commemorate the second and third anniversaries of the RDP earned widespread criticism from those who were forced to vacate their homes to make way for the new construction, and by those civil servants coerced into taking up residence in relatively expensive state-owned houses and apartments. Nevertheless, Sankara addressed these criticisms in 1987, with the construction of new subdivisions on the outskirts of Ouagadougou, to mark the fourth year of the revolution, by building cheaper houses from local materials.

The Popular Front made declarations acknowledging the severe shortages of housing in the capital, promising to rent out these homes in March 1988. But there was no indication as to whether the Front intended to go ahead with more such projects, or to enforce CNR rulings about construction of new homes in the country, rules which required that certain sanitation and safety standards be met.

Health

The Popular Front gave no indication that there would be a significant change in the strategy for health improvement in Burkina Faso. The construction of over 2,000 primary health posts, massive vaccination programmes, and significant gains in the areas of developing traditional pharmaceutical drugs and training primary health care workers were applauded in the national debate on the first four years of revolution. No new policies were specified by the Popular Front.

Education

The reinstatement of 1,400 teachers fired in 1984 for striking against the CNR government earned approval from trade unions and teachers in general. Apart from that the main programmes begun by the CNR—literacy campaigns, school construction in rural areas and research with practical local applications—were to be continued by the Front.

Environment

While the Popular Front called for the 'intensification' of the all-important fight to save the environment from further desertification, the evidence pointed to a relaxation of this struggle. The three-pronged 'Trois Luttes' programme, launched in 1986 which controlled the cutting and selling of firewood, the grazing of animals and the lighting of bush fires, with severe sanctions against those who break the rules, seemed to have been all but forgotten, except by the official press. Furthermore, a more centralized approach was adopted towards rural development and the disbursement of aid; this was not welcomed by foreign aid agencies or the peasantry.

Until the rise to political prominence of Captain Thomas Sankara in 1983, the external relations of Upper Volta (as it was known until 1984) were based on close cooperation with France and the cultivation of links with other states that would help the country in its search for economic assistance. Successive governments since independence had developed a high level of economic dependence on France while also attracting small amounts of aid from the People's Republic of China and a number of international development agencies. A plethora of aid agencies had established regional headquarters in Ouagadougou.

In regional terms, the country was close to Côte d'Ivoire because of the need to rely on its transport network and the high level of imports from there, especially fresh fruit and vegetables. Upper Volta also had good links with other former French colonies in the region and cooperated with them in regional economic organizations. The country was also a member of the Economic Community of West African States (ECOWAS), a grouping which included all states in West Africa.

Historical links with Arab countries north of the Sahara, developed over centuries of caravan traffic across the Sahara, meant that Voltaic governments also cultivated relations with the states of the Mediterranean littoral. From the early 1970s onwards, this involved Upper Volta in a far from smooth relationship with Libya. Under Colonal Gadaffi, Libya was seeking to develop relations with and gain influence over the Sahel states. It both offered economic aid and supported anti-government movements from the Sahel states. The aid offers were often extravagant but were rarely honoured. Support for opposition and exile groups was uneven and fluctuated according to Gadaffi's changing priorities. In 1981, Upper Volta had a minor diplomatic row with Libya when the latter attempted to turn its embassy in Ouagadougou into a People's Bureau—a move which had implications of a more activist and less diplomatic role in the host country. The Voltaic government refused to accept the change in designation. The Foreign Minister of Upper Volta, Félix Tiemtarboum, said at the time that: 'The threats of destabilization which are weighing down on countries that have common borders with the Libyan Arab Jamahiriyah—some of whom are our direct neighbours—concerns us in many ways. What we may call the Chadian tragedy cannot leave us indifferent' (*African Contemporary Record*, 1980–1, pp. A43–4). This led to a cooling of relations between Ouagadougou and

Tripoli and increased Libyan interest in relations with opponents of the Voltaic government. Such a policy accorded with that of other Francophone states (notably the influential Côte d'Ivoire) and with that of France.

The change in policy towards countries such as Libya, not to mention towards France and conservative states in the region, began after Sankara was appointed as Prime Minister in late 1982 by the then President, Major Ouedraogo. Sankara had served as a Minister of Information in a previous regime and had gained the reputation of a radical reformer and an admirer of Jerry Rawlings of Ghana as well as Gadaffi. In the brief period between his appointment as Prime Minister and his arrest in May 1983 on suspicion of working to subvert Ouedraogo, Sankara made contact with the Libyans and met Gadaffi in Tripoli in February 1983, where the latter agreed to supply Sankara with military aid for the Voltaic armed forces. Gadaffi also offered Upper Volta aid worth $6 million and put forward plans for a joint Libyan–Voltaic Bank and joint companies. Sankara arranged a visit to Ouagadougou by Gadaffi on 30 April. The first the President knew of it was when a hundred Libyan security men arrived in the country. Ouedraogo was furious and this was one factor in his decision to sack and then detain Sankara.

Soon after the Gadaffi visit, Libyan arms dispatched to Upper Volta went directly to troops loyal to Sankara and one of his supporters, Captain Blaise Compaore, at Po paratroop base.

Following Sankara's arrest, his supporters in the army, led by Compaore, freed Sankara and deposed Ouedraogo. Sankara was appointed head of state and chairman of the National Council of the Revolution (CNR). Immediately after the coup, which was executed on 4 August 1983, Libya promised to support the new revolutionary government and sent a present of weapons to Ouagadougou by plane. The weapons had not been requested by the regime and Sankara did not want to give the impression of being a Libyan stooge so he sent the arms back and said openly that he had 'politely asked the Libyan authorities to refrain from continuing this airlift which we had not requested' (Ouagadougou Home Service, 8 August 1983).

Once firmly in power, Thomas Sankara set about a major realignment of the country's foreign policy, basing it on radical anti-imperialism and improved links with Libya, Cuba, Ghana (under the radical regime of Jerry Rawlings), Benin, Congo and the Soviet Union. The CNR set up Committees for the Defence of the Revolution (CDRs) both to act as organs of political control and as channels for popular involvement in government. Although established and structured according to the needs of the revolutionary government, the CDRs were similar to the Libyan people's committees and revolutionary committees, the Cuban revolutionary defence bodies and mass organizations and the committees for the defence of the revolution established in Ghana under Jerry Rawlings and the Provisional National Defence Council. In an interview with the author in November 1987, the Minister of Peasant Affairs, Jean-Leonard Compaore (who held this portfolio under Sankara and then under Blaise Compaore), said that in creating the CDRs nationwide and emphasizing their importance in rural areas, the Voltaic leadership had benefited from the experiences of Libya, Cuba and Ghana and had discussed methods of operation with leaders of the relevant bodies in those states. But Compaore stressed that the CDRs in his country were not copied from those in the other three states (interview with Jean-Leonard Compaore in Ouagadougou in November 1987).

Soon after the coup, Sankara allowed Libya to open a people's bureau in Ouagadougou to replace the embassy closed during the dispute about its status. Libyan military advisers were said by sources in Ghana to have been sent to Upper Volta within weeks of the coup along with large numbers of copies of Gadaffi's Green Book. Relations with Libya were aided by the close personal and political ties which developed between Sankara and Jerry Rawlings of Ghana, already a friend of the Libyans.

Soon after Sankara's rise to power, close cooperation and warm personal friendship began to develop between Sankara and Rawlings. They pursued similar radical, populist policies and had foreign programmes based on opposition to imperialism and neo-colonialism. Cooperation took the form of regular consultations over political, foreign and economic policies and frequent joint exercises by the armed forces of the two countries.

The developments caused panic among their conservative neighbours, who feared that a bloc of pro-Libyan states on their doorsteps would lead to attempts to subvert their regimes—Côte d'Ivoire and Togo were particularly suspicious of the growth of radicalism in Ghana and Upper Volta and of their friendship with Libya and Cuba. As a result of their fear, the two states were stridently critical of Rawlings and Sankara and began to give support to opponents of the two regimes. However, there was never a clear break between Upper Volta and Côte d'Ivoire, as there was between Ghana and Togo, because of the strong bilateral economic links which were of great value to both countries.

In late 1983, the Voltaic and Ghanaian armies held joint exercises at which Libyan advisers were reported to be present. In April 1984, Upper Volta hosted the quadripartite summit, attended by the leaders of Upper Volta, Benin and Ghana and Major Jallud of Libya. Although the meeting pledged the four to close cooperation and coordination of policy, the three sub-Saharan states were disappointed with Libya's failure to come up with significant offers of financial aid. This was made clear to the author during visits to Burkina Faso and Ghana in November 1987 (unattributable interviews with government officials and diplomats). One of the most trenchant criticisms of Libya's failure to come up with the hoped for aid came from Beninois President Mathieu Kérékou (and his views were certainly shared, though not voiced so openly, by Voltaic and Ghanaian leaders). Kérékou stated that after the four-way summit in Ouagadougou in April 'it became clear, more than ever before, that each of our countries should first rely on its own strength and resources to accomplish the gigantic task of production and national reconstruction, despite the difficult economic climate' (Cotonou Home Service, 28 April 1985). The President's remarks were an admission that Libya was unable to meet the extravagant promises of aid which it made to friendly West African countries during the oil boom of the 1970s.

Sankara's relations with radical states—notably Ghana, Libya and Cuba—continued to develop well in 1984 and 1985, although Sankara and other leaders were steadfast in asserting the country's independence. On the anniversary of the coup which brought him to power, Sankara announced the renaming of the country as Burkina Faso—'the land of dignified men'. Libya welcomed the change in name and Libyan delegates were present at celebrations of the anniversary. At this time links were established between the CDRs in Burkina and the revolutionary committee in Libya. Similar ties were also established with the defence committees in Ghana and revolutionary bodies in Cuba, the latter also providing training for members of the Burkina's CDRs. The idea was for the CDRs to exchange experiences and develop cooperative relations with their counterparts in friendly states. However, French sources reported in 1984 that the Burkinabe leadership was growing increasingly critical of Libya's failure to supply aid that it had promised and that relations between Ouagadougou and Tripoli had cooled. This problem in relations was one exploited by Côte d'Ivoire, which in 1984 offered drought relief and came to an agreement with Sankara on the upgrading of Bobo Dioulasso airport.

In 1985 functional cooperation continued with Libyan youth delegations visiting Burkina to promote links between the youth organizations of the two countries with the aim of cementing 'anti-imperialist unity' (Ouagadougou Home Service, 9 July 1985). The delegation which visited in July 1985 held talks with the head of the Burkinabe CDR movement, Pierre Ouedraogo. The result of the talks was the establishment of a permanent commission to encourage cooperation between the revolutionary organs of the two countries. The following month Libya sent a consignment of cross-country vehicles, uniforms and communications equipment for use by the Burkinabe CDRs.

In December 1985, Sankara hosted an official visit to Burkina by Gadaffi, an event designed to cement their alliance and increase cooperation. The visit had almost the opposite effect, for while openly the two sides pledged themselves to strengthen relations, the practical effect of the visit and of Gadaffi's behaviour in Ouagadougou was to sour relations and start a gradual decline.

The first mistake the Libyan leader made on his arrival in Ouagadougou was effectively to snub Sankara. Informal in his approach to ceremonial functions, Sankara met Gadaffi at the airport and planned to drive back to the Presidential Palace in Sankara's own modest Renault 5—Sankara and his ministers had abandoned the use of expensive limousines in favour of small, more economical and less pretentious cars which they usually drove themselves. Gadaffi rejected Sankara's idea and walked from the airport into Ouagadougou at the head of his large contingent of armed bodyguards. Sankara was highly offended by Gadaffi's high-handed reaction to his welcome (information received in interviews with former press aide to Sankara and Western journalists and diplomats who were present in Ouagadougou during Gadaffi's visit).

The next mistake the Libyan made was to patronize the Burkinabes and belittle their revolutionary achievements during his keynote speech in Ouagadougou. He implied that the Burkinabe revolution was modelled on the Libyan one and made violent and unrestrained attacks on neighbouring states (ones of which Sankara was critical but which he had no intention of offending unnecessarily).

Relations were further damaged when Gadaffi failed to live up to his promise to provide Libyan financial aid for development in Burkina Faso. During a visit to the military base at Po, Sankara asked Gadaffi about a request he had made some time earlier for funds to expand the airport at the town. Gadaffi had not given complete approval at the time of the request but later his deputy, Major Jallud, and senior army officers talked him into an outright refusal of aid for the scheme. According to a Western ambassador serving in Burkina Faso (interviewed in Abidjan in November 1987), the aid was refused because the Libyans feared that if Sankara was overthrown or reversed his critical stand towards France, then the expanded airport could be used by the French as a staging post for an air support base for operations in Chad. Diplomatic sources in Ouagadougou and Abidjan believed that Burkina Faso received little more than $500,000 in disbursed, as opposed to pledged, aid from Libya between 1983 and 1988.

Relations declined still further after the visit when Sankara turned down a Libyan offer of $30 million for the building of mosques and Islamic cultural centres in Burkina Faso. Not only was the offer worth more than all other Libyan aid to Burkina Faso, but it was to be used solely for religious purposes. Sankara was not a Muslim and anyway wanted funds for development not religion. Diplomats and journalists in Burkina believe that the offer was viewed by Sankara as an attempt by Gadaffi to set up the foundations for an 'Islamic party' in Burkina that would be under Libya's influence and funded by it through Libyan-backed religious institutions.

The next opportunity for Libya to aid Burkina was during the brief Burkina–Mali border war of December 1985. The conflict was the result of a long-running dispute over a strip of land along the border in the Gorom area of Burkina Faso. Clashes started on 20 December and lasted until the end of the year. They ended following Libyan and Nigerian mediation. Sankara was said to be angered that instead of supporting him, Gadaffi had sought to mediate and so had not lived up to all his promises of fraternal aid to Burkina. The dispute was later patched up through the International Court of Justice. However, a further example of Libya's failure to live up to its promises had occurred.

Despite this setback, Sankara was still willing to offer moral support to Libya when it came into conflict with the United States over the naval exercises in the Gulf of Sirte. Sankara strongly attacked the United States over its 'provocations' and pledged to fight the sole enemy—imperialism.

Although regular contacts and exchanges of visits took place in 1986, there was no evidence of the establishment of warmer relations or of Libyan aid to Burkina. At a press conference in Ouagadougou on the third anniversary of Sankara's seizure of power, Sankara denied that Burkina had received CFA fr. 25 billions' worth of arms from Libya.

Another setback in relations occurred in April 1987 during a visit to Tripoli by Sankara. At a ceremony in the Libyan capital on 7 April, Gadaffi suddenly announced that he had promoted Sankara to colonel from captain. Libyan sources said that Sankara was deeply touched by the gesture. However, Burkinabes told the author in November 1987 that Sankara had been insulted by Gadaffi, as the ceremony seemed to imply that Gadaffi was the superior and was thus in a position to 'promote' the President of another country. Sankara never used the title colonel, something confirmed two days after the ceremony by sources in the Burkinabe army high command.

Prior to his death in a coup on 15 October 1987, Sankara had made an attempt to restore good relations with Libya by attempting to reconcile the warring factions in the Chadian GUNT and had also attempted to mediate between Habre and Libya. Goukouni Oueddei and Acheikh Bin Oumar were both in Ouagadougou at the time of Sankara's murder and Blaise Compaore has since tried unsuccessfully to reconcile the two. Sankara's attempt at mediation failed because of Habre's suspicion that the Burkinabe leader supported the Libyans. This had certainly been true at one stage, but diplomats in Ouagadougou and Abidjan told the author that Sankara had been very impressed by Habre's victories over the Libyans and had altered his opinion of the Chadian leader accordingly; he had previously viewed him as little more than a French puppet, but the victories led Sankara to view him as an able military leader worthy of respect.

After Sankara's death, Libya made swift moves to cement good relations with Blaise Compaore—Sankara's deputy who had taken over the leadership of the country in the name of the Popular Front. Within days of the coup the Libyans sent a gift to Compaore of an undisclosed number of bullet-proof Alfa Romeo cars. In mid-November, the Libyan Foreign Secretary turned up in Ouagadougou for talks and was received by Compaore and other leaders of the new regime. In early January 1988, Compaore paid an official visit to Libya for talks with Gadaffi. By all accounts the visit was a success and Gadaffi and Compaore established better working relations than had existed with Sankara prior to his demise. This was surprising in a way as from the start of his rule Compaore had sought to improve relations with Togo and Côte d'Ivoire—the more conservative states in the region which had been extremely hostile towards Sankara at times.

Burkina Faso's relations with the Soviet Union and the socialist states were cooperative and friendly, if not particularly close. Burkinabe foreign policy under Sankara was welcomed by these states as it centred on criticism of capitalist, particularly French and American, exploitation and domination of Africa. Small-scale economic projects in Burkina were assisted by the Soviet Union, which also gave some aid in the form of scholarships. None of the socialist countries played a major role in supplying economic or technical aid and political relations were good though not particularly close. Sankara visited Moscow during 1986, but his talks with Gorbachëv and other leaders while friendly did not lead to any great changes in the relationship.

Cuba was much more important to Burkina than the Soviet Union and did serve to a limited extent as a source of inspiration for bodies such as the CDRs, although Burkinabe leaders have always been at pains to reaffirm that although they have benefited from the experiences of other radical states they have not just copied them. Towards the end of his life, Sankara grew closer to the Cubans, perhaps because of the need for allies in the wake of the cooler relationship with Libya. A former Sankara aide told the author in November

1987—a month after Sankara was killed—that Cuban security personnel had advised Sankara and had served with his personal guard. The aide said that the Cubans were saddened and angered by Sankara's murder and were unlikely in the short term to be willing to establish close links with Compaore.

Compaore met with the Soviet ambassador to Burkina in late November but the reports of their talks gave no indication of any particular change in relations following the death of Sankara. However, the more pragmatic foreign policy being formulated by Compaore is likely to be viewed less positively than was Sankara's.

Under Compaore, stress has been put on rebuilding relations with Côte d'Ivoire and Togo, to which Compaore paid important visits in 1987 and 1988. Close economic ties were the main reason for the visits, but Compaore was keen to diversify Burkina's foreign links and to end the radical phase of policy. As a result of this policy and of Ghanaian regret and anger over Sankara's murder, Ghanaian–Burkinabe relations can at best be described as cool. At times, a note of hostility has been evident. The killing of Thomas Sankara brought to an end the hopes for integration and ever greater cooperation between the two states. Under Compaore, Burkina enjoys better relations with Côte d'Ivoire than with Ghana.

Because of the emphasis on diversified relations, Compaore has improved Burkina's ties with France and dropped much of Sankara's criticism of France and other Western nations. In speeches in early 1988, he dismissed much of Sankara's policy of anti-imperialism as rhetoric that achieved nothing while damaging the country's economic relations with neighbouring states and with France.

Effectively, Compaore has returned foreign policy to the pre-Sankara pattern. The only 'radical' state with which Burkina now has friendly links is Libya—partly because Gadaffi adopted a more cautious and less strident foreign policy himself in 1988.

Relations with other radical states in Africa have declined in importance under Compaore. Those with the Congo, which were warm when Sankara was alive, have become distinctly hostile since 15 October 1987. The Congolese government and government-sponsored student groups were bitterly critical of the killing of Thomas Sankara, while the new Burkinabe regime rejected their criticism as uninformed and unwarranted interference in Burkinabe affairs.

Under the Popular Front, Burkina's regional relations have improved as a result of the toning down of revolutionary and anti-imperialist rhetoric. Many West African states had been wary of the CNR policy of 'expanding the revolution', carried out by Burkinabe residents living in such capitals as Libreville and Dakar, who formed Committees for the Defence of the Revolution. This caused diplomatic tension between Sankara and other heads of state.

Sankara's relentless condemnation of corruption and torpidity in African organizations, such as the Francophone West African Economic Community (CEAO), Air Afrique, the Organization of African Unity, earned him the guarded respect (but fear) of several of his counterparts in the region. In 1986 when Burkina Faso finally had its turn at the helm of the CEAO, Sankara wasted no time in bringing the community's top bureaucrats to trial in the TPRs, for embezzling funds. In April that year Mohamed Diawara, an Ivorian businessman, Moussa Diakite, former Director of CEAO's funding organ, and Moussa Ngom, former general secretary of CEAO were sentenced to prison in Ouagadougou for embezzling a total of CFA fr. 6.5 billion. In 1987 when Sankara put himself forward as a candidate to preside over ECOWAS, the Economic Community of West African States, in Nigeria, he was blocked by presidents fearful that he would apply similar embarrassing measures to their economic organization (interview with Sankara, June 1987).

The Popular Front considered this kind of belligerent foreign policy ridiculous for landlocked and impoverished Burkina Faso. Early on Compaore made it clear that he was out to make amends for his predecessor's outspokenness. But not everyone in Africa was impressed. Heads of state seemed anxious not to stir up anger among their own youth who had come to regard Sankara as a hero, and avoided endorsing the new regime. When Compaore visited Nigeria in April 1988 the popular press proclaimed him a 'murderer'.

Later that month he headed a Burkinabe delegation on a whirlwind tour of three Front Line states in southern Africa: Angola, Mozambique, Zambia, with a stopover in Gabon. Once again, Compaore received only a lukewarm welcome on this tour.

This southern African mission was intended to put into practice the second stated intention of the Popular Front's foreign policy: 'to develop relations based on peace and justice with all countries regardless of their political and economic system', with mutual respect for territorial independence and sovereignity', with 'non-interference in internal affairs' on an equal footing. The Popular Front promised to 'consolidate relations in particular with countries, parties, and revolutionary organizations and to throw support behind national liberation movements and social emancipation struggles' among peoples of the world. Compaore has repeatedly said this means support for the independence struggle in Namibia, the anti-apartheid fight in South Africa, the Sandinista government in Nicaragua and the Palestine Liberation Organization in Palestine.

However, this revolutionary line was not congruent with actual politicking. Shortly after the *coup d'état*, Burkina Faso abstained from a United Nations vote on independence for the French colony, New Caledonia—a complete turnaround from its position under Sankara, when Burkina Faso was one of the most outspoken opponents of continued French presence on the island.

Similarly, the Front's repeated support for the anti-apartheid movement in South Africa amounted to little more than idle rhetoric. Sankara's stated anti-apartheid stance was matched by his flamboyant move at the OAU summit in Addis Ababa in 1986, when he called on African nations to donate arms to the African National Congress, and his outspoken condemnation of French President Mitterrand during a state visit to Ouagadougou in 1986, for having allowed South Africa's foreign minister onto French territory earlier that year. Shortly before his death in 1987. Sankara presided over an anti-apartheid forum in Ouagadougou, in which he called once more for action against the Pretoria regime. While the Popular Front continued to aim harsh words at the 'racist regime' in Pretoria, it is significant that Compaore was careful not to direct strong words at countries which invest in South Africa—Japan and West Germany in particular, since these are both nations with which the Popular Front seemed intent on developing strong economic ties. Indeed, shortly after Compaore's visit to the Front Line States, Minister of Economic Promotion, Captain Henri Zongo visited Japan looking for more Japanese investment in Burkina Faso.

In April 1988 Compaore was reportedly poorly welcomed at the annual OAU summit in Addis Ababa, and was taken to task by several heads of state for press reports that Mariam Sankara, widow of the former president, had been harassed by security forces and blocked from leaving the country. Shortly before leaving for this summit, it is noteworthy that Compaore finally gave orders for the construction of a proper tomb for his predecessor, and on his return agreed to a request from Gabonese president, Omar Bongo, that Mariam Sankara be allowed to leave Burkina Faso on a special plane to be sent from Libreville for her and her two children. These moves were evidence of the kind of pressure Compaore was under from other African heads of state, to make amends for the violent death of his predecessor. They also support the widely accepted belief that Compaore is intent on making himself and his regime popular anywhere he can, on and off the African continent.

Bibliography

Food and Agriculture Organization (FAO) 1984. *Production Yearbook 1984*, Vol. 38. Rome, FAO.

Gregory, Joel W. 1979. Underdevelopment, dependence and migration in Upper Volta. In Shaw, Timothy M., and Heard, Kenneth A., *The Politics of Africa: Dependence and Development*. London, Longman.

Udo, Reuben K. 1978. *A Comprehensive Geography of West Africa*. Ibadan, Heinemann.

World Bank 1986. *Financing Adjustment with Growth in Sub-Saharan Africa 1986-90*. Washington, DC.

Periodicals

Africa, London
Africa Contemporary Record, London and New York
Africa Now, London
African Business, London
Modern Africa, London
Sidwaya, Ouagadougou
West Africa, London

Index for Benin

Index for the Congo

Index for Burkina Faso